T0382695

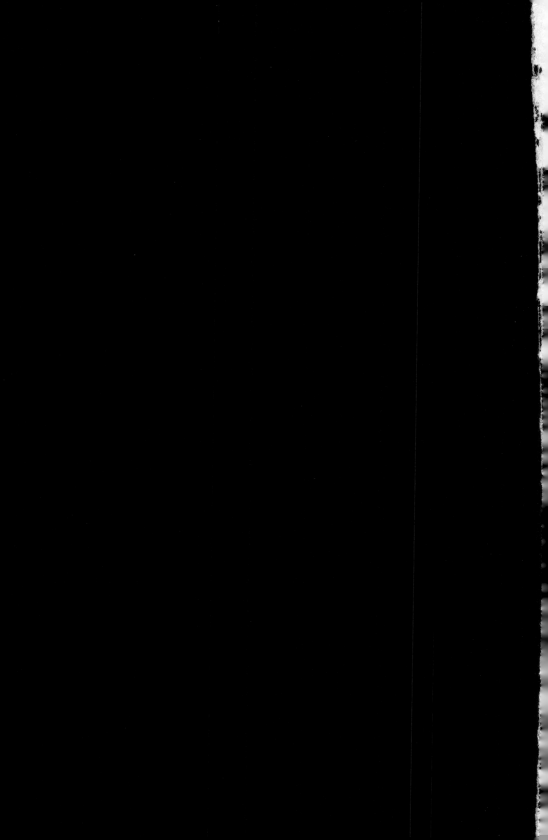

MALCOLM
LIVES!

MALCOLM LIVES!

The Official Biography of Malcolm X for Young Readers

IBRAM X. KENDI

Farrar Straus Giroux
New York

Farrar Straus Giroux Books for Young Readers
An imprint of Macmillan Publishing Group, LLC
120 Broadway, New York, NY 10271 • mackids.com

The publisher thanks the Schomburg Center for Research in Black Culture of
the New York Public Library and the Charles H. Wright Museum of African
American History for their generosity in supporting the creation of this project.

Our books may be purchased for promotional, educational, or business
use. Please contact your local bookseller or the Macmillan Corporate and
Premium Sales Department at (800) 221-7945 ext. 5442 or by email at
MacmillanSpecialMarkets@macmillan.com.

Library of Congress Cataloging-in-Publication Data
Names: Kendi, Ibram X., author.
Title: Malcolm lives! : the official biography of Malcolm X for young readers /
    Ibram X. Kendi.
Other titles: Official biography of Malcolm X for young readers
Description: First edition. | New York : Farrar Straus Giroux, [2025] | Includes
    bibliographical references. | Audience: Ages 10–14 | Audience: Grades 7–9 |
    Summary: "Compiling the definitive speeches, sermons, and correspondence
    as well as some never-before-seen original material, this comprehensive
    narrative biography of American icon, Malcolm X, will be the definitive
    reference volume for young readers" —Provided by publisher.
Identifiers: LCCN 2024012784 | ISBN 9780374311865 (hardcover)
Subjects: LCSH: X, Malcolm, 1925–1965—Juvenile literature. | African
    American civil rights workers—Biography—Juvenile literature. | Civil rights
    workers—United States—Biography—Juvenile literature. | Black Muslims—
    Biography—Juvenile literature. | United States—Race relations—History—20th
    century—Juvenile literature.
Classification: LCC E185.97.L5 K46 2025 | DDC 320.54/6092 [B]—dc23/
    eng/20241205
LC record available at https://lccn.loc.gov/2024012784

First edition, 2025
Book design by Trisha Previte
Printed in the United States by Lakeside Book Company, Harrisonburg, Virginia

ISBN 978-0-374-31186-5
10 9 8 7 6 5 4 3 2 1

TO A YOUNG MALCOLM,

to all you overcame,
to all you wanted
our world
to overcome

MALCOLM LIVES!

NEBRASKA
HISTORICAL MARKER

MALCOLM "X"

El-Hajj Malik El-Shabazz was born Malcolm Little at University Hospital in Omaha, Nebraska, May 19, 1925. He was the son of Earl and Louise Little, 3448 Pinkney Street. Reverend Little helped organize the Universal Negro Improvement Association. After threats by night riders, the family moved to Milwaukee and later to Michigan, where Reverend Little allegedly was murdered. During his mother's illness, Malcolm was sent to Boston, then to New York, where he committed burglary. While serving a six and one-half year prison sentence, he became self-educated and converted to an American sect of Islam.

After leaving prison, Malcolm took the name Malcolm X, studied under Elijah Muhammad, and became outspoken about mistreatment of Blacks. His *Autobiography of Malcolm X* was published in 1964. During a pilgrimage to Mecca, he converted to orthodox Islam. He abandoned concepts of racial antagonism and counseled the need for human brotherhood and international cooperation. Malcolm X formed the Organization of Afro-American Unity in 1964 and became renowned as an articulate spokesperson for human rights.

Malcolm X was assassinated February 21, 1965, in New York City. His teaching lives on.

City of Omaha
Malcolm X Memorial Foundation   Nebraska State Historical Society

The historical marker at Malcolm's first childhood home:
3500-3598 North 34th Avenue, Omaha, Nebraska

INTRODUCING MALCOLM

Today, there is a huge open field. There are paths to walk around the spot where a house once stood. There is green and brown grass in the distance. There are trees beyond the grass. There is enough space to play tag here. Or football. Or dodgeball.

There is an empty stone bench on some concrete. A visitor can sit down on the bench and look up at the Nebraska historical marker here at 3463 Evans Street in Omaha. On the marker is the life story of someone who lived here as a kid. The marker states he "became renowned as an articulate spokesperson for human rights." What does that mean? Malcolm X later explained what it means: "I'm for truth, no matter who tells it. I'm for justice, no matter who it is for or against. I'm a human being first and foremost, and as such I'm for whoever and whatever benefits humanity *as a whole.*"

History is boring when it is dead. And interesting when it is alive. "His teaching lives on," the marker states after describing Malcolm's death. His teaching lives on all around us today. This book shows how. This book tells the story of a single life navigating racism on a course to be antiracist—to revolutionize society, to be free. Malcolm teaches us all along the way of his life. We learn from our lives. We learn from others' lives. Life stories are the greatest teachers.

Before one can teach what's right for humans, one must learn what is right. Before one can stand up to what's wrong, one must learn how to stand up to what's wrong. Even in oneself. And for this antiracist spokesperson for human rights, Malcolm X, it all began here in Omaha, Nebraska, at this historical site.

It feels so calm. So peaceful. So quiet right now. But it wasn't that way one hundred years ago.

Chapter 1

LOUISE

Maybe they rode through the rustling trees in the distance. Maybe not. But the six or so White men on horses were now outside the farmhouse. Malcolm had not been born yet. But his life story had already begun with his parents. All life stories begin with our parents. Whether we know them or their life stories or not.

It was the year 1925. Exactly one hundred years before the publication of this book you're holding. The horsemen carried torches that fired up the night sky. They looked like the White supremacists who marched in Charlottesville, Virginia, in 2017. That march prompted Joe Biden to run for president of the United States. Racism has not faded into history, as some people will tell you.

"Little!" one horseman yelled.

The rebel yell had to shock Louise Little. Maybe she was finishing feeding her three children. Preparing them for bed. Now she had to prepare her children to remain in the house and be quiet.

Best believe *she* wasn't going be quiet. Or stay inside. She wiped her hands. She opened her front door. Louise likely yelled at the horsemen, "My husband is not home!"

Her belly was big. The horsemen could see she was pregnant.

And they could see her light skin. So light she could pass as one of their White wives. But they hated Louise because of her color? And loved their wives? How? Because they were different races? How can race exist when two people who look the same are considered different races? Race doesn't exist. Racism does. Racist ideas keep people hating other people who look the same or don't look the same.

Race is a power construct. Powerful Portuguese writers constructed *race* in the 1400s to justify the enslavement of peoples in Africa. The Portuguese were enslaving all these different peoples who spoke different languages, dressed differently, practiced different cultures, lived in different communities in Africa. But Portuguese writers looked at their darker skin colors and called them one race of people, one Black race, one inferior Black race. Portuguese writers said this inferior Black race should be enslaved. They constructed the Black race—and soon the White race—to defend slavery for Black people and freedom for White people. They stamped slavery and inferiority onto dark skins. They stamped freedom and superiority onto White skins.

These stamps were made up. Race is made up. Race is not a biological reality. Whether it is the Black race or the White race or the Native race or the Middle Eastern race or the Latino race or the Asian race. Below our different hair textures and skin and hair colors and the shapes of our hair, eyes, noses, and lips, experts can't find any biological or genetic differences. How humans appear— from the colors of their skin to the colors of their clothes—doesn't mean anything about who humans are, whether inferior or superior.

But Black people like Louise could not ignore race even though it was made up. Because racial inequity was everywhere. Because people were still judging people by their skin colors. And since racism made people from Africa into one race, soon some of them started seeing themselves as one race. As Black people. To understand why they were being mistreated as Black people. To come together. To fight racist mistreatment. To protest rules that enslaved and segregated and excluded Black people. To push back against the idea that Black people were inferior. To defend themselves against Klansmen who hated Black people.

Staring angrily at Louise, the men got down off their horses. They announced themselves as the "knights" of the Ku Klux Klan. They held up their rifles and shotguns.

Louise Little probably was not surprised the Klan was making all the noise. Only the Klan came around this time of night. The Klan had begun night-riding and terrorizing like this when the organization formed after the end of slavery. They often wore hoods and looked like ghosts. The Klan and other racist mobs had kidnapped thousands and thousands of people and lynched them. The violence of enslavers to force Black people to accept slavery—which they never did—became the violence of the Klan to force Black people to accept racism. Which they never did. Louise never did.

Her birthright to Malcolm.

• • •

Louise was born in St. Andrew, Grenada, in 1897. This small island nation in the Caribbean is not close to the United States like Cuba. Grenada is north of the mainland of South America, close to Venezuela. Rumor was her White father had raped her Black mother. Louise never knew her father. Her mother died when she was young.

Louise was raised by her strict grandmother and aunt. She worked hard at her religious school. She learned discipline and became wicked smart. She wanted more than her small island could provide. In 1917, she moved to Montreal, Canada. She found a job as a housekeeper and seamstress for White families. Racism and sexism shut Black women out of other jobs.

Louise had moved to Canada with her uncle, who told her about Marcus Garvey. From the Caribbean like Louise—Jamaica, to be exact—Garvey moved to the United States and built the Universal Negro Improvement Association (UNIA). The UNIA started a newspaper, the *Negro World*. (Before the 1960s, Black people commonly self-identified as Negroes.) Garvey called for Black people to come together and fight for their freedom from racism. White people controlled many Black people through racist rules and Klan violence. So Garvey wanted Black people to gain control of their *own* homes, neighborhoods, and nations. "Up, you mighty race," Garvey declared.

Garvey wanted Black people to love their *own* skin color and their *own* culture. If racist ideas taught White people they were better than Black people, then racist ideas taught Black people they were less than White people. But Garvey told his followers: "I am the equal of any white man; I want you to feel the same way." Garvey's antiracist words were music to the ears of Black people . . .

Migrating North from the South . . .

Coming home from Europe after fighting in World War I . . .

From the Caribbean like Louise.

● ● ●

Garvey's words gave Louise courage to face the Klan that day in Omaha. Remember: Courage is not the absence of danger. It is the strength to do what's right in the face of danger.

"Get that [N-word] out here, now!" a Klansman yelled.

The Klansmen were looking for Louise's husband, Malcolm's father, Reverend Earl Little Sr. He was preaching five hundred miles away in Milwaukee, Wisconsin.

Chapter 2
EARL

Earl Little was basketball tall. About six foot four. Very dark-skinned. He had only one eye. He was from Reynolds, Georgia, a small town about one hundred miles south of Atlanta. Earl didn't complete school, like Louise. Maybe finished third or fourth grade. Racist White landowners and cotton manufacturers did not think Black kids needed to go to school. They only wanted Black people to learn how to pick cotton and maintain White homes as maids and cooks. In many ways, Black people were still enslaved in Georgia when Earl was growing up there.

Earl escaped this new slavery by learning to be a carpenter. Being a carpenter made him independent of White rule. His independence caused problems. Racist White people did not like that Earl acted as if he was equal to any White man. His family became worried for his life.

In 1909, Earl married Daisy Mason. They had three children: Ella, Mary, and Earl Jr. But Earl had all sorts of trouble with Daisy's family. All the criticism from Daisy's family and all the violent threats from racist mobs became too much. In 1917, Earl left his wife and kids. He left town. He joined the Great Migration of nearly six million Black people who moved from Southern towns to cities up North during the first half of the twentieth century.

Earl settled in Montreal, Canada. A chapter of Garvey's UNIA had just been founded there. One day, the UNIA held a meeting. Earl and Louise attended. They met. They fell in love with Garvey and each other. They got married. They left Canada. After stops in Philadelphia and Reynolds, they moved to Omaha, Nebraska, at the urging of Earl's brother.

The Littles started a UNIA chapter in Omaha. The local klavern took note. Local groups of the Klan were called klaverns. These klaverns also terrorized Asian Americans, Native Americans, and Latino Americans. Even White Americans, especially Catholics and Jews and union organizers and antiracists.

By 1925, the Ku Klux Klan had risen to the height of its power. Months after six Klansmen showed up at the Littles' home to terrorize this Black family, around forty thousand Klansmen marched down Pennsylvania Avenue in Washington, DC, to terrorize all Black families in the United States.

• • •

Louise stared down the Klansmen. Folded her arms. They waved their guns. A Klansman spurred his horse. Nothing fazed her. Louise yelled that her family didn't cause no trouble in Omaha. Didn't bother nobody. Didn't harm nobody.

The Klansmen gripped their guns harder. Shot back threats. They warned Louise that her family better leave town. Because "the good Christian white people" were not going to stand for them "spreading trouble" by teaching Black people the words of Marcus Garvey and by living in a "Whites only" neighborhood.

As calm as it is today, as quiet as it sounds today, it is hard to imagine how full of terror this place was for Louise and her children. But Louise didn't back down to these racist bullies. The baby she was carrying would one day become known around the world for refusing to back down too.

One Klansman took his rifle and smashed the front window of the Littles' house. Louise's baby, Philbert, started crying. Her young daughter, Hilda, tugged at her housedress in fear. Her oldest child, Wilfred, watched behind another window.

The Klansmen climbed back on their horses. They rode away into the night. They left behind a crying baby, two dazed kids, pieces of glass everywhere, and an angry pregnant woman. But Louise probably felt some relief. Many Black people didn't live when the Klan showed up at their homes. She lived. The baby inside her lived. She gave birth weeks later, on May 19, 1925. Named the boy Malcolm Little.

Maybe Louise did not feel any relief as she saw the Klansmen gallop away. Maybe she worried they may come back later in the night. No threats. Just gunshots.

She needed to reach her husband immediately. But only rich people had phones in those days. Louise went to a rich friend's house. She called Earl and told him everything. He boarded the next train from Milwaukee back to Omaha.

Malcolm speaking on Marcus Garvey Day, 1958

Chapter 3

LANSING

Earl and Louise struggled to build the UNIA chapter in Omaha in 1925. But they weren't alone in their struggles to build the Universal Negro Improvement Association. Their leader, Marcus Garvey, had entered prison that year. Instead of investigating the lynchings of the Ku Klux Klan, the police investigated Garvey. Klan attacks on Black people were not dangerous? But Garvey's empowering of Black people *was*? That's what the Federal Bureau of Investigation thought. For years, FBI agents tried to find a law Garvey broke. To put him in jail. And deport him. To stop his movement. They finally found one: mail fraud.

With Garvey behind bars, local leaders shifted their attention to getting Garvey released. But most of Earl and Louise's attention was likely on easing the fears of their Black neighbors in Omaha. Black people feared being harmed by members of the local Klan if they joined the UNIA. They heard about those Klansmen who came to the Littles' home when Earl wasn't there. They probably thought if Earl had been home, he would have been killed. People around town remembered the lynching of a Black man named Will Brown in Omaha in 1919.

When Louise called him, Earl was in Milwaukee, Wisconsin. Milwaukee seemed like a better city in which to build on Garvey's message. Factories were hiring Black workers left and right. Black workers were being paid better than in other cities. Black people were realizing Garvey's vision. They were coming together and starting their own organizations and businesses. A thriving UNIA chapter existed.

So Earl and Louise moved to Milwaukee from Omaha in December 1926. Malcolm was barely walking at one and a half years old. Earl Little became the UNIA chapter's new "spiritual adviser." Louise continued her secretarial and writing duties for the chapter in Milwaukee that she began in Omaha. Perhaps Louise drafted Earl's letter to the president of the United States on June 8, 1927. Maybe a two-year-old Malcolm looked on, curious.

In the letter, Earl asked President Calvin Coolidge to "release Marcus Garvey from the five-year sentence without deportation." It would be "your priceless gift to the Negro people of the world." But federal law stated that conviction of a crime like mail fraud made an immigrant like Garvey subject to deportation. In 1927, President Coolidge ordered that Garvey be immediately released from prison and coordinated with immigration officials to ensure that Garvey would be deported "promptly" and "by operation of the law." Garvey never came back. The UNIA lived on. But never recovered.

Earl and Louise taught their children all about Garvey on Saturdays. One Garvey lesson: Black people have five fingers on each hand and a brain in their head like everyone else. So they are equal to everyone else. And Black people cannot let White racism stop them from believing in themselves and doing for themselves. Malcolm, at two years old, was already taking in these lessons. His siblings noticed all his "mental energy." Malcolm spent a lot of time as a toddler searching and discovering and seeking to understand.

Milwaukee became Earl's new base. He regularly left town to travel and preach and encourage Black people to join Garvey's UNIA. But soon after they had settled in Milwaukee, the Littles were moving again. They made their way to Albion, Michigan, where Earl's brother had moved from Omaha.

When the Littles lived in Albion, Earl worked for a time at a factory where metal objects are made. He found a similar job in Lansing, the state capital of Michigan. The family moved from Albion to Lansing in January 1928.

In Lansing, Black people were forced to live in an overcrowded area of town White people called the "[N-word] section." The Little family stayed with friends in that Black neighborhood only for a short time. They bought a one-and-a-half-story farmhouse in an all-White area just west of Lansing. They were tired of moving. Tired of moving away from the Klan or moving toward jobs. Malcolm moved three times before he turned three years old. He wanted to be settled. His family wanted to be settled. Their hopes for being settled were dashed.

A racist sign posted by White residents
of Detroit in the early 1940s

Chapter 4

2:30 A.M.

White men arrived. No noise. No horses. No gunshots. No sheets over their heads. No more threats like last time in Omaha. Just cartons of gasoline in their hands. Matches in their pockets. Hateful ideas in their minds.

This time Earl Little was home.

The White men poured gasoline around the back of the wood-framed farmhouse. It was around 2:30 A.M. on November 8, 1929. They lit a match.

Boom! The explosion of fire woke everyone up. Earl jumped up. He looked out the window. He saw two White men running through the fields. He grabbed his gun. He ran outside. Shot at the men. Missed.

Earl did not recognize the men. But he probably figured out quickly *why* they firebombed his new home.

A deed is a document that says who owns a property. The deed of the Littles' new property in Lansing had a racist covenant. A racist covenant is a sentence on the deed stating that only a White person can occupy a property. One stated in 1921, "Said lot shall not be occupied by a colored person." Racist covenants were the main way White Americans kept Black people out of all-White neighborhoods in the 1920s. In 1922, the Michigan Supreme Court ruled that racist covenants were legal. The justices said they could be used to keep out or force out Black families like the Littles. The

US Supreme Court did not rule racist covenants to be unenforceable until 1948.

But after 1948, racist covenants remained on many deeds across Lansing, Michigan, and the United States. In 2019, a Michigan state legislator from Lansing introduced a bill to remove racist covenants from deeds. Three years later, Rep. Sarah Anthony had yet to get her initial bill passed. But in December 2022, Michigan governor Gretchen Whitmer signed into law a bill sponsored by Anthony that made it easier for people to remove the racist covenants.

Malcolm's parents did not know of the racist covenant on their new property. Some White neighbors came by to notify Louise. The White neighbors offered to buy back the property, probably at a lower price than the Littles paid for it. Louise said no.

The White neighbors filed a lawsuit to remove the Little family. A judge ruled in the neighbors' favor due to the racist covenant. Earl secured a lawyer who filed an appeal. The Littles were not going to leave easily! Maybe this angered some of the White neighbors. Maybe they were the men who set fire to the home. Maybe these same men were running away from Earl's gunshots.

Earl ran back inside the home. The fire seemed to be everywhere. Smoke seemed to be everywhere. Hot all of a sudden. No one could see. The kids started running from the fire into walls, into each other. Louise and Earl were yelling for their kids by name. Probably coughing from the smoke. They found each child. They found four-year-old Malcolm. Everyone had on pajamas. No time to change. Earl and Louise rushed all their children out of the fire, out of the smoke, out of the house.

Now outside looking back at their burning home, they could see there was not a lot of fire. There was not a lot of smoke. Because it was a small house. On a small amount of land. Enough for the growing family. The Littles did not have much.

• • •

Earl quit the factory job to earn more money as a carpenter in Lansing. But local White construction companies would only give him work as a lesser-paid carpenter's helper. Racist White carpenters would start trouble if their bosses gave Earl and other Black men equal wages and equal work. It all angered Earl. How racist White workers pushed Black people out of their unions and professions.

All the racism made no sense to Earl. He did not believe the Whiter the person, the better. But did Earl believe the lighter the person, the better? Is that why he was also attracted to Louise? Did Louise reverse it? The darker the person, the better? Is that why she was so attracted to Earl? No one knows. But in those days, just like today, too many people adore people due to their skin color. And they hate people due to their skin color. Hate causes them to set houses on fire. Then and now.

A page from Malcolm's datebook detailing his musings on hard work and success, 1961

Chapter 5
BLAME

Two White neighbors from nearby houses came to help. With the fire starting in the back of the house, the Littles and their neighbors had a little time to save some stuff in the front of the house. The adults rushed back inside to grab bedsheets and quilts and whatever else they could. They dropped it all onto the porch and then onto the yard. Louise placed Yvonne, her three-month-old baby girl, on a pillow in the yard. She ran back in for more stuff. At some point, a quilt probably landed on top of the baby, covering her up.

Louise did not see her baby, forgot where she put Yvonne down. She looked into the house. Flames everywhere. She started to run back in to save her baby. The other adults grabbed her. She probably fought them until they heard Yvonne cry.

Louise removed the quilt. Picked up her crying baby. She probably wanted to cry too. She stood there with Earl and their seven children and two neighbors. Freezing in the winter air, only in their nightwear. But the cold was an afterthought. They watched their home and almost everything they had burn. Imagine the horror Malcolm and his siblings experienced. Imagine the pain their parents felt. Imagine the terror.

• • •

A White neighbor asked the owner of a nearby gas station, Joseph Nicholson, to call the firefighters. He did. But the Lansing Fire

Department refused to come. Fire did not separate by skin color. But firefighters did. The Littles paid taxes that paid for the firefighters. It did not matter. Only racism mattered. Racism is worse in times of tragedy. If you are Black, the agencies designed to help you will ignore you or hurt you. Ask Black residents of New Orleans who survived Hurricane Katrina in 2005. Ask houseless Black people near you. Ask Black people who called the police when their loved one was having a mental health crisis—and the police came and killed them.

The public will blame you when things are taken from you if you are Black. When Black people are harmed, racist ideas claim Black people harmed themselves. Which allows for the denial of racism. Which is exactly what happened here, to Malcolm's family.

Neighbors knew that racist covenants had failed to get this Black family out of this White neighborhood. Neighbors knew that the Littles were appealing the judge's order for them to leave. Neighbors had tried everything to get the Littles out. But the Littles were refusing to leave their home. When racist rules and cases fail, violence is around the corner.

But all this was denied.

Rumors spread like fire that Earl torched his own home with himself, his wife, and seven children inside. Why? To get insurance money. If a family has insurance on their home and possessions, if they are lost in a fire, then a family will get some money.

Local police wasted precious time investigating Earl. Even arrested him. But Earl and Louise did not get down on themselves. They carried on. They stayed with friends for a month and then relocated to a house in a White neighborhood near East Lansing—Michigan State University is about two to three miles from that address. Faced with constant harassment from racist neighbors, Earl and Louise moved their family out of town. They found a six-acre property south of Lansing.

Finding no evidence against Earl after nearly four months, the local prosecutor dismissed the case. The police never did find the actual White men who torched the home. They didn't even seem to look.

Maybe the racist White men stood in the distance as the fire burned. Maybe they knew they'd get away with it. Maybe they felt satisfied for burning almost everything this Black family had. All for what? Because Louise and Earl dared to live like they were free and equal in a country that claimed to be about freedom and equality? Because they raised their children to respect themselves and disrespect racism? Because they demanded that Black people be treated as human beings?

For four-year-old Malcolm, this was "the nightmare night in 1929, my earliest vivid memory." Another nightmare night was coming for Malcolm. It would be even worse.

As-Salaam-Alaikum

My Dear Sister Henrietta,

How are you and the family? I pray this finds all of you well and enjoying the best of happiness. I have started to write to you many times but somehow I always put it off. This place is making me the master of procrastination, and that isn't a good "trade" to be master of (smile).

You wrote to me last in October. At that time you were enjoying the remains of your garden...and now it is time to plant all over again. How time flies! Let us hope that this year the weeds will not outgrow the vegetables. Tell Phil that I said he never was much of a farmer(smile). So, if he needs advice just write to "Farmer Malcolm"...he will remember that I had my own garden at home. He used to swipe some of my crops and then he and I would fight all over the yard. Of course, I always lost, but it was lots of fun, now that I look back on it... once after he had given me a good beating, I took a pot shot at him with a 22 rifle. You should have seen the spanking Mom laid on me...I couldn't move for a week. But as soon as I recovered from one spanking, I would earn another one (smile) until finally Mom decided that she was wasting her time. We certainly were some very mischievious sons. I don't know who received the most spankings between Phil and me, but I was the most mischievous so it must have been me. Besides, Phil could always run faster than I, and he out ran the whip. (smile). You really married

A letter from Malcolm to his sister-in-law Henrietta reminiscing about his childhood, March 25, 1951

Chapter 6

BULLIES

Have you ever seen adults argue? Well, Malcolm saw Earl and Louise argue a lot. Many days, Earl came home angry from the racism he experienced. On some nights, he took his anger out on his wife and children. Earl hit Louise sometimes. Earl and Louise spanked their kids too. And Malcolm almost always tried to get out of it. Earl did not spank Malcolm. He always asked Louise to do it. Maybe because Malcolm had become Earl's favorite child. Maybe he saw himself in Malcolm. Or because Malcolm was the lightest child? Many people treat light-skinned Black kids better than dark-skinned Black kids. Kids face racism too.

When these spankings happened, Malcolm would scream for help. "If anybody was passing by out on the road, she would either change her mind or just give me a few licks," Malcolm remembered. "So early in life, I had learned that if you want something, you had better make some noise."

On September 28, 1931, Malcolm saw his parents argue over dinner. Earl came into the house and into the kitchen from the farm. Earl carried vegetables he had picked and a dead rabbit.

Earl ordered Louise to cook the rabbit. He wanted rabbit stew. He did not ask Louise. He knew she'd say no. Louise believed rabbits were unclean animals. She believed God did not want humans to eat rabbits. But Earl had grown up eating rabbits in Georgia.

Louise did not like rabbits and did not like being ordered around.

Earl liked rabbits and liked ordering Louise around. They argued in the kitchen. The more they argued, the angrier they became.

• • •

Malcolm was likely one of the children in the kitchen. He was separating the farm crops that they would eat from the crops they were going to sell.

There were seven children in the household by now. Wilfred, the oldest. Hilda, the next oldest. Then Philbert and Malcolm. Reginald, Wesley, and Yvonne were younger than Malcolm.

Malcolm, at five years old, had started school earlier in the year, in January 1931. Malcolm, Wilfred, Hilda, and Philbert had to walk two miles to school. Through farms. Over fences. Through woods. They walked each weekday to Pleasant Grove Elementary School in southwest Lansing. The only Black people they saw were each other. All the teachers and other students at the school were White.

A book used at Pleasant Grove was *The Story of Little Black Sambo*, written and illustrated in 1899 by Helen Bannerman. It is about a little boy in the country of India. He gives his clothes and umbrella to tigers so those tigers won't harm him. The tigers start fighting among themselves, and Sambo is able to get his belongings back. In many editions of the book, Sambo has very dark skin, very white teeth, very white eyes, a very big nose, and a very big smile. To Americans, Sambo looked like a "pickaninny." That is like the N-word. It is a slur. A pickaninny is a racist picture of a Black child who is outdoors and thoughtless.

Malcolm's White classmates thought *The Story of Little Black Sambo* was funny. They teased Malcolm that he was Sambo. Malcolm did not think it was funny. The book hurt him. The teasing hurt him. His classmates hurt him when they kept calling him the N-word.

The racist bullies only went so far. The Little children got a reputation for defending themselves. The more they fought, the less the bullies messed with them.

Still, Malcolm told his mother about the racist bullying. Louise reminded him about Garvey's teachings. She said to Malcolm something like, "If you feel the White kids are better than you, then they will treat you that way. If you feel you are equal to them, then they will be forced to treat you as their equals. Even if they make fun of your skin color and your race, don't ever think there's something wrong with your skin color or your race. There is something wrong with what they are saying—not you."

Louise told Malcolm he should never let the bullies see him hurt. Because they would soon realize they couldn't hurt him and would stop trying.

Maybe this is why Malcolm's mother did not show fear when those Klansmen came. Maybe this is why Malcolm's parents did not let the burning of their house stop their family.

But Malcolm's parents were not invincible. Human beings can be hurt. They can hurt each other.

• • •

Malcolm's mother backed down. She grabbed the rabbit. She removed the rabbit's skin.

Earl left the kitchen in a huff. Maybe the argument stole his appetite. Or did he leave the kitchen after eating? Whatever happened, he did feel the need to leave the stuffy house. Stuffed with anger. Maybe he remembered some people in town owed him money for chickens he had sold them.

Earl washed up. He changed out of his dirty farming overalls. He put on some cleaner clothes.

He came out of his bedroom still angry. Malcolm saw him walk straight to the front door. Earl told Louise he was going to get some "chicken money." Louise was shocked. The children too. No one expected Earl to go out that night.

Marcus Garvey during a parade in Harlem, 1922

Chapter 7
A VISION

Malcolm probably wanted to go along. He was used to joining his father at Garvey UNIA meetings. Most of the meetings were held at night. Sometimes the meetings were held during the day. Daytime meetings happened in "sundown towns": the most violent towns in the country for Black people. Sundown towns were places where Black people were threatened with violence (sometimes even death) by racist White people if found outside after the sun went down. Lots of Midwestern towns were this way. Nearby East Lansing was this way.

One day, Malcolm went to a daytime meeting in a sundown town named Owosso. It was forty miles away from Lansing. Black people called the town "White City."

These secret meetings were usually held in a Black family's home in and around Lansing. Never more than twenty people. Packed in someone's living room. Everyone crowding around Malcolm's father. His father saying, "Africa for the Africans," "Ethiopians, Awake!" Earl saying it would not be long until Africa was run by Black people again. Africa meant more than the continent of Africa. It also meant Black nations, Black neighborhoods, Black homes in the United States. It meant no more Klan. Freedom from White racism. "No one knows when the hour of Africa's redemption cometh," Earl would say. "It is in the wind. It is coming. One day, like a storm, it will be here."

Earl then handed out shiny photographs of Marcus Garvey.

Maybe Malcolm helped pass them out. The photographs showed what seemed like millions of Black people in a parade. They were marching behind Garvey riding in a nice car down a street in Harlem, New York. Garvey was dressed in a bold uniform with gold on it and a nice hat. Garvey looked like a king. He almost looked like Moses to Black people, leading his people to freedom.

As the people stared at these photographs, Malcolm stared at them too. Maybe he dreamed of seeing Harlem. Maybe Malcolm dreamed of leading Black people like Garvey in Harlem. Malcolm had no idea his dream would one day come true.

After the pictures were shown off, the meetings would end the same way every time. Earl shouting again and again: "Up, you mighty race, you can accomplish what you will!"

It all made Black people feel good when times were so hard. Not as hard for the Littles as other Black families. Earl worked out a crop-sharing arrangement with a White neighbor with more land. Meaning the two families planted different vegetables and shared them with each other. They planted and shared corn, potatoes, spinach, peppers, string beans, and squash. The Littles purchased a cow and a goat for milk. They raised chickens for eggs. They raised rabbits in a pen. When home, Earl woke up early to work on the farm. He expected all his children to work. Nothing angered Earl and Louise more than laziness, than old and young people who didn't want to work long and hard. The family collected walnuts from the trees on their property and sold them along with other crops. Louise made and sold clothes. Malcolm remembered his mother "always working—cooking, washing, ironing, cleaning" and taking care of her seven children. When he came of age, Malcolm would be remembered as always working like his parents.

Earl was always leaving to preach at Baptist churches, to speak at UNIA meetings, to do carpentry work around town, to collect money. Louise had a lot of work to do when Earl was there. Then all his work fell to her when he left. Doing all his work and her work was hard. Worrying about his safety, with the hateful Klan out there, was hard.

Never this hard. Louise tried to stop Earl from leaving this time. She didn't feel right about him going out. But Earl kept walking. She followed him out of the house, pleading with him to not go.

As she watched him walk over the yard and into the road, Louise had a vision. She saw the death of her husband. She "had always had a strong intuition of things about to happen," Malcolm remembered. All her kids did too. "When something is about to happen, I can feel something, sense something," Malcolm wrote when he was older. Louise felt something, sensed something.

She grabbed her apron and ran through the yard and onto the road. "Early! Early!" she screamed. Earl was already far down the road. But he heard her. He turned around, waved, and kept on.

Louise walked back into the house, upset. She hoped she was wrong. She wanted to get her mind off the pain. So she worked and the children worked with her. Malcolm and his siblings hand-washed clothes. They squeezed out the water. They hung them to dry on lines outside.

All those hours, all that washing, she could not wash away the fears. Earl did not come back. Louise probably stayed up late waiting for him. Or maybe she went to bed early. Because the waiting was too hard. At some point, Louise and her seven children went to bed.

The uniform and weapons of the Black Legion

Chapter 8

ACCIDENT?

E arl had gotten on a streetcar. He reached for his money to pay. He realized he did not have his overcoat. His money was in his coat pocket. All that money he had collected for his chickens since he left home.

He asked the driver to let him off. He got off the streetcar to go find his coat. The streetcar left.

It took Earl a while to find his coat out there east of Lansing. He decided to go home. He came upon the streetcar stop at the intersection of East Michigan Avenue and Detroit Street. Today, the train tracks are gone. There's a Chevrolet dealership on the corner. Cars are bought and sold. Cars speed on by. It is a busy intersection. People drive by every day not knowing what happened here in 1931.

What may have happened there is Earl ran to catch the streetcar. It was the last car that night. He did not want to have to walk miles home. As he approached the streetcar, he slipped on something wet. He fell. The streetcar ran over him. The driver said later he didn't realize he had run someone over. Because he did not stop.

Earl lay there on the tracks. Badly hurt. Leg smashed. He tried to get up. He couldn't. Sometime later, someone saw him. Called the police. A young Michigan state police officer named Lawrence G. Baril arrived. Earl told the officer what had happened, told him where he lived.

Or at least that is the story Officer Baril told Louise. That is the story Officer Baril told the local newspaper. But that story may be a lie. Police sometimes lie. Especially to cover up when they harm someone, when they break the law. In those days, racist police officers lied to cover up the murders committed by the Klan. In those days, many police officers were secretly Klansmen too. It is the same today. Too many police officers are secretly White supremacists.

Around the time Malcolm was born in 1925, Michigan had around 75,000 Klansmen. About half of them lived in Detroit, and Lansing had its own active chapter. But with the publicity surrounding the murder conviction of Indiana Klan leader David C. Stephenson in the shocking death of a young woman that year, Klan membership began to decline around the Midwest.

Former Klansmen were recruited into a new terrorist group, the Black Legion, even more secret than the Klan. Black Legionnaires wore black robes rather than white. Like the Klan, they targeted Black people, Jewish people, Catholic people, and labor unions. The Black Legion grew into a large organization due to the work of a former Detroit police officer named Isaac "Peg Leg" White. Peg Leg helped bring many police officers and public officials into the secret society. The Black Legion was lurking the day Earl Little was hurt.

Some Black people in Lansing did not believe the police report. They did not believe the newspaper report. One of Malcolm's brothers was told that someone pushed his father and placed his father under the streetcar. "Negroes in Lansing," Malcolm said, "have always whispered that he was attacked, and then laid across some tracks for a streetcar to run over him."

Earl did tell his wife that he was traveling to North Lansing to collect the chicken money. They found his body on those train tracks east of Lansing. Not many Black people lived out there. It was near the sundown town of East Lansing. Why was he there? A group of Black Legionnaires could have beaten him up. And left him on the train tracks to make it seem like an accident. The police officer could have helped. This is what Malcolm believed when he got older. But some of his brothers and sisters did not. They believed it was an accident.

• • •

Earl was taken to the local hospital. He fought to live. Or at least to see his wife one last time. It probably pained him how he had left the house.

Officer Baril and his partner drove to the home of the Littles. They didn't think they had much time.

Maybe the bright lights of the Lansing police car woke everyone up. Definitely the loud knock on the front door. Louise came to the door in her nightwear. She opened the door and saw the officers. Her heart probably dropped. They told her about her husband being at the hospital. Tears fell.

She went back in her bedroom. Dressed quickly. Wilfred, her oldest child, had to take care of his brothers and sisters. By the time Louise arrived at the hospital, her forty-one-year-old husband was dead.

Malcolm slept through most of the night. He learned the terrible news in the morning. He noticed that his mother could not stop crying. About what happened. About what was going to happen.

12-12-49

As-Salaam-Alaikum

In the Name of "Allah", the True and Living God; and in the
Name of His True Servant and Apostle, the Honorable Mr. Elijah
Muhammad...All Praise is due to "Allah."

My Dear Brother,

    Your letter arrived tonight catching me quite by surprise,
its promptness being so unexpected; but your quick reply was
delightfully soothing in all ways.

    Reginald wrote to me Saturday, and much of the facts
disclosed to me by him coincided and harmonized with your letter
tonight...proving to me, that despite the material miles that
separate you...you are still joined together spiritually, making
you both intellectually one.

    It makes me feel good (incouragingly) to hear the Brothers
there think I was in contact with Islam before my seclusion...
for they are correct. We were taught Islam by Mom. Everything
that happened to her happened because the devils knew she was not
"deadening" our minds. When she refused those two pigs from
Mr. Doane that time I thought she was crazy myself (as hungry
as I was); and they sowed their lying seeds in our heads...but
she sufferred the abuse of all...even incurring the worst degree
of the devils fury...unto death, all for our sake. Tis true,
that my accomplishments are yours, and yours are mine...because
we are all brothers and sisters...but all of our achievements are
Mom's...for she was a most Faithful Servant of Truth years ago.
I praise "Allah" for her. The love that exists in our family

A letter from Malcolm to his brother Philbert acknowledging
their mother's early refusal to eat pork, December 12, 1949

Chapter 9

GREAT DEPRESSION

E arl died on September 28, 1931, during the Great Depression. By 1933, almost half of US banks had closed their doors. Without access to money from banks, many businesses did not survive. Black businesses generally had fewer resources than White businesses and were often quickly forced to shut their doors during the Great Depression, with White businesses taking over their customer base and properties. When businesses closed up or cut costs, people lost their jobs. Black workers had often been the last hired. So they were often the first fired. When they kept their jobs, racist White people called for Black workers to be replaced with White workers who needed jobs. In Northern and Midwestern cities, White unemployment reached as high as 25 percent. In many places, more than half of Black workers were out of jobs. Close to fifteen million people were out of work by 1933. When people lost their jobs, they did not have the money to buy things. With fewer people buying things, more businesses closed up and more people lost their jobs. That was the vicious cycle of the Depression.

At first, Louise thought her family would be fine. Earl had been paying for two insurance policies. Just in case he suddenly died. He had a $1,000 life insurance policy. Meaning if he died for any reason, then his family would get $1,000. Louise used this money to pay for his funeral. She also received $18 per month from this policy. But it only lasted a few years.

Earl had also been paying another insurance company for a

$10,000 accidental death insurance policy. The Lansing medical examiner, newspapers, and police ruled his death an accident. But the insurance people refused to pay Louise the $10,000. Not because they thought Black Legionnaires killed Earl. The insurance people ruled that Earl's death was likely a suicide.

You got that right. A suicide! Imagine how mad Louise was. She needed that money to feed her children. The insurance people probably knew her husband did not die by suicide. But they probably figured Louise did not have the money to hire a lawyer to sue them. And even if she did, an all-White jury would rule against her. In the end, the insurance company cheated this Black woman out of her money.

The family needed money to survive. Wilfred, the oldest, quit school. He went to work. He'd work all day. Come home all tired. Give all the money to his mother.

Hilda, the second oldest, took care of the babies. Which allowed Louise to go into Lansing and find work. She'd clean the homes of White people. Work up to ten hours. Receive fifty cents.

She'd sew for White people. Her White employers sometimes thought she was White. They would find out she was not—or learn she was the widow of the "troublemaker" Earl Little—and *fire* her. Another racist act.

Louise would "come home crying, but trying to hide it," Malcolm remembered.

Malcolm and his brother Philbert "didn't contribute anything." Then again, they did contribute more stress on the family. They were fighting all the time. Fighting each other at home. Fighting classmates at school.

Young people often misbehave when they are very sad. To be very sad *all the time* is to be depressed.

One thing that makes young people depressed is when they are separated from a parent.

When a parent is incarcerated.

When a parent leaves like Earl left his family in Georgia.

When a parent is separated from a child being sent to foster care.

When a parent suddenly dies, like Earl.

Has this ever happened to you? Any of these things can make young people feel abandoned. Deserted. Like there is something wrong with them *when there is nothing wrong with them*. Truly, there is nothing wrong with them.

There is nothing wrong with you.

Imagine how bad the depression can be if the child is very close to the parent. No child was closer to Earl than Malcolm. His seventh born. Earl's pride and joy. The child Earl would take to the Garvey UNIA meetings. Malcolm loved those trips with his dad. Oh, the joy filled Malcolm at six years old. But now his dad was gone. Now Malcolm's joy was gone. Now his anger had arrived. Anger at *everybody*. Including his family. Is that why he did not help them in this time of need?

There was another reason Malcolm was angry. The deep poverty. What comes with very deep poverty? Hunger. Malcolm was not alone, then or now. One in eight households in the United States today struggles to put food on the table. Meaning if you were to go outside and count eight homes, one of them would have people who were hungry like Malcolm. Black children are more likely to go hungry than White children. If you were to go outside and count *one hundred* White homes with children, *eight* would have kids who do not get enough to eat. Eight is eight too many! But it is even worse for Latino and Black families. If you were to go outside and count one hundred Latino homes with children, you would find *twenty* have hungry kids. If you were to go outside and count one hundred Black homes with children, you would find *twenty-three* have hungry kids like Malcolm. Isn't that unfair? Black households with children should not be nearly three times more likely to have hungry kids than White households with children! There should not be *any* hungry kids.

Have you ever been so hungry it put you in a bad mood? Like a really bad mood. The more your belly hurt, the angrier you were. When you were really hungry, you would get dizzy. You couldn't even think straight. See straight. How could you not be angry? There is a word some people use for being hungry and angry now: *hangry*. That is how Malcolm felt. *Hangry. All the time.*

When there was nothing else to eat, the Littles would eat those yellow weeds that grow wildly around our homes sometimes. Louise went and picked those dandelions. Boiled a big pot of dandelion greens. They are very nutritious plants packed with vitamins, minerals, and fiber.

Many people don't know that. To many people, eating dandelions is like eating grass. Actually, a neighbor told people in town that the Littles were eating dandelions. At school, kids teased Malcolm for eating "fried grass." It all made Malcolm madder.

Sometimes Malcolm would be so hangry after school, he would not go home. No food there. He ate dinner at the home of a churchgoing Black couple named the Gohannases. Or he walked two miles to Lansing. Malcolm searched for food stores with apples and other treats on display. He watched the owner, waited, and then went for it. Stole a treat. Ran away. Found a place to eat it quickly. Stole some more food. Until he was no longer hangry. Until he got what he wanted. The poverty caused him to wait for food. Malcolm remembered, "I never wanted to wait for anything."

Louise never wanted her children to wait for food. Watching her kids be hungry made Louise feel very sad. Sadder and madder than Malcolm. Mad at all the racism that dragged her family into poverty. Sad about how badly the poverty hurt her children. It all made Louise feel very depressed. Do you know how a disease can take over someone's body? Depression can do the same to someone's mind. On a cold day in 1938, Louise's mind was taken.

6-11-52
Wednesday night

In the Name of Allah, the Great Living God!!!
Consider the Time. Most surely man is in
loss, except those who believe and do good
deeds, by teaching their Brothers The Truth
and the Power of Patience. In the Name of
His Holy Messenger, the Honorable Mr.
Elijah Mohammed.

As Salaam Alaikum

Dear Sister Beatrice,

In this Final Day Almighty Allah is showing we who have
long thought that we were all alone in this world that we have many
Brothers and Sisters, and the Love He has instilled within us is
drawing us all together into His House, where we have One Mind,
One Love, and One Goal.

Surely you are a blessed Sister, for look at your wonderful children. All grown up, strong and healthy. My love for you
began when I heard how your sons chose prison rather than the
devils' Army, and my love for you was strengthened a million fold
when I heard how you yourself chose jail rather than let the devil
indoctrinate your children in his school with his lies...surely
Allah shall reward you greatly for a strong-minded mother has strong
minded children, and if your children will even now look around
them at the weaknesses in other families, they will thank Allah
abundantly for having had a Mother like you...

For the past 14 years my Mother has been in seclusion,
a mental asylum. When I was six(in 1931), my Father was found all
ground up beneath the wheels of a street car. He was a rabid
Garveyite, and must have also heard the Teaching in Detroit, for
he began to preach (already being a minister) something that had
the whole town of Lansing Michigan in a stir...so one night he met
met his death; you can imagine what happened to him. The devil
went to the "colored Masons" and told them my Father was giving out
their secrets, so they did the devils' dirty work...that left my
Mother with seven hungry mouths to feed, and we starved.

One day the man next door butchered his hogs and offered
two of them to her free, and she refused them. Everyone had been
saying she was crazy, and when she refused all that meat I began to
believe what everyone was saying. In 1938 they came to the house
and put her in an institution. Until I heard Islam four years ago,
I had thought she was in the wrong. So you can see how I feel today
having condemned my own Mother for nearly ten years, just because
the devil constantly whispered in my ear(as a child) that she was
crazy. This should be a lesson to all Muslims: beware of that
devils' forked tongue, for if one listens to him long enough, one
will end up doubting even those who are nearest and dearest to him.

There are many things that need to be done, but so few
to do the task. I have looked around and wondered why more of our
people aren't being awakened. There is no one to awaken them.
The Apostle needs many servants to go forth throughout the land with
this wonderful Truth, but those who have the capabilities are married, with families, and thus have to stay home to provide food
for their hungry mouths...thus our people who have never heard The

A letter from Malcolm describing his father's death and
his mother's subsequent mental illness, June 11, 1952

Chapter 10
COLD

Christmas approached in 1938. Snow covered the roads outside. Cold colored the air. Leaves on trees were long gone. Crops and animals on the farm were long gone. But not the distress inside the farmhouse.

On this December day, nobody was watching Louise. Nobody perhaps heard Louise mumble about taking the baby for a walk. Into the snow and the cold. Nobody heard her because perhaps she didn't say it aloud. Perhaps because no one was home except Louise and her baby boy, Robert.

She had given birth to Robert, her eighth child, earlier in the year. August, to be exact. The child's father "looked just like my father," Malcolm's oldest brother, Wilfred, remembered. "If someone didn't know my father was dead, and saw him in the house, they'd think it was my father. He was the same height, same color, same everything."

Very big. Very dark. Very proud. Like Earl. His name, Edgar Page.

Malcolm and his siblings giggled about the relationship. They watched their mom get all dressed up before Edgar came to the house. And Louise acted differently around him. Not sad like many days since Earl had died. She laughed with this man who reminded her of Earl. Louise sometimes did not smile around her kids. Let alone laugh out loud.

Malcolm and his siblings liked seeing their mother happy. Even if it was when Edgar was around. Even if as soon as he left, her happiness left with him. Edgar had recently left her for good. Did it feel like Early leaving all over again?

Maybe Louise was thinking about Edgar or Earl when she walked out of the house into the snow. No shoes. Only her bare feet.

None of her children saw her leave. None of her children saw her walk barefoot onto the snow in their yard. None of her children saw her walk onto the snow-covered road. Her children were likely at work or school.

Perhaps she walked up the same road that Earl walked up the last time she saw him alive. Maybe his wave to her was grabbing her attention. Not the coldness of the snow on her toes. Not the freezing air right before Christmas in Michigan in 1938. Not her baby boy on her chest. Not, perhaps, his cries.

She did not seem to feel any of it. The cold. Her baby. She just walked along the road. Sometimes a person has been hurt so badly for so long they stop feeling in moments.

• • •

Nothing hurt Louise more than having to depend on people outside her family. Marcus Garvey urged Black people to be self-reliant. Meaning to rely on themselves. Not to rely on White people. Louise wanted to be self-reliant. That's why she tried every which way to get a job. That's why Wilfred traveled to Boston and worked a job there. That's why he sent back the money he made. But Malcolm and Philbert stole the money from the mailbox. They had gone from bringing stress on the family from all their fighting to bringing stress on the family from stealing money. All this stress came down on their mother like punches to her heart.

Malcolm never forgot how his stealing contributed to the pain. Perhaps that is why when he grew up and became famous, he never talked about his mother. If anyone spoke ill of her, he'd want to fight them. He'd want to fight them because he could not go back and fight himself at thirteen years old. Louise hated depending on others, just as much as White people around town hated that she was so independent. Hated that she didn't treat White people as if they were better than her. But racist White people treated her that way. They would speak down to her. "They were trying to get her to kneel," her oldest son, Wilfred, recalled.

Especially the White welfare agents. The state of Michigan provided financial support to impoverished mothers. But the state only gave around $1.75 per week per child. And sometimes, mothers with eight children like Louise received funds for *only three kids*! How is that fair? And since Louise was a Black mother taking care of so many Black children on her own, welfare officials saw her and her kids as people they needed to police, not simply as people who needed more food and money. Welfare officials were constantly coming to the home to inspect what they assumed was the problem. For racist Americans, the problem is Black people.

When his White classmates found out Malcolm was on welfare, oh, did they harass him. It was horrible. The jokes kept coming at school. The jokes kept stinging Malcolm. The more the jokes hurt him, the more he didn't want to be on welfare. The more he didn't want to be on welfare, the more he took food and other items from stores. And the more he broke the law, the more he got caught. And the more he got caught, the more welfare officials came to his home. Welfare officials ignored the problem that poverty creates for families. Malcolm's unlawful activity became proof there was a problem.

Welfare officials were "as vicious as vultures," Malcolm remembered. "They had no feelings, understanding, compassion, or respect for my mother." They seemed focused on breaking up this family. They really wanted to take Malcolm away. Nothing upset Louise more! "Take away my child?" she probably shouted at them. "Malcolm is my child! I can raise my own children!"

In 1938, months before she went out walking barefoot in the

snow, the nightmare happened. Welfare officials took Malcolm. Placed him into foster care with the Gohannas family, where he would eat dinner sometimes after school. Louise resisted but couldn't stop it.

The stress of her husband dying was too much.

The stress of having no money was too much.

The stress of the racist welfare workers was too much.

The stress of Malcolm getting in trouble with the law was too much.

The stress of Malcolm being taken was too much.

The stress of having another mouth to feed after her eighth child arrived was too much.

The stress of the father of her eighth child leaving was too much.

It all became too much in 1938.

• • •

A neighbor probably saw Louise walking barefoot in the snow with her child. She needed help. But too few people had truly helped since Earl died. That was why she was here: cold to the cold around her. Because the racist world had been cold to her.

No one came to direct Louise back home. Ensure she received treatment from a doctor. Someone called the police instead. They came and took her away. A doctor diagnosed her as having a "paranoid condition, probably dementia praecox." That is what is now called schizophrenia. It is a serious mental health condition and a leading cause of disability.

People are taught to be ashamed of people with disabilities. But there is nothing to be ashamed about. People with disabilities are people. Just as normal as anyone else. They don't need pity. All they need are accommodations: changes that allow people with disabilities the equal opportunity to live in society. Changes like ramps for wheelchairs or walkers. Changes like flexible work hours.

Changes like assistance to help a mother feed her eight children. When a person acquires a disability after years of racist trauma, what is shameful is the racist trauma, not that person.

But Louise may not have had schizophrenia. It seems as if the doctor overlooked the effects of Louise's recent pregnancy. She could have been experiencing what's called postpartum depression. This illness causes some mothers who just gave birth to withdraw from family and friends. It can cause mothers to have less of an ability to think clearly and make good decisions. It can cause mothers to be restless.

Or the situation may have been more serious. She may have been suffering from postpartum psychosis. This rare condition causes mothers who recently gave birth to be confused or paranoid or to have hallucinations and delusions. That is seeing things that aren't there. That is like dreaming while awake. Is this what happened to Louise in those final months of 1938? It is hard to know all these years later.

What's known is that she was taken against her will to a psychiatric facility in Kalamazoo, Michigan, on January 31, 1939. And state officials split up her children. Wilfred, now back in Michigan, and Hilda, the oldest, stayed at the family farm. State officials placed Philbert with the Hackett family. Reginald and Wesley were sent to the Williams home. The McGuire family was allowed to take in Yvonne and Robert. Malcolm remained with the Gohannases.

The state of Michigan deemed Malcolm's mother the problem. Rather than the conditions that depressed her, that broke her. Louise Little would be at that psychiatric facility for the next twenty-four years. Malcolm would rarely see her. His mother's mind, gone. His father's body, gone. His parents, gone. His anchors, gone. Gone.

Soon Malcolm was gone.

Malcolm, 1964

Chapter 11

HOMELESS

When police took away his mother, a thirteen-year-old Malcolm grew angrier and sadder. He had no way of dealing with the pain of it all. Except to act out. Maybe Malcolm questioned what was truly right and wrong. Authorities breaking up his family considered right? His parents teaching Black people they were equal to White people considered wrong?

Malcolm did whatever he felt like doing, whether right or wrong. A dangerous way of living. But he didn't care. Growing tall and redheaded, he looked older. Hung out with older teens. He smoked and sold marijuana. He stole money and cigarettes and candy from stores. Partied with girls at nightclubs and dance halls and pool halls. Went to the movies. Played sports at the Lincoln Community Center.

He rarely went to school. He despised West Junior High School in Lansing or, more likely, all the teasing about his poverty from his classmates. He had been permanently suspended from his previous school, Pleasant Grove, for his absences, and because White teachers and school officials believed he was disobedient and disrespectful to them. His absences showed up in his grades. In seventh grade, he earned four Cs. Seven Ds. Two Es. (Educators used to use E instead of F to mark a failing grade.)

Malcolm hardly slept at the Gohannas home. Sometimes he'd see his brothers and sisters at the family farm. Spend the night. But he spent many nights on the streets. Sleeping on benches in parks. Sleeping in abandoned cars. Sleeping at the houses of people he hardly knew. He was, in many ways, more than houseless. He was homeless. Nowhere felt like home. Nowhere felt like home because his parents weren't anywhere around town.

Maybe a part of him wanted to be gone too. There was that day Malcolm and a friend were talking to two White girls at a downtown corner in Lansing. That was a no-no then and, with some people, now. Racist Americans did not want Black boys hanging with White girls. Officer Knapp and Officer Griffin noticed it. Office Knapp walked up to Malcolm, pulled out his gun, and pointed it at Malcolm's head. His friend froze, frightened of dying. Not Malcolm.

"Go ahead, pull the trigger, whitey," Malcolm said.

"Ah, it ain't even worth it," said Officer Griffin, lowering his partner's arm and gun.

Or that time Malcolm wore a hat into a classroom. The teacher did not privately ask Malcolm to take off his hat or ask him why he wore a hat against the rules. He ordered Malcolm to keep the hat on and walk around the classroom until he told Malcolm to stop. "That way," he said, "everyone can see you. Meanwhile, we'll go on with class for those who are here to learn something."

Malcolm kept walking around the classroom, distracting his classmates who likely couldn't learn anything. Malcolm passed by the teacher's desk as the teacher wrote something on the blackboard. Malcolm saw a thumbtack. Placed it on the teacher's chair. Kept walking. He reached the back of the room. The teacher sat down. The teacher hollered! Soon after, Malcolm was expelled from school.

In August 1939, Malcolm was expelled from Lansing, too, after breaking rules outside school. A judge ordered him to be placed in a detention home. These homes had been organized in almost every state because adults assumed that misbehaving kids, like Malcolm, were the problem. When kids today come to school hungry and the hunger causes them to misbehave, should you put them in detention for misbehaving instead of ensuring they have enough food to eat? Is that right?

Black boys were more likely to be forced into detention homes than White boys. That is still the case today. People believe it should be that way. Because people believe Black people are bad parents and Black children are behavior problems. These are racist ideas. Like all racist ideas, they aren't true.

A state official arrived at the Gohannas home. Malcolm stuffed the few items he owned into a small box. He didn't cry. Maybe Malcolm was looking for a change, a new environment, a new school like Mason Junior High School and new teachers like Mr. Kaminska.

THE YALE POLITICAL UNION
Yale's Largest Student Organization

BOX 1951 ● YALE STATION ● NEW HAVEN ● CONNECTICUT. 06520

President
JOHN F. KERRY

Vice President
JOHN F. SOUTHWORTH

Secretary
JACK H. DUNN

Treasurer
ALLEN C. BARRINGER

Speaker
A. LEE LUNDY, JR.

Corresponding Secretary
HARVEY H. BUNDY, III

August 15, 1964

Mr. Malcolm X.
Theresa Hotel
New York, New York

Dear Sir:

I am writing on behalf of the Yale Political Union to extend an invitation to you to speak at Yale this fall. The Political Union, a nonpartisan organization, is the largest student group at Yale and each year it undertakes to bring a number of outstanding national and world leaders to speak before the students on issues of great importance and interest. Some of those who have appeared before the Yale Political Union in the past few years include Archbishop Makarios of Cyprus, Winston Churchill, Krishna Menon of India, former President Harry Truman, Adlai Stevenson, Barry Goldwater, Hubert Humphrey, and many other Senators and Congressmen. We would be very honored to have you participate in our program this fall.

Since we are only just beginning to formulate our schedule, we have a good number of dates to offer, and remain very flexible to any suggestions which you might have. I am enclosing a pamphlet which gives a full description of our meetings and the format which our guests may expect. Generally, we try to hold a press conference in the afternoon with the Yale Daily News and the local papers. Then after a reception for the members of the Union, there is a dinner which is followed by the meeting and the address or talk by the guest speaker. I am sure that if you are able to accept the invitation, we will have no trouble working out the details.

In closing, may I stress how much we would like to have you come and address the Union. In the past there has been a strong tendency to rely on Capitol Hill for our speakers and I am anxious to get away from that trend by bringing the most able representatives of other fields to our platform. I am sure that a speech or talk here by you would be met with great interest. Hoping that you will be able to join us, with all best wishes, I am

Sincerely yours,

John F. Kerry

John F. Kerry, President
Yale Political Union

John F. Kerry (future US senator and secretary of state) inviting Malcolm to speak at the Yale University Political Union, August 15, 1964

Chapter 12
MR. KAMINSKA

Mr. Kaminska was Malcolm's eighth-grade English teacher at Mason Junior High School. Mason is a town in Michigan about fifteen miles south of Lansing. The school no longer exists, but back then, it sat at the top of a small hill. The brown brick building is now Jefferson Street Square Senior Housing: small apartments for people fifty-five and older. Hardly any kids around Malcolm's age, around your age. No teachers today walking up the hill to their classrooms like Mr. Kaminska.

Malcolm liked Mr. Kaminska. Maybe because this teacher reminded Malcolm a little of his parents. Tall and mustached, Mr. Kaminska seemed more like a hard-nosed basketball coach than a tender teacher. He expected students to follow the rules. And follow him. He had strong opinions. Didn't mind sharing them with his students. Sometimes turned students off. But other students listened to him. Because he listened to students.

Students respected that about Mr. Kaminska. Malcolm too. Until the day Mr. Kaminska and Malcolm were alone in the classroom together.

Mr. Kaminska sat at his desk. Malcolm faced him from a student's desk. Maybe Mr. Kaminska dismissed the class early and asked Malcolm to stay to talk. Malcolm did not feel uneasy about being alone in the classroom with Mr. Kaminska. If anything, Malcolm felt uneasy about how his classmates joked on their teacher. The more Mr. Kaminska advised students on how to become a "success," the more it became clear he didn't expect them to find "success" in Mason. So the students joked on Mr. Kaminska for still teaching in Mason, for not listening to his own advice, for not finding himself success outside Mason. Malcolm made these jokes too. But on this day, Malcolm was all ears for Mr. Kaminska's advice.

"Malcolm, you ought to be thinking about a career," Mr. Kaminska said. "Have you been giving it thought?"

Malcolm had been giving it some thought. The future seemed oceans away. He had spent the last few years living hour to hour, and now he was adjusting to a new town and the detention home of Mr. and Mrs. Swerlein.

Older White people, the Swerleins couldn't be more different. Mrs. Swerlein: large, talkative, rude at times. Mr. Swerlein: thin, quiet, and usually polite. Malcolm had his own bedroom for the first time in his life. He had regular meals for the first time since his mother's money and mental health started failing. The Swerleins found him a job washing dishes at a local restaurant after school. For the first time, he had regular money.

Malcolm became popular almost from the moment he walked into Mason Junior High School. White students were always happy when he came around. Always wanted to play with him. It became hard to get through a school week without a classmate asking Malcolm to join their club. He never turned anyone down. Malcolm loved the attention. He played on the basketball team. He was elected class president.

Malcolm could have been giving more thought to a career. Because he had completely turned his grades around. He had always been capable. Now he did not battle hunger and living in the streets. He could focus on applying himself in middle school. Got among the highest grades in Mr. Kaminska's classes, in the whole school.

Malcolm sat there thinking about what he wanted to become. A profession popped in his head. A profession his family had leaned on many times. When the family first arrived in Lansing and their White neighbors tried to force them out. When his father died and the insurance company refused to give his mother the money. And all those times in court when he had broken a law or the court had removed his mother or siblings, the Littles needed a particular professional.

"Well, yes, sir," Malcolm said to Mr. Kaminska, "I've been thinking I'd like to be a lawyer."

In 1940, there were only sixty-one Black male lawyers in the state of Michigan. Then and now, there have been all sorts of racist barriers preventing Black people from becoming lawyers. Law schools not admitting Black students. Black people not having the money for law school. Teachers not encouraging them.

Mr. Kaminska looked surprised. He leaned back in his chair. He placed his hands behind his head. He half smiled.

"Malcolm, one of life's first needs is for us to be realistic. Don't misunderstand me now. We all here like you, you know that. But you've got to be realistic about being a [N-word]. A lawyer—that's no realistic goal for a [N-word]. You need to think about something you *can* be. You're good with your hands—making things. Everybody admires your carpentry shop work. Why don't you plan on carpentry? People like you as a person—you'd get all kinds of work."

This stunned Malcolm, coming from Mr. Kaminska. From the teacher who had given Malcolm high grades for using his *mind*. From the teacher who encouraged another student who wanted to be a veterinarian, another classmate who wanted to be a nurse. But all those students Mr. Kaminska encouraged were White. Mr. Kaminska had high expectations for them. Not Malcolm who got *better* grades? Just because he had brown skin? How is that fair?

This situation forced Malcolm to see what he did not want to see. Why he had become so popular in a town with a few dozen Black people amid nearly three thousand White people. Why so many White people in Mason were so nice to him. Malcolm's popularity had little to do with who he was on the inside and more to do with what Malcolm looked like on the outside.

His teachers, the Swerleins, many of his classmates, didn't treat him as another teenager. They treated him more like a favorite pet. A pet is something you care for and enjoy. Maybe you love it. Maybe you even respect it. But you don't treat it like a human because it isn't human. In White people's eyes, Malcolm wasn't human.

Take the Swerleins, who were big-time in town. Politicians and other powerful people were always coming over. Their favorite topic of discussion at dinner: Black people. All the things *wrong* with Black people. They would speak horribly about Black people with Malcolm *right there*. Call them N-words with Malcolm *right there*. Unbelievable? Believe it.

Thinking about this as an adult, Malcolm said, "It just never dawned upon them that I could understand, that I wasn't a pet, but a human being. They didn't give me credit for having the same sensitivity, intellect, and understanding that they would have been ready and willing to recognize in a white boy in my position."

The White judge who sentenced Malcolm to the detention home sometimes came by. The Swerleins would fetch Malcolm from his room. He felt like the Swerleins were showing him off. The judge's face beamed as he looked Malcolm up and down. Like a finely bred horse? Or dog?

In the same way, Mr. Kaminska refused to see that his best student wanted to be a lawyer. He saw the school's pet saying he wanted to be a lawyer. Which sounded impossible. Unrealistic. But his reaction was real to Malcolm.

Malcolm finally saw what racist White people saw in him. He

finally saw their racist ideas. It all hurt Malcolm. Almost like his father dying and mother being taken away all over again.

"It was then that I began to change—inside," Malcolm later said. It was then he started withdrawing yet again from school and society. It was then he started drawing away from White people. He could no longer be their pet. He no longer appeared happy to be played with. He became more distant. His teachers, his classmates, and the Swerleins had no idea what had come over him. Kept asking, "What's wrong?" He kept saying, "Nothing."

Malcolm had to get out of Mason. Before long, he was gone again.

A Legacy of Color, mural in Boston by local artists
Geo "GoFive" Ortega and Luis "Take One" Taforo, 2024

Chapter 13
ELLA

In the spring of 1940, before Mr. Kaminska hurt him, Malcolm had another life-changing moment. For the good. Ella visited Malcolm in Mason. One day, when he got home from school, she was there. At the Swerleins' place. Ella grabbed Malcolm. Hugged him tightly. Stood back. Took Malcolm all in. Malcolm looked at her.

Ella was Malcolm's half sister.

Remember his father, Earl, had married and had kids in Georgia before fleeing. Malcolm's father always lit up when he spoke about his daughter Ella. She had fled Georgia too. As a teenager. Early in the Great Depression. That time in the 1930s and the early 1940s when it was hard to find jobs and make money. Especially for Black people.

Ella landed in New York City. She worked as a security guard at a department store. Five feet nine and 145 pounds, she was asked by store leaders to scare away people from stealing stuff from stores. She did. But she also learned the tricks to shoplifting. When she moved to Boston, she always seemed to be in a store somewhere, taking food or clothing and exchanging it for money or giving it to hungry and unclothed relatives arriving in town. With all Ella's shoplifting and arrests, Malcolm's older brothers and sisters were not overly excited about her. But they knew she had saved and invested in real estate and had stopped breaking the law as much. They knew she cared about Malcolm much more than the

Swerleins in Mason. They knew Malcolm had a lot of relatives in Boston.

Ella and her relatives fled Georgia for the same reason Earl fled Georgia. To get away from racism. Especially the violence. The lynchings. Racist White people were so violent around Reynolds, Georgia, that the Littles kept guns to protect themselves. His father's sisters, Sas and Gracie, told Malcolm all about the terror. Aunt Gracie told him that a White mob murdered the young man she had planned to marry. His offense? Acting equal to the White people around town. But Ella and her relatives did not find a place without racism in Boston or anywhere else in the North.

Malcolm's father told him no lies about Ella. She was just like Earl. Ella presented herself to the world as a woman who led people, who did what she wanted, who got what she wanted. A grand woman. Large. Larger than Mrs. Swerlein, probably. Dark-brown skin like their father. Love for her skin, for herself, for her family, for Black people, radiated out of her like sunshine. What Malcolm saw his father try to put into people at those Garvey meetings. Looking at her, Malcolm probably felt the presence of their father. Joy filled him up after so many empty, sad days.

On that day when they first met, Malcolm told Ella about his high grades, his being elected class president. Ella showered down praise. Motherly praise, not sisterly. And Malcolm loved it. Ella shared about his relatives in Boston. How she had made it for herself there. How she turned around and helped other Littles come to Boston. How they in turn helped other Littles. "We Littles have to stick together." These words squeezed him. A teenager whose immediate family had not been stuck together for years.

Before leaving, Ella asked Malcolm to write to her. He did. The letters led to a summer trip to Boston in 1940. The Black community there happened to be a revelation. There were 23,679 Black people in Boston, about 676 times as many as the thirty-five Black people in

Mason. In certain neighborhoods of Boston, Malcolm did not stand out because of the color of his skin. He blended in because of the color of his skin. He liked that feeling (what his White classmates felt in Mason). He liked not being treated as a pet. He liked being treated as another human being.

When he got back to Mason, Malcolm felt unsettled about being the only Black person around. He did not like being treated like a favorite pet. He did not like all the racism. And then Mr. Kaminska shot down his dream of being a lawyer. Afterward Malcolm started writing almost every other day to Ella, telling her he wanted to come and live with her. She made it happen in February 1941. The fifteen-year-old boarded his second Greyhound bus to Boston.

HARVARD UNIVERSITY
INTERNATIONAL SEMINAR

CONDUCTED UNDER THE AUSPICES OF THE
HARVARD SUMMER SCHOOL
OF ARTS AND SCIENCES AND OF EDUCATION

6 DIVINITY AVENUE
CAMBRIDGE 38, MASSACHUSETTS

HENRY A. KISSINGER, *Executive Director*

5 June 1964

Mr. Malcolm X
Mohammed Temple of Islam
Temple 3
116th Street and Lenox Avenue
New York, New York

Dear Mr. X:

I am writing to ask if you might be able to come to
speak to the Harvard International Seminar, which is a program I have directed for the last several years.

The Seminar originated in 1951 in the belief that existing
exchange programs failed to provide an opportunity for the group
of individuals who were on the verge of reaching positions of
leadership in their own countries and many of whom were too active
to leave their countries for extended periods of time. These influential people find themselves so overwhelmed by the pressures
of day-to-day concerns that they hardly have the opportunity to
understand the purpose of these activities. Moreover, international
tensions and the confusion connected with newfound independence
have led to a situation in which, though communication has never
been easier technically, the ablest and most active people have become more and more isolated from one another. The result has been
either extreme nationalism or a sterile incantation of ideological
stereotypes. It is our belief that a meeting of the most promising
representatives of this group in an atmosphere of tolerance created
by a privately sponsored program would go far to promote a better
appreciation of common problems and of America's deeper values.

Among our former participants are the Congolese Ambassador to
London and former Minister of United Nations Affairs; the Japanese
Minister of Atomic Energy in the Cabinet before the present one;
Secretary General of the Christian Social Party in Belgium; the
French Finance Minister; the shadow Cabinet Minister for Civil
Aviation of the Labour Party of Great Britain, as well as the shadow
Air (Defense) minister; the editors of leading newspapers in Germany,
France, Israel, Japan, and many other countries; Deputy Prime Minister
of Turkey; academicians in leading universities all over the world,
and senior government officials from India, Uganda, Pakistan, Indonesia,
Ghana, and other nations.

An invitation from Henry Kissinger (future national
security advisor and secretary of state) for Malcolm to
attend a symposium at Harvard University, June 5, 1964

Chapter 14
BOSTON

It was Malcolm's second day in Boston when Ella sat him down for a talk.

"You don't have to start hunting for a job right away," Ella said. But she did give Malcolm chores. Washing the family car. Shopping for household goods. Walking the dog.

Malcolm was surprised. He had already started thinking about a job. Ella had enrolled Malcolm in a school downtown. But when he learned on the first day there were no girls there, he walked out. Never to return. He did not want to deal with any more teachers like Mr. Kaminska.

Not being in school wasn't unusual for Black teens. Back then, fewer than 20 percent of Black people finished the eighth grade. Only about 4 percent finished high school. Many Black teens did not have the option to go to high school like Malcolm. Many towns' high schools were for "Whites only." Or many Black teens needed to find work to support their poor families.

Ella told Malcolm what she told all the family members she brought to Boston. "Take your time. Walk around. Take the buses and the subway. Get a feel of Boston before you tie yourself down with work somewhere. Because once you start working, you will never again have the time to really see and get to know the city you are living in."

Malcolm liked what he was hearing. "I'll help you find a job when it is time for you to go to work," Ella said. And that was that.

He felt free to do what he loved to do. Travel. Explore. Learn. A school away from school.

Malcolm walked around the neighborhood of Roxbury, an area of Boston fast becoming a Black community. Immigrants from Europe had long lived in Roxbury and, before them, of course, Native Americans, namely the Massachusett people. But when Malcolm arrived, the Black population in Roxbury was increasing fast. Black migrants were coming to town almost daily, like the Littles from Georgia. Boston was 96.7 percent White and 3.1 percent Black in 1940. But most of these Black people were crowding into Roxbury and especially the nearby South End.

Ella lived in Sugar Hill, a section of Roxbury around Waumbeck Street and Humboldt Avenue. Where the middle-income Black people lived. In the 1940s, racism shut Black people out of almost every high-paying job. But some Black people found jobs as teachers, preachers, nurses, police officers, and cooks. Black people worked as maids for rich White families. Black people worked as waiters, errand runners, and janitors at White-owned businesses like hotels. Regular pay for regularly serving White people, keeping them out of poverty, putting them on the Hill.

They were known as "Hill Negroes." Malcolm couldn't stop staring at their quiet homes sitting back from the streets, overlooking yards. Big homes with yards of grass all cut and pristine. Malcolm couldn't stop staring at these Black people. As he walked, he stared at them standing, sitting, moving along sidewalks to work, to shop, to socialize, to attend church. The way they dressed. The way they talked. The way they looked at him. Some of them reminded Malcolm of racist White people back in Michigan: the people who didn't think he could become a lawyer. Some Hill Negroes tried to lift up other Black people as they climbed up the Hill. Other Hill Negroes acted like they were at the top of a hill and other Black people were down below them. Some Hill Negroes looked down on Malcolm. Because they thought they were better than Black migrants from other cities and countries. They thought they were better than low-income Black people. Actually, Malcolm saw some of these Black middle-income people as trying to be White. So White people would open the doors of opportunity for them rather than them forcing open the doors of opportunity for themselves. Malcolm did not like that. And he did not like those Hill Negroes.

Malcolm didn't spend much time walking around the Hill. He ranged out into the rest of Roxbury and then into the rest of Boston. In one of America's oldest cities, Boston's historic buildings and markers and plaques and statues of famous events and people kept his mouth open. Even today, you can't walk far in Boston without seeing a historical marker from the 1600s or the 1700s or the 1800s. Boston is a city to sightsee history.

Malcolm liked history but didn't like history class back at Mason Junior High School. Because he didn't like the history teacher. Didn't like his insulting jokes about Black people. And the textbook this history teacher used only had a single paragraph on Black American history. As if Black people had no history. The teacher read it aloud, laughing and joking between lines. The paragraph said that Black people were enslaved, then they were freed, and now they were lazy and unintelligent. Such racist ideas about Black people were common in textbooks at this time. Take a history textbook recommended by the head of public education in Michigan around that time: It described Black people after emancipation as "millions of illiterate freedmen, ignorant, lazy, and often vicious." Black people would "perhaps" never be equal to White people because they lacked "ambition to *do* something and to *be* somebody," the textbook said. "Vast numbers of the southern blacks are of the listless, aimless class who aspire to nothing, who are content to live in squalor and ignorance."

Imagine reading this as a Black student.

Imagine reading this if you were Malcolm.

This stuck in Malcolm's mind. He still remembered it as an adult.

One day, Malcolm became stuck when he explored Boston Common. Boston Common is the oldest city park in the United States. It was established in 1634. Malcolm stopped when he came across the twenty-five-foot-high and ten-foot-wide Crispus Attucks monument. He stared. He couldn't move. The monument had been built about five decades before Malcolm saw it, in 1888. The monument is still there today.

The monument honored Crispus and the four other victims of the Boston Massacre. When British soldiers opened fire on angry colonists on March 5, 1770. The Boston Massacre only increased the American hunger for independence from Great Britain.

Looking at the monument, Malcolm saw a woman holding a broken chain in her right hand. This symbolized freedom. In her left hand, she is holding an American flag. Malcolm saw her right foot stomping the crown of the British monarchy. Next to her left foot, the eagle—the symbol of the United States—preparing to fly. She is the spirit of the revolution.

Malcolm looked up above her and behind her on a huge rounded column. He read the five names: Crispus Attucks, James Caldwell, Patrick Carr, Samuel Gray, and Samuel Maverick. Below the woman is a portrayal of the Boston Massacre, showing Crispus Attucks lying dead on March 5, 1770. From his hair to his facial features, Crispus looks like a Black man. Malcolm had never heard of Crispus Attucks. He had never known that the first person to die in the Boston Massacre that set off the American Revolution was Black. Too astonished to say anything, Malcolm stood there in awe.

Malcolm did not know this, but Crispus was also Native American. His mother was a member of the Wampanoag Nation. Black history is American history. Native history is American history.

When you don't know Black American history, when you don't know Native American history, you don't know American history. But today, instead of teaching Black and Native American history in schools, people are trying to erase American history.

Boston Common is near downtown Boston. Malcolm probably spent the most time exploring there. Downtown Boston had the biggest stores he had ever seen. Like Filene's in Downtown Crossing. He walked on the cobblestoned streets. He saw boys shining the shoes of businessmen. He saw "sandwichmen" hawking their food. He saw townhomes pinned together, where everyone lived on top of each other. He saw the movie theaters! Malcolm told himself he'd see every movie that came. He saw the gigantic Roseland State Ballroom. The big posters outside its doors sharing the famous White and Black bands that were COMING NEXT WEEK! That first time, he saw that Glenn Miller's band was coming. It had just formed in 1938 and quickly became world-famous.

While walking, Malcolm noticed that Boston had two huge railroad stations: North Station and South Station. He couldn't understand why the city needed two. It was that big! At both stations, he stood outside and just watched people go in and come out, arrive and depart. Malcolm stood there wondering where they were going. Maybe wanting to go on a train himself? Maybe wondering where he was going?

Malcolm walked down by Boston University, a couple of miles from North station. He took in the Boston University that Martin Luther King Jr. would attend in a decade. Malcolm probably saw the Charles River that separates Boston from Cambridge and then wraps around downtown Boston. On another day, Malcolm took the subway for the first time. He rode it over the Charles River into Cambridge. He walked to Harvard University. He saw the entire campus. Maybe while walking by the college students, Malcolm daydreamed about attending Harvard or Boston University. Maybe the dream turned into a nightmare when he remembered what Mr. Kaminska had said about him being a lawyer, a career he needed to go to college to do. "You've got to be realistic . . . Why don't you plan on carpentry?" Maybe he got upset all over again. Maybe his anger remained when he arrived back at Ella's place on the Hill in Roxbury. Or maybe he was happy to be done with school and racist teachers like Mr. Kaminska.

Ella did not like that Malcolm did not hang around the Hill much. She did not like that he did not hang out with "nice young people" at a drugstore near her house. She did not like that he kept going down the Hill to the South End and Lower Roxbury, where the low-income Black people lived. That's where he spent most of his time sightseeing all the pawnshops, cheap eateries, bars, store-front churches, barbershops, beauty salons, poolrooms, and bars. All the games being played. All the sounds. The jazz firing out of clubs like the Savoy Café. It was all so alive! How could it not be alive? After working hard in service jobs all day long, all week long, for low pay, Black people had to blow off steam. At nights. On weekends.

After being told what to do, they wanted to do what they wanted to do. Like Malcolm.

They spoke their Ebonics, an African American language. Malcolm gobbled up words like *stud* and *cat* and *chick* and *cool* and *hip*. These words were spoken by the young Black men who hung out on corners, in bars, in poolrooms.

There, at the bottom of the Hill, people did not sneak around. Not even interracial couples. What was done behind closed doors in White communities and up the Hill was done out in the open. There, the people did not try to cover up who they were. They did not try to cover up their actions. They did not need to cover up their actions to cover up who they were, to claim they were better than other people. There, Black people did not look down on others.

Malcolm felt at home with them. "Even though I did live on the Hill," Malcolm said later as an adult, "my instincts were never—and still aren't—to feel myself better than any other Negro."

After a while, Malcolm stopped roaming alone around town. He started going out with three much older friends. And getting into trouble.

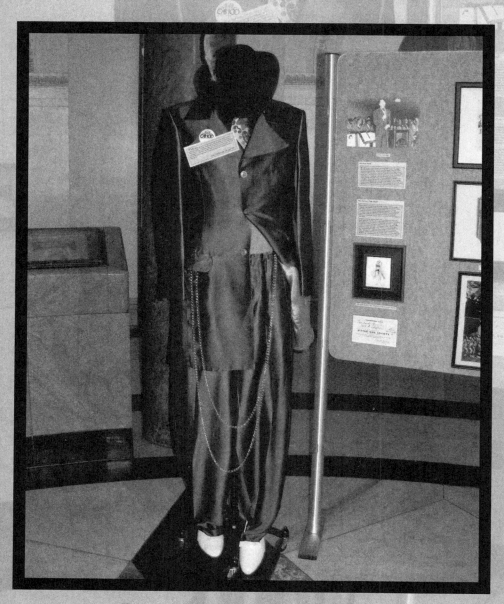

Zoot suit worn by jazz star Cab Calloway

Chapter 15
NEW LOOK

Malcolm probably went around town with one of the first people he clicked with: his half brother, Ella's brother, Earl Little Jr. About thirteen years older than Malcolm, Earl Jr. was hip and stylish and flashy and running the streets and getting in trouble with the law.

Before Malcolm hit the streets, he had to sound like he belonged. He spoke in a deeper voice to sound older. Malcolm had to look like he belonged. Young, low-income, urban Black, Latino, and Asian men were wearing zoot suits in the 1940s. A look that became identified with the famous dance, the jitterbug, and popular jazz musicians like Cab Calloway.

The suit pants: high-waisted and wide-legged. The suit jacket: wide padded shoulders and long, down to the knees. Usually brightly colored. Malcolm's first zoot suit: sky blue. The huge jacket flared out below his knees. He got a matching sky-blue hat with a feather and a four-inch brim.

He modeled it for Ella when he got home. She looked long and hard and said, "Well, I guess it had to happen."

Malcolm got the major accessory to the zoot suit: the conk. Short for "congolene," the conk straightened the kinky hair of Black men. Earl Jr. had a zoot suit and a conk. He likely gave Malcolm his first conk at home. Malcolm got the ingredients from the grocery store and pharmacy: Red Devil lye, eggs, potatoes, Vaseline, and soap.

Earl Jr. mixed the ingredients. Had Malcolm sit down. Rubbed

Vaseline through his hair and over his scalp and neck and ears and forehead. Combed in the congolene. It felt warm. Then Malcolm felt like his hair was on fire. It burned like the stove. Malcolm's eyes watered. His nose ran. He squeezed a nearby table in pain. Soon, he couldn't take it anymore. He ran to a sink. Washed the conk out of his hair. Earl Jr. took over and washed the rest out.

Malcolm saw in the mirror that his hair texture had changed. He saw a smooth sheen of straight red hair. He grinned. His joy buried his pain. All worth it. So worth it. Staring in the mirror, Malcolm vowed to never again step outside his home without a conk.

Malcolm reflected on this moment when he got older. "I endured all of that pain, literally burning my flesh to have it look like a white man's hair. I had joined that multitude of Negro men and women in America who are brainwashed into believing that the black people are 'inferior'—and white people 'superior'—that they will even violate and mutilate their God-created bodies to try to look 'pretty' by white standards."

But Malcolm and Earl Jr. were not thinking about all that. They were thinking about looking good. And to them, to look good was to look White.

Earl Jr. was trying to break through as a singer. Many of the major jazz singers had their hair conked. He performed in Boston's dance halls. Until one day, tuberculosis caught him. It was a deadlier disease back then. He died within months of Malcolm's arrival.

Earl and Earl Jr. now dead. Malcolm probably took it hard. All the loss of life probably caused this sixteen-year-old to care less about living. It all probably caused Malcolm to want to drive through life more recklessly. But with Earl Jr. gone, Malcolm still needed a driver. He didn't know the Boston streets. He found a new friend in a pool hall.

Chapter 16

OTHER MALCOLM

One day, Malcolm approached a pool hall on Humboldt Avenue in Roxbury. On his walks around town, Malcolm found his way to this hall many times. He stared inside its window many times.

The window to the pool hall was like a television. Malcolm gazed at the show. At the guys standing around the big green tables. All looking so cool.

Malcolm wanted to surprise Ella by finding a job. This seemed like the place where he wanted to work. He saw the guy who collected the balls for the pool players. He seemed nice. Another day, he had come outside. Saw Malcolm standing there, staring in the window. "Hi, Red," the guy said to Malcolm. Everyone had been calling Malcolm "Red" because of his red hair.

On this day, Malcolm slipped inside the pool hall. Quietly. He walked past the pool players to the back. The worker was filling up a can with powder that the pool players put on their hands. It helped them grip the stick better.

Malcolm asked how he could get a job like this. "If you mean racking up balls," said the man, "I don't know of no pool joints around here needing anybody. You mean you just want any slave you can find?"

In Black Boston, "slave" meant work, a job.

At some point, they probably exchanged names. The worker's name: Malcolm Jarvis. Malcolm Little told Malcolm Jarvis his name. Malcolm Jarvis nearly dropped the can and spilled the powder.

"My homeboy! Man, gimme some skin!"

And with that handshake they became friends. Over time, *best* friends. Malcolm Little called his fellow Malcolm by his last name: Jarvis.

Jarvis worked in the pool hall to support himself. But Malcolm learned Jarvis's real passion: the trumpet. He aspired to form a small band. He did not want to play around the country. "There's a lot of bread to be made gigging right around here in Roxbury," Jarvis said. "Bread" meaning money. "Gigging" meaning playing.

Jarvis hit the numbers way back. The numbers then are like the lottery today. But the numbers were illegal; the lottery today is legal. Jarvis used the money to buy his trumpet. Now Jarvis played the numbers every day. Hoping to hit again. So he could get the money to start his band and not have to work at the pool hall.

At least this is the story Malcolm told about how he and Jarvis first met. Jarvis recalls a different first meeting at the pool hall. They were both there. Near each other. The leather strap on Jarvis's expensive watch broke. His watch fell to the floor. Someone quickly scooped it up. The robber made sure Jarvis didn't see them. Jarvis accused Malcolm: He had a reputation for being slick.

"Give it back," Jarvis screamed at Malcolm, as he backed him against the wall.

Someone tapped Jarvis on the shoulder. "Man, he doesn't have your watch; the cat that got it split."

Jarvis apologized to Malcolm. A potential fight became a lasting friendship.

However they first met, what mattered is that Jarvis was raised in Boston. He knew the nightlife around the time that Malcolm ached to know.

So did Kenneth Collins, Ella's husband. Kenneth was from Lansing. He knew Malcolm's older brothers from when he lived in Lansing. Ella and Kenneth had probably connected on this. Now

Malcolm and Kenneth connected on this. When Malcolm mentioned names and places in Lansing, Kenneth remembered. Malcolm and Kenneth hit it off almost immediately. But Kenneth and Ella's relationship was on the outs. They argued a lot about Malcolm.

Malcolm's curfew was midnight. But when Malcolm started going out to nightclubs with some combination of Kenneth, Jarvis, and Earl Jr., he rarely made it home in time. Sometimes Ella would rush into the nightclub and grab Malcolm, screaming at her husband and brother. Eventually, Ella stopped. She could not stop Malcolm from doing what he wanted to do. Just as no one could stop her from doing what she wanted to do.

Jarvis continued to look for jobs for Malcolm. But it was Kenneth who found Malcolm the job of his dreams. Shining shoes at the Roseland State Ballroom. Malcolm had long imagined what it would be like to be inside. He wanted to witness the greatest bands in the world!

Ella relayed the news when Malcolm got home one day. The ballroom needed him to start that night. She wasn't happy. "Malcolm, you haven't had any experience shining shoes," she said. What she really wanted to say was that she didn't want him taking a nightlife job. But Malcolm was excited! So excited he could not wait to get there. He didn't even eat dinner. Malcolm left.

Ella's home in Roxbury, 2024, where
Malcolm lived from 1941 to 1944

Chapter 17
BALLROOM

The ballroom's bright lights were shining like stars when Malcolm arrived that night. A White man at the door was letting in the human stars—Benny Goodman's band. Malcolm approached the doorman and said he was there to shine shoes. The doorman directed Malcolm to the second-floor bathroom. That was where the shoeshine stand was located.

But Malcolm first had to go downstairs. He had to get a glimpse of the ballroom: the largest waxed wooden dance floor he'd ever seen! Under the rose-colored lights at the far end, the band members were setting up their instruments. Talking. Joking. Getting ready.

Malcolm headed upstairs. He found the second-floor bathroom. Kenneth Collins was likely there. He had likely just hit the numbers. Didn't need this job anymore. But he came to train Malcolm on how to shine shoes, how to get tips, how to hustle.

Kenneth was busy setting up his stand and sharing his skills. "Get here early . . . your shoeshine rags and brushes by this footstand . . . your polish bottles, paste wax, suede brushes over here . . . everything in place, you get rushed, you never need to waste motion."

Malcolm observed Kenneth closely watching men leave the urinals. Kenneth rushed over. He offered a small white hand towel. "Your towels are really your best hustle in here," he told

Malcolm. "Cost you a penny apiece . . . you always get at least a nickel tip."

Kenneth advised Malcolm to bring shoelaces. "Buy them for a nickel a pair, tell cats they need laces if they do, and charge."

Kenneth sold customers illegal drugs from the bathroom. Anything legal or illegal the men wanted. And Malcolm soon learned to do the same.

But as much as Malcolm loved the hustle, the money he made, nothing compared to the music and the musicians. Star musicians like Duke Ellington, Count Basie, and Lionel Hampton came. Malcolm shined their shoes before they hit the stage. When it got slow in the bathrooms, that meant the bands were rocking in the ballroom. Meant Malcolm had to see the action. Five exhilarating minutes felt like five hours.

Most of the dances at the Roseland had White bands. Only White people were allowed at these dances. Segregation was not just in the South. "Whites only" was in the North, too, in the 1940s.

What a racist rule. Black people could shine shoes or clean up the ballroom afterward. But they could not watch the White bands? How is that fair?

Black people had to wait until the Black bands came to town. They were allowed to come on these nights. These dances were not Black only. All racial groups came out to see the Black bands. Interracial couples came out. Everyone having a good time. Malcolm loved sneaking away from the bathroom to see these Black bands and interracial dances. He loved to watch the Lindy-Hopping dance. "Some couples were so abandoned," he remembered, "that you couldn't believe it. I could feel the beat in my bones, even though I had never danced."

Sometimes Malcolm stood there inside the door. Jumping up and down. Moving all around. Feeling it all. The manager would see him. The manager would order Malcolm back up to the bathroom and his customers.

For a while, Malcolm had dreamed of what it would be like to be in the Roseland State Ballroom. Now that he was inside, he dreamed of being out there on the dance floor. Soon, Malcolm quit his job. And he was there. Out there on the dance floor with girl-friends. Out there in the Roxbury streets. Everywhere at night.

But the excitement of it all got old. After he'd done it all, seen it all, Boston got much smaller. He wanted to branch out. He wanted to be gone again.

Harlem YMCA exterior, 2024. Malcolm and key
figures from the Harlem Renaissance stayed here.

Chapter 18

GIRLFRIEND

Malcolm had pleased Ella when he quit the shoeshine stand at the Roseland State Ballroom. Made her happier still when he took a full-time job at the soda fountain of the Townsend Drugstore near Ella's home. It was on the Hill in Roxbury. Where Black youngsters from the Hill hung out. They were going to high school and working toward a career.

Ella hoped Malcolm would befriend some of them. Turn his life around. Turn away from the nightlife and the illegal activities with Kenneth Collins and Malcolm Jarvis. Maybe go back to school and go on the path to becoming a lawyer.

Malcolm did befriend a high school junior he named "Laura" in his autobiography. She looked like his mother. A very nice girl who was in her books, not the streets. She wanted to make something of her life. She wanted to be a nurse. In no time, they became boyfriend and girlfriend. And Ella loved it.

But Laura did not rub off on Malcolm. She did not get Malcolm back into school and becoming a lawyer. Malcolm rubbed off on her. He got her into the nightlife. She stopped studying. She started lying to her grandmother, who took care of her. She started sneaking out at night to go to the Roseland State Ballroom with Malcolm to dance the night away.

One night, Malcolm and Jarvis were hanging out at the Savoy Café. A night spot in the South End. Malcolm spotted a brown-haired White woman sitting with a friend. When she pulled out a cigarette, he walked over to light it. Her name, Beatrice Caragulian. Malcolm bought Beatrice and her friend Kora a drink. Malcolm and Jarvis sat down and started talking to them. They all really hit it off.

Malcolm did not care that racist Americans were against inter-racial dating. In fact, legislation had been introduced in Massachu-setts to prohibit interracial marriage in 1913 and 1927. Interracial marriage was banned in the South. Malcolm did not care about that. All he knew was that among the young Black men he hung with, they gave you more praise when you dated a light-skinned Black girl than when you dated a dark-skinned Black girl. They gave you even more praise, the most praise, when you dated a White girl instead of a light-skinned Black girl. Because they had internalized the racist idea that the lighter and Whiter, the more beautiful. Plus White women had money, and Beatrice had lots of it.

Dating White women was off-limits to Black men. But Malcolm was daring, always doing things that would get him in trouble. Now and later, breaking the laws of racism.

That night was the beginning of their relationship. And the end of Malcolm's relationship with Laura. But Laura did not move back into her studies and a path to college and nursing. She fell deeper into nightlife. Into drugs. Into liquor. In and out of prison. She became "a wreck of a woman." And Malcolm regretted it all when he got older. He had wrecked her life. He was a wreck of a young man.

Malcolm also wrecked his relationship with Ella. Because he dropped a Hill Black girl for a White girl. He paraded this White girl into bars in Roxbury like she was a queen and Black girls were not. Ella hated Malcolm's zoot suits, his conked hair, the crowds he ran in. She hated that he lived for nights of dancing and gambling and drugs. "He was a real honest-to-goodness mess," she said later.

Ella had to get him out. Get him away from his White girlfriend. Get him away from disrespected and low-paying jobs like busing dirty dishes at a hotel where he worked after the drugstore. Get him away from the nightlife and drugs and illegal activities.

At that time, jobs were opening up everywhere. The United States entered World War II on December 7, 1941. The government started drafting men over twenty years old and sending them to Europe, Asia, and Africa to fight with troops from the United Kingdom, France, the Soviet Union, and other countries on battlefields against Nazi Germany, Japan, and Italy. These drafted men were leaving behind jobs. Malcolm was only sixteen years old, though he passed for being in his twenties.

Ella called a friend who worked at the Brotherhood of Sleeping Car Porters. A. Philip Randolph organized this union of Black railroad workers in 1925. Randolph would go on to lead the March on Washington in 1963, where Martin Luther King Jr. gave his "I Have a Dream" speech.

Ella's friend secured Malcolm a job loading up trains on the Boston railroad. He moved on to washing dishes for a train headed from Boston to Washington, DC.

Until the day came.

The Yankee Clipper to New York needed a sandwich man. It had a layover every other day in New York City. Malcolm jumped at the opportunity in 1942. He wanted it to be permanent. He became so good at carrying a box of sandwiches, candy, and ice—as well as a heavy coffeepot—up and down the aisles of the Yankee Clipper, he got a new nickname: Sandwich Red.

Malcolm did as he did as a shoeshine boy at the Roseland. He smiled wide and long for racist White customers to get bigger tips. From the days of living in Mason, Malcolm knew that racist White people loved smiling, happy-go-lucky Black servants. They had no problem rewarding smiling Black servants with money and attention. Anything that covered up their racism made racist White people feel good. Any anger that exposed their racism made them feel bad.

What made Malcolm feel good was arriving in New York City that first time.

Chapter 19

HARLEM

Malcolm had already changed into his zoot suit before the first passenger got off the train. He could not contain his excitement. The train had parked at Grand Central Terminal located around 42nd Street and Park Avenue. Midtown Manhattan. New York City! The place with the skyscrapers and the biggest of them all, the Empire State Building, which was just eleven years old.

Malcolm was not interested in seeing some of the tallest skyscrapers in the world. He had other sightseeing in mind. The neighborhood in Manhattan without the skyscrapers. But its history, its culture, its reputation in 1942 hovered over the Black world like a skyscraper.

Malcolm walked quickly up the stairs out of the station. The cooks from the train kept up. They all jumped in a cab. The cab driver sped off. Going uptown. Toward the reason why Malcolm took this train job, toward the neighborhood of his dreams: Harlem.

When Malcolm rode uptown that first time in a cab, he noticed that almost everyone walking the streets was White. Around 110th Street, people's skin color changed. He started to see nothing but Black people. He was here, in Harlem. Where huge numbers of Black people celebrated in the streets whenever heavyweight boxing champion Joe Louis won another fight. Where the jazz musicians who came by the Roseland and Roxbury told him to go. Where Marcus Garvey, dressed like a king, had led throngs of Black folk in a parade. Malcolm could still remember the pictures of the parades that his father showed off at Garvey meetings to open mouths and sighs.

Now Malcolm's mouth was open. Now Malcolm kept sighing.

Harlem was the Roxbury of New York City. In the 1940s, Black Southerners were still migrating away from racist White Southerners and into Harlem and Roxbury and watching racist White Northerners move out. In New York, fleeing White people usually moved back downtown where Malcolm had just come from.

Malcolm and his escorts, the cooks from the train, got out at 135th Street and 7th Avenue. It was still early, around 6:00 P.M. But they had to take Malcolm to their favorite night spot in Harlem. Malcolm looked at the gigantic sign: SMALLS. Between the tinier signs of CABARET and BAR. He was here. The one and only: Smalls' Paradise.

Malcolm walked through the double doors. He saw about thirty or forty mostly Black men sitting around a large, circular bar. It looked luxurious. The men were drinking and talking. All quietly. They weren't wearing loud zoot suits either. They weren't trying to call attention to themselves. To cover up for their insecurities. They weren't trying to flash their money. To cover up for their lack of money. They weren't performing for anyone. To cover up for their inability to find themselves. They looked like the epitome of cool. That epitome of cool: being yourself, comfortable within yourself. On another level from Lansing and Roxbury. What Malcolm wanted to be. Where Malcolm wanted to be.

Malcolm sat down at the bar. "Within the first five minutes in [Smalls']," Malcolm later said, "I had left Boston and Roxbury forever."

Malcolm later learned there were as many zoot-suiters and loud talkers and flashing-money types and performers in Harlem as anywhere else. The people he mingled with at the bar this first time were the more mature and successful men in Harlem running legal and illegal businesses. Almost like the mobsters of Harlem. The regular nightlife crowd was just getting off work, just eating dinner.

After leaving Smalls', Malcolm took a taxi ten blocks to 125th Street. He had to see perhaps the most famous Black theater in the world: the Apollo Theater. He noticed that Jay McShann's band was playing that night. On the other side of 125th Street, he saw one of the tallest and grayest buildings in Harlem: the Hotel Theresa. Visiting Black celebrities and dignitaries stayed there since they were barred from staying at White hotels in downtown and midtown in the 1940s. Or these Black people got rooms at the Braddock Hotel on 126th Street. The huge bar at the Braddock Hotel was a hangout spot for Black celebrities. Malcolm, of course, went in. It was jam-packed. He saw stars like trumpet player Dizzy Gillespie and singers Billie Holiday, Ella Fitzgerald, and Dinah Washington. He stood in awe again of Harlem.

Malcolm just sat there and watched the stars like he was looking through the pool hall window again back in Roxbury. As Dinah Washington was leaving with her friends, he overhead someone say they were headed to the Savoy Ballroom to see the jazz great Lionel Hampton perform. Malcolm followed them up the fifteen or so blocks to 140th Street and Lenox Avenue. He did not think any ballroom could top the Roseland. But when he walked into the massive and stunning Savoy Ballroom, Malcolm forgot about the small and shabby Roseland. He "had never seen such fever-heat dancing," he said later.

Malcolm got a room at Harlem's YMCA on 135th Street. The highrise building had 254 dorm rooms. Everyone who is anyone in Harlem stayed there at some point. Malcolm gazed at Aaron Douglas's iconic "Evolution of Negro Dance" mural near the entrance. The Harlem YMCA was an "incubator for the Harlem Renaissance," a burst of creativity by Black writers, musicians, and visual artists that captured African American culture, spread messages of Black pride, and inspired antiracist activism. Writers Langston Hughes, Ralph Ellison, Richard Wright, and Alain LeRoy Locke all stayed or worked there.

Malcolm kept coming on the train to New York City. And staying the night. When he couldn't get a room at the YMCA, he stayed at rooming houses. Where the owner let you rent a room for a night or two.

The more he stayed over in Harlem, the more he explored. He ventured to Harlem's Sugar Hill, where the wealthier Black people like Duke Ellington and Billie Holiday lived. He walked to the apartment houses where the low-income people lived but the rats were in control. Where garbage cans overflowed.

Malcolm heard choirs and pastors shouting from storefront churches. He smelled the aromas coming from greasy restaurants. He walked by beauty shops and barbershops firing kinks into straight hair with conks. It was hard to walk a single block without someone urging Malcolm to come over to their table and buy what they were selling.

Or inviting him to join a labor union or learn about how capitalism or racism was oppressing him.

Or inviting him to "rent-raising parties," which Harlemites were always throwing to raise money to pay rent costs that were as high as the number of rats.

Malcolm did go to a rent-raising party. He probably did buy a copy of the *New York Amsterdam News*, Harlem's Black newspaper.

The more Malcolm explored on layovers, the more he fell in love with Harlem. The more he fell in love with Harlem, the more he hated having to get back on the train to Boston the next day. The more he had to head back to Boston, the more he hated his railroad job. The more he hated his railroad job, the longer he'd stay out at night. The longer he stayed out at night, the more he did drugs and alcohol. The more he came onto the train drunk or high the next morning, the more hostile he became.

Racist White customers wanted their Black sandwich boys submissive, humble, quiet, and smiling. But the more the Harlem nightlife took hold of Malcolm, the wilder, louder, and brasher he became. Almost all his words were curse words. Customers complained. By the fall of 1942, Malcolm had been fired. He was still dating the nightlife and Beatrice. Even though Beatrice had married, and if her White husband found out, there was no telling what he would do.

Ella was surely angry. Malcolm was lost.

After being fired from his railroad job, Malcolm received his last paycheck. He also still had his railroad ID that could get him free travel. So he decided to go home. Not Boston. *Home*, home.

You know this made us well pleased, and we are getting set now to turn them out as fast as our finances will allow.

I wrote to Bill McLaurine last week. It has been over a year since he last heard from me, but I have some "overlaid" styled chests that I want him to try and sell for me. I'm quite certain he'll try to do so.

Hilda was here yesterday, and as usual we had a nice chat. She's getting along fairly well, and I think her nervous condition is improving.

Lionel Hampton was in town last week, and his trombonist, Al Hayse, came by to visit me. T'was the first I'd seen of him in six years. He's from Detroit, in fact I brought him by to meet Wilfred, Bertha and Wesley. He brought me up to date on that particular life, and though he admits they're all dying like flies from fast living, he's still living a fast life himself. I studied him, as he talked, and learned how lucky I've been. He's aged tremendously!

His impression of Islam has been formed from his observations of the various Muslims (so called) in show business who say one thing and do another, thus I didn't press the subject. But someday I shall introduce him to some real Muslims (be it the will of Allah). Hamp! too.

How is Henrietta? When I see her I'm going to give her and Sister Ruth a piece of my mind for their failure to write. I hope they are well.

My eyes are killing me, (I have much trouble with head-aches) so I'd better close.

All here send love.

As-Salaam-Alaikum
Your Brother,

Malcolm X. Little

Malcolm describing the "fast life" of his
youth in a letter to his brother

Chapter 20

HOME, HOME

To his brothers and sisters—and especially people in Lansing, Michigan—when Malcolm arrived, he appeared to be from outer space. He'd walk up to relatives and old friends, stick out his hand: "Skin me, daddy-o!" He told the most outrageous stories of Roxbury and Harlem. They saw his wild conk. His four-inch-brimmed pearl-gray hat over his conked hair. His wilder, oversize zoot suit with the wildest shark-gray color.

One time, he caused a traffic accident. A driver suddenly stopped the car and gazed at Malcolm. The driver behind crashed into the back bumper.

Mrs. Swerlein's emotions crashed when Malcolm appeared at her front door in Mason. She couldn't believe what she was seeing. Her mouth all open. It was the same when he went to a school dance his last night in town. Other teens—even the band—were amazed watching Malcolm dancing like he was at the Roseland or Savoy, showing his steps, flinging girls over his shoulders and around his hips. He signed autographs "Harlem Red."

Malcolm only toned it down when he visited his mother in Kalamazoo. She did not fully recognize who he was. Likely hurting him deeply. Maybe he partied hard—and spent all his money—to cover up that pain.

Malcolm returned to his new home, Harlem, New York. No job. No money. He went to the railroad office. Railroads still needed workers, with so many men off at war. He got a job on the Silver Meteor train to Florida. The gig didn't last long.

But somehow, someway, another dream job found him. A job that allowed him to fall into the abyss of lawbreaking. That afternoon after he was fired, he walked into his favorite hangout spot: Smalls' Paradise.

Chapter 21
SEVENTH HEAVEN

A bartender at Smalls' Paradise called Malcolm over. The bartender said a day waiter had been drafted into the army and asked if Malcolm would be interested in his job. Of course Malcolm was interested!

But wait. Worry overtook him. Ed Smalls, the bar's owner, and his brother Charlie would never hire Malcolm if they knew how wicked he had been. On the streets in Roxbury and Harlem. On the railroads. But they did not ask around. They had seen Malcolm in Smalls' Paradise many times. Just sitting at the bar. Very quiet. Observing. Malcolm got the job!

During the 1920s and 1930s, Smalls' Paradise was the top Black-owned nightclub in Harlem and had an interracial group of customers. Some White owners of Harlem clubs barred guests of color, kind of like the Roseland in Boston and its "Whites only" dances.

Smalls' Paradise had two levels. The bar on the main level. The club in the basement. In the basement, guests sat at rows and rows of tables watching performers onstage. Or they danced it up on a wooden floor in the middle. The club could hold up to 1,500 people. Many nights it did.

If you walked by this block today, you would never know Smalls' Paradise used to be here. You would never know it was the center of Harlem in the 1940s. There is no trace of it. Where the bar used to be was most recently an IHOP restaurant. The rest of the building holds Thurgood Marshall Academy, a public school for grades six to twelve. Kids your age there are reading books as you read this one.

Charlie Smalls told Malcolm the rules for employees. No lateness. No laziness. No stealing. No hustling people, selling them stuff. Especially army men in uniform. Everything Malcolm had done in his life and at his previous jobs. But Malcolm pledged to follow the rules. He knew he'd never be late. So excited, he'd get there early. Smalls' Paradise was "Seventh Heaven," he said.

Malcolm got to know Harlem's top illegal moneymakers at Smalls' Paradise. Men named Black Sammy and Bub Hewlett and King Padmore and West Indian Archie and Cadillac Drake and Dollarbill and Sammy the Pimp. The men who always liked when Malcolm brought around his White girlfriend from Boston. The men running the numbers, the local lottery—which Malcolm played almost every day with his tips. The men dealing drugs. The men stealing things. The men gambling. The Black men making the most of these illegal activities. Precisely what Malcolm wanted to do and be. His days of wanting to be a lawyer were over. Whenever they started talking, Malcolm started listening and learning. Especially to Sammy the Pimp, who became Malcolm's best friend in Harlem. Smalls' Paradise became his college, and the customers his professors.

One day, Malcolm served a Black soldier. The soldier claimed he had just come up from the South. Malcolm served him four or five drinks. The soldier sat there looking pitiful for a long while. Looking lonely. Malcolm felt sorry for him. He came up close. Asked if he wanted a woman. The soldier cheered up. Yes, he did. But connecting soldiers to women for money was against military rules, was against the rules at Smalls'.

Malcolm got caught. This wasn't a lonely soldier. But an undercover military officer. Malcolm was fired on the spot. Taken to the police station. Into a back room. In the next room over, Malcolm heard officers beating up somebody. "Please! Please don't beat my face!" Soon after, the police let Malcolm go.

Worse than being fired. Worse than going to the police station. Worse than listening to someone get beat up. Malcolm was barred from Smalls', from "Seventh Heaven." It was downhill from there.

CLOVER LEAF BAR AND CABARET

SMALL'S PARADISE, 135th STREET and 7th AVE., NEW YORK CITY

Smalls' Paradise around 1942, the year Malcolm first visited

Chapter 22

CRAZY RED

World War II still raged abroad. Malcolm wanted none of it. He had no interest in joining the US Army to prove to White Americans that he was just as American as they were. That he loved his country as much as they did. Because he did not love the country that killed his father, took his mother away, broke up his family, and kept him poor. He had no interest in what the Black press was calling the Double V campaign. Victory over fascism abroad and victory over racism at home.

Malcolm had already joined an army back in Harlem after being fired at Smalls' Paradise. An army of people trying to survive in Harlem. This army was at war against hunger and houselessness and poverty. Moving through all these poor people, Malcolm had learned a lesson that served him later in life when he became the world's fiercest soldier against racism. Many people engage in illegal activity. Not because they want to. But because they don't see any other way to survive. Or make money. Racism closes legal pathways out of poverty for certain people. Good-paying jobs were rare for Black people in Harlem (as in Roxbury). Racism meant "almost everyone in Harlem needed some kind of hustle to survive, and needed to stay high in some way to forget what they had to *do* to survive," Malcolm later wrote. "All of us—who might have probed space, or cured cancer, or built industries—were, instead, black victims of the white man's American social system." That system: racism.

Malcolm at eighteen years old should have been starting his first year of college, if only. Instead, he started selling marijuana as he had as a thirteen-year-old back in Lansing. A lot of jazz musicians coming to Harlem were smoking marijuana. They became regular customers of Crazy Red, as Malcolm was known in those days. Wherever they were in Harlem, Malcolm was there. He rarely slept. Because he worked nights. But he had money in his pocket. He felt free. He used his freedom during the day to go to the movies. Watch movies all day. Sometimes with his friend Sammy.

One day, Malcolm's sixteen-year-old younger brother, Reginald, came to town in uniform. Reginald was in the Merchant Marine, which transports cargo in and out of the United States. His ship came into New York for repairs.

Malcolm and Reginald got a nice hotel room. They talked all night about Lansing and the family. Malcolm told his brother stories about their father and mother that he didn't remember. Reginald shared what was going on with their brothers and sisters.

In the coming days, Malcolm showed Reginald all around Harlem. Malcolm was probably closer to Reginald than to any of his other brothers or sisters. Malcolm tried to get him to stay in Harlem. Reginald could not. He had orders as a Merchant Marine to ship out.

These were some disappointing days for Malcolm. The freedom and easy moneymaking did not last long. As they never do when dealing illegal drugs. After a while, the police figured out Malcolm was selling drugs. Started trailing him. Trying to find drugs on him.

Arrest and jail stalked Malcolm. He needed a way out. His friend Sammy suggested he use his railroad identification card. Travel with the bands along the East Coast and sell to them. Malcolm did. Soon, the heat on him cooled. Police officers thought he had left town.

One day, Malcolm got into a huge fight during a card game at Grand Central Terminal. He was barred from the station and the railroads.

First Smalls'. Now the trains.

Malcolm's world seemed to be closing in on him. He couldn't sell drugs anymore. So Malcolm got a gun. Started robbing stores and people. Started sniffing cocaine to cover up his pain from all the pain he was causing. He played the lottery. Hoping to score big. Sometimes he did.

Reginald's ship came back to Harlem. The two young men got closer. Discussed family a lot. Talked about how their book-loving oldest brother, Wilfred, had little opportunity to go to one of the big universities. Because he was Black. This time Reginald's ship sailed off without him.

Malcolm got some legal jobs to cover up his illegal activity. Like at Jimmy's Chicken Shack.

He had just turned eighteen years old on May 19, 1943. On their eighteenth birthday, men were required to register for the Selective Service System. This is a government record of all the American men eligible to be drafted into the military. Malcolm registered two weeks after his birthday. Soon, he received a classification: 1A. Meaning available for military service. He was ordered to report to the induction center for an examination.

Malcolm received these orders from the New York draft board. Because he registered from his new home: Harlem.

among us is strong...more so than in any other I know...and the
devils kept us split up for years...so think what it would be
after obtaining perfect unity...to surpass the love I now feel for
for my brothers and sisters would indeed be real paradise, for it
is that love that wracks my entire being, and shakes me into
submission to perfect peace and truthful contentment.

Yes, I'm aware many Brothers were put into the federal
institutions for not taking active part in the war. Surely
you must remember I would have taken imprisonment first also...
though I knew nothing, consciously, by Truth...I was even at that
time aware of the devil and knew it to be foolish for "yours truly"
to risk his neck fighting for something that didn't exist..
especially for the devils. Seclusion is the greatest thing in
the world for bringing out the Truth that lies inherent in all
of us...but we never take time to seek it.

Bertha was one in a billion. She's the only woman I
know who could sit and write page after page of nothing but Truth.
I miss her. All other women want to either talk romancing
holes in my clothes, or gossip.

Your facts are quite clear because you construct your thoughts
wonderfully, rhetorically perfect. You and Hilda had more schooling
than the rest of us. Reg is really doing fine, and I notice how
he becomes more adroit with his english usage as time passes.
For the entire family, everything seems to be working toward a
certain goal of perfection.

Is the story of the tower of Babel the explanation for the
english language? I notice the word fits in many ways to things
of this civilation, and so does the story. Likewise, if Edom

Malcolm writing about his draft dodging in a
letter to Philbert, December 12, 1949

Chapter 23

ACTOR

Malcolm approached the New York City Induction Center. It was eight stories high. Located on the other side of the long rectangular island of Manhattan from Harlem. It was where Malcolm and Black people rarely went in the 1940s: downtown.

Malcolm probably gathered himself as he looked at the building's granite, sandstone, and redbrick surface. Countless protests against wars, against the US government forcing people to fight in wars, and the first gay rights demonstration in US history, were staged outside this building. Maybe Malcolm caught a glimpse of the nearby Statue of Liberty. Likely not. He was focused. Focused on his act. An act to get out of being drafted into the army. And going to Europe, Asia, or Africa to fight against Nazi Germany, Italy, and Japan. And possibly dying.

Malcolm wore the wildest zoot suit in his closet. With bright-yellow shoes. He had rubbed his hands all through his hair. It looked frizzled and unkempt. What he figured the White examiners wouldn't like.

Malcolm did not walk into the building. He made sure everyone saw him *skipping* in. Skipping was associated with gay men back then. He knew the examiners were homophobic. He knew they did not want gay men in the army. He skipped up to a White soldier at the reception desk. "Crazy-o, daddy-o, get me moving," Malcolm said. "I can't wait to get in that brown." The White soldier looked stunned. Malcolm's plan was working.

There were all sorts of Black undercover military men in Harlem. Not just at Smalls' Paradise. Not just getting waiters in trouble. These spies reported to the induction office about who was or was not fit for service. For days before going to the induction center, Malcolm made sure to act the wildest around them. He wanted the military spies to think he was eager to join . . . *the Japanese army*. You read that right: the enemy of the US Army. He told everyone he could easily join the Japanese army if the US Army drafted him, trained him, gave him weapons, and brought him to Asia. Just a matter of running to the other side of the battlefield.

Malcolm told this again to everyone in the waiting room at the induction center. The forty or fifty potential inductees grew quiet. Listening to Malcolm's curse words—all his words, running his mouth a mile a minute. About how eager he was to be drafted. About his plans to fight on all fronts. For the Japanese, for the Germans, for the Americans. In all places. How he wanted to be a general.

The line moved along. Soon, Malcolm was getting a physical exam. Taking off his clothes. But it didn't slow his mouth before the white coats.

After his physical examination, Malcolm was ushered to the office of the person he had been waiting to see: the army psychiatrist.

The receptionist for the psychiatrist was a Black nurse. A young woman in her early twenties, she thought like a Hill Negro in Roxbury. She took one look at Malcolm. Became sick to her stomach. Malcolm, being Black, probably embarrassed her. She probably thought all Black individuals were supposed to represent the race well around White people. But no individual Black person—no individual of any race—is a representative of any race of people.

Maybe Malcolm was thinking about this as he sat and waited outside the psychiatrist's office. Probably not.

Malcolm heard a buzz at her desk. The nurse did not wave Malcolm into the psychiatrist's office. She went in. She probably made clear to the White male psychiatrist that she did not like Malcolm. Everybody was likely saying the same at the induction center. That Malcolm was not fit for service. But the psychiatrist had to see for himself.

The psychiatrist asked Malcolm questions in the quietest, steadiest tone. Malcolm responded in the loudest tone. Rambled for three or four minutes. About how eager he was to join the army. The psychiatrist sat there listening intently. He doodled with a blue pencil.

Just Malcolm and the psychiatrist were in the room. The two doors were closed: the door to the room and the closet door. But Malcolm kept turning around in his chair as if someone was listening in. He looked and sounded so very anxious.

All of a sudden, Malcolm jumped up from his chair. He skipped over to the closet door, got down on his knees, looked under the door. Did the same for the other door. He seemed satisfied. Malcolm came back to the psychiatrist and whispered fast in his ear: "Daddy-o, now you and me, we're from up North here, so don't you tell nobody . . . I want to get sent down South. Organize them [black] soldiers, you dig? Steal us some guns, and kill us [some white people]!"

Malcolm saw the blue pencil drop onto the desk. The psychiatrist looked up at Malcolm like Malcolm held a gun to his head. The psychiatrist fumbled for a red pencil. Malcolm had him. "That will be all," the psychiatrist said.

That was all for Malcolm with the army. His deception worked. The report of his examination, dated October 25, 1943, said, "The subject was found mentally disqualified for military service by the reasons of psychopathic personality inadequate, sexual perversion and psychiatric rejection."

He had avoided the army. But Malcolm could not avoid something else he was afraid of.

Harlem storefronts, 1938, on Lenox Avenue,
later conamed Malcolm X Boulevard

Chapter 24

HUNTED

It happened days after Malcolm went to the induction center. A violent rebellion in Harlem in August 1943. That year violent rebellions broke out in forty-seven cities around the country. Detroit. Los Angeles. Mobile, Alabama. Now New York. Usually from the same causes. Black people had grown frustrated with the soaring prices of food and housing. The bad treatment of Black soldiers. And perhaps most of all: police violence.

On August 1, 1943, a White police officer named James Collins mistreated a Black woman named Marjorie Polite in a place Malcolm knew well: the lobby of the Braddock Hotel in Harlem. Robert Bandy, a Black army private, intervened. Collins shot him. Bandy did not die. But Black people were angry. They stormed into White-owned stores and smashed windows. They took everything they needed or wanted and did not have. Everything they could grab and carry: food, jewelry, furniture, clothes, liquor. Black-owned businesses, like Smalls' Paradise, were spared. The Black rebels went after the White-owned businesses that they felt were exploiting them. Charging them too much money.

About one-third of New York City's cops came to Harlem to stop the rebellion. And they were joined by eight thousand members of the National Guard.

When it was over, six Black people had been killed and at least 185 people injured. Police arrested nearly six hundred people. In the aftermath, New York officials blamed the immorality of the people for the rebellion. Blamed people like Malcolm, who were engaged in illegal activity. They ignored the police violence, the high cost of living, and the poverty that drove people to violence. So the poverty and police violence and inadequate housing persisted. They persist to this day.

• • •

Malcolm got out of being drafted into the US Army. But he could not get out of the dangers of doing illegal things to make money. Robbing stores and people with his friend Sammy. Buying stolen items at low prices and reselling them for higher prices. Betting big money on card games. He even worked as a numbers runner. Meaning he collected the illegal lottery numbers people played.

But Malcolm fell on bad luck. A tall light-skinned Black man with a stocking mask robbed a Harlem bar. Possibly the same tall, light-skinned Black man who robbed Italian mobsters in the Bronx. In both cases, people suspected Malcolm. The bar manager hired some people to find the robber. They kicked down Malcolm's door one day. Malcolm convinced the men it wasn't him. When they left, Malcolm left town. He went back to Michigan until Sammy called. They had found the bar robber.

But the Italian mobsters were still looking for Malcolm. When he got back from Michigan, he was talking to someone in a phone booth at a Harlem bar. Two mobsters with guns came in. Then a cop walked into the bar. Allowing Malcolm to escape.

But there was no way Malcolm could escape the dangerous man everybody in Harlem knew as West Indian Archie. He had been running numbers for a long time. At sixty years old, nobody who wanted to live messed with West Indian Archie. Malcolm claimed he had hit the lottery for $300. So West Indian Archie paid him. But when West Indian Archie checked his records, it did not square. He thought Malcolm lied and thus stole $300 from him.

West Indian Archie heard Malcolm was at his friend Sammy's home. He showed up. West Indian Archie gave Malcolm until noon the next day to pay him back his money.

Malcolm borrowed Sammy's gun. Went about his day. He was at La Marr-Cheri on St. Nicholas Avenue when West Indian Archie came in. Armed. Cursing. Screaming. Demanding his money. Telling Malcolm and everyone listening about the deadline.

The code of the streets: No one shoots at each other in a crowded bar. Malcolm walked outside. Hands in his pocket on his gun. Malcolm waited five minutes. But West Indian Archie did not come out. Malcolm left.

The noon deadline came and went. Malcolm had no intention of paying West Indian Archie. Because Malcolm did not cheat him. Or he didn't have the money. Or he did not want to back down. But Malcolm was rattled. Scared. Felt he was being hunted by West Indian Archie. And the Italian mobsters.

His friend Sammy decided to save Malcolm's life. He called Malcolm Jarvis in Boston. Told Jarvis the situation. Asked him to get on the road and pick up his friend.

Jarvis arrived early the next morning. Went to Sammy's place. Sammy answered the door. "I don't know where Red is—he hasn't been here all night," Sammy said. "Cruise down there around La Marr-Cheri, sometimes he hangs around there. You get him. Don't even come back for his clothes. Hit the road."

Sammy did not want the two Malcolms to come back. Gunmen were probably watching the house. Sure enough, Jarvis saw Malcolm walking down the street around La Marr-Cheri on St. Nicholas

Avenue. Jarvis honked the car horn. Malcolm got scared. Then he noticed who it was. Malcolm ran over and got into the car.

"Man, am I glad to see you," Malcolm told Jarvis in the car. "Let's get out of here."

Within minutes, they were out of Harlem. Headed back to Boston. Back into Malcolm's old life there.

Chapter 25

DARING

It was early 1945. The year World War II ended. Saturday night. So you know a nineteen-year-old Malcolm was out at a nightclub with his best friend, the other Malcolm. Jazz music pounded from the heart of a nightclub.

The sound came from the intersection of Columbus Avenue and Massachusetts Avenue. In Boston's South End. One of the first major nightclubs in the area was named Little Harlem. The club was owned by a White man named Eddie Levine. In 1937, Boston leaders decided to "clean up nightlife." They created a rule that nightclubs had to close by 1:00 A.M. and could not sell liquor after hours. They did not use the rule to go after the all-White clubs in downtown Boston. No, they went after Little Harlem and other interracial clubs. Police stationed outside Little Harlem at 1:00 A.M. Police caught the club breaking the rule. The city forced Little Harlem to close in the spring of 1937.

By August of that year, another club had opened in its place. Little Dixie. That is the club where Malcolm and his friends were likely hanging out. There were so many famous jazz clubs near this historic intersection in the 1940s.

Today, you would never know that jazz once thumped out of clubs at this intersection of Columbus and Massachusetts Avenues in Boston. Because the night resembles the day. You see people pumping their gas at the Shell station. You see people holding coffee and treats coming out of Dunkin'. You see people ordering at New

York Pizza. A few doors down from the pizza shop is the only trace of what a young Malcolm saw in his day. A brownstone with a bright-red door on the lowest level. A sign swings announcing WALLY'S CAFÉ JAZZ CLUB. Before, it was called Wally's Paradise. Joseph L. Walcott, who went by Wally, founded Wally's Paradise. Probably inspired by Smalls' Paradise in Harlem, where Malcolm had worked. Wally's Paradise was the first Black-owned nightclub in New England.

Wally created his paradise in 1947, two years after Malcolm found himself at this intersection, in another club.

There was an interruption. Someone interrupting Malcolm and his friends from having a good time. A woman who had had too many drinks of alcohol. Someone called the police.

A White Boston police officer known for harming Black people showed up. He grabbed the drunk Black woman. Started dragging her headfirst out the door of the club. It all angered Malcolm. The racist police brutality. Malcolm walked up. Pushed the cop off the Black woman.

"Look, if that was your mother, or your sister, you wouldn't handle her like that," Malcolm said. "So don't put your hands on her like that again."

Malcolm would go on to become one of the fiercest critics of police brutality in history. The man who inspired people who spoke out against the murders of George Floyd and Breonna Taylor and Tyre Nichols. The man who inspired those three Black women who first said: BLACK LIVES MATTER.

But no one around Malcolm at the club knew that was in his future. They just thought he was daring and reckless and wild. Living on the edge. Indeed, he was. He had been running from death for a while in Harlem. When he arrived back in Boston, he was exhausted. Tired. Spent most days sleeping. When he wasn't sleeping, he was listening to jazz records. And smoking cigarettes. Three packs a day!

He was still with his White girlfriend, Beatrice, despite his time away in Harlem. She had made regular trips to Harlem to visit him.

Now Beatrice supplied him with cash to buy his cigarettes. He gambled her money on card games. He could not stop gambling with his money and his life. Or traveling back to Harlem to buy stolen items and resell them in Roxbury. Or stealing things himself. He stole a fur coat from Ella's home. Got $5 for it. Ella called the police. Had him arrested.

Malcolm also robbed someone back in Lansing. Was again arrested. Embarrassing his family both times. Neither time, though, did he go where he feared the most: prison.

It took Ella some time to believe what her eyes saw. What her brother had become in Harlem. Same thing for Jarvis, whom Malcolm lived with in Roxbury. Malcolm didn't wear zoot suits anymore. He didn't dance anymore. He had no time for showboating. He talked about all the dangerous things he had done in Harlem.

Malcolm felt the need to back up his reputation, so he wore guns like other men wore ties. He played with death like many people play in life. He consumed drugs like other people consume food. Jarvis was astonished by Malcolm's smoking. How often Malcolm put himself in dangerous situations. How fearless Malcolm seemed. Malcolm believed that a man "should do anything that he was slick enough, or bad and bold enough, to do."

Including shoving a White police officer! As much as Jarvis and Ella did not like how much Malcolm had changed, they admired his rebellion against the world. Against everything. Including what harmed Black people: racism.

After Malcolm shoved him, the officer stepped back. Probably shocked. Jarvis and their other friend, John, surrounded the officer.

They reached for their weapons. Ready. The officer looked at them. Back at Malcolm. The officer began to reach for his own gun.

"Oh, we've got more than that," Malcolm said.

The officer ran out of the club. Called for backup. Malcolm helped the woman into a cab. Paid her cab fare. He and his friends rushed into their car. And away. By the time backup arrived, Malcolm and his friends and the woman were gone.

But Malcolm and his friends became marked men. Meaning word went around police precincts that he and his friends were heavily armed and dangerous. What were really dangerous at the time were police brutality and racism. World War II had just ended in September 1945. The US government had passed the GI Bill in 1944. This bill provided government welfare to returning soldiers who fought in World War II. Money to go to college. Money to buy a home. Money to start a business or farm. But Southerners in Congress insisted that these benefits should be administered locally so that segregation could be maintained. These lawmakers got their wish, and racist local officials blocked many Black veterans from receiving benefits. White veterans used this welfare to move into the middle class. Black veterans struggled to carry on. Then racist ideas said Black people remained low-income because they were lazy. Racist ideas always cover up racist bills, like the GI Bill.

Many of the people who avoided the draft like Malcolm probably had an even harder time carving out a living than veterans. Remember how many people had found work during the war because so many White men were overseas fighting? When those soldiers started returning to the United States, things went back to normal. Meaning Black workers were the first fired. Meaning Black workers struggled to find jobs. Or good-paying jobs. Because racist rules allowed White workers to receive the jobs. Or the best-paying jobs.

The unemployment rate for workers of color more than tripled. When Black workers did get jobs, they still got paid less than White people working the same job. A government report in June 1946 warned that "the wartime gains of Negro, Mexican-American and Jewish workers are being lost through an unchecked revival of discriminatory practices."

Malcolm could only find difficult, low-wage jobs in and around Boston. But these jobs hardly paid for his rent or gambling or drugs. One night, Malcolm and his friends were possibly sitting around drinking at Beatrice's home. Jarvis. Malcolm. A friend they called Sonny. Beatrice. Her younger sister, Joyce. And Beatrice's friend Kora. These three White women all had money, just as Malcolm and his friends struggled to get by. These three White women were almost as daring as Malcolm. They did not seem to enjoy hanging out with Rudy, Malcolm, and Jarvis for who they were as human beings. They seemed to enjoy the thrill of hanging out with three "bad" Black men. Bad boys who broke the law. But they had gotten bored of just hanging out with people who broke the law. They wanted to break the law too. And get away with it. At one point, Joyce apparently said, "I'm bored." "Let's break into a house," someone, perhaps Beatrice or Kora, suggested.

Prisoners' cage in Middlesex County Superior Court,
where Malcolm and Jarvis were held during their trial

Chapter 26

ARREST

Everybody looked at each other. Joyce, Beatrice, and Kora wanting to do something daring. Jarvis, Rudy, and Malcolm wanting, above all, money. They all agreed to do it. They each had their roles. The White women scouting homes for what valuables they had. The Black men breaking into the houses and stealing the valuables.

They robbed their first home on December 11, 1945. By January 10, 1946, they had stolen nearly $10,000 worth of valuables from about a dozen homes in and around Boston.

At one home in Dedham, a town south of Boston, they took a wedding band with initials on it and an expensive watch. The owners filed a police report of what had been stolen. The police likely alerted jewelry shops and pawnshops in the area. *Be on the lookout for these items.*

When they stole things, the group normally sold them to a fence. A fence is someone who buys stolen items and resells them. Something Malcolm had done for years. But Malcolm wanted to keep the expensive watch. It needed fixing. So he dropped it off at a jewelry shop on Warren Street in Roxbury to get it repaired.

When Malcolm returned to pick it up, three policemen were waiting for him. The police arrested Malcolm. He had a gun on him that day. An additional charge.

The police brought Malcolm back to the precinct. Interrogated him. The police told Malcolm that if he gave up the rest of the crew, they would not add the gun charge. It was a lie. Malcolm named his accomplices in the burglary ring. Police arrested Jarvis. The White women too. They got out on bail since they had money. Malcolm and Jarvis remained in jail, awaiting trial.

The police officers, the lawyers, and the court officers were more upset that these rich White women were hanging out with these Black men than they were about the robberies. They tried to get the White women to say that they had been raped. A long line of White women had lied about being raped when caught with their Black boyfriends. A long line of Black men had been lynched as a result of these lies.

But these White women refused. The White women did testify that the Black men forced them to participate in the robberies. They lied to save themselves from going to prison. Remember, the robberies were possibly their idea. At the very least, they had eagerly taken part.

Ella thought a short prison stay might "teach him a lesson." So she decided not to secure Malcolm a lawyer. When defendants can't pay for a lawyer, the state assigns them a public defender. Most public defenders have too many clients and don't have the time to provide each with an adequate defense. But Malcolm's lawyer did not provide an adequate defense for another reason. "You had no business with white girls!" he told Malcolm at one point.

The judge read the sentences. Probation and no jail time for Kora and Joyce. Beatrice received a five-year prison sentence but served only seven months. The sentence for Jarvis and Malcolm: *eight to ten years*. Malcolm later claimed that two years was the average burglary sentence for someone who hadn't been to prison before. But the judge gave Malcolm and Jarvis longer sentences because they had broken the racist rule: Black men could not have relations with White women.

After the judge read the sentences, all hell broke loose in the courtroom. Jarvis rocked the cage he and Malcolm were sitting in. Their relatives stood up and shouted in anger. Ella screamed, "You're sending my boy to prison." Eight to ten years, five minimum, would destroy him, not teach him. Ella had probably thought he'd get a year and be out in months.

The judge ordered everyone out of the courtroom. An officer grabbed Ella's arm. Ella threw the officer against the wall. A riot squad came in. Forced everyone out. Malcolm stayed silent through it all. Stunned. Eight to ten years in the place he had long feared.

Malcolm was twenty years old. He should have been preparing to go to law school. Instead, he was preparing to go to prison. And its horrors.

But Malcolm held out hope that Beatrice and her money and her contacts would come to save him. At a second trial for robberies in a different county, Beatrice again testified that she did not love Malcolm. That Malcolm had threatened her. That she had been forced to rob houses.

Malcolm blew up at her in the courtroom. He shouted that she had been a willing participant. That she had selected the homes to be robbed. That she had stolen money from her family to rent the Cambridge apartment where they stored the stolen goods. But racist ideas cause people to believe the lying White women and disbelieve the truth-telling Black man.

Malcolm left the courtroom betrayed. By the woman he had dated for four years. To Malcolm, nothing angered him more than betrayal. Even as he betrayed Jarvis. Malcolm filled up with rage. A rage always there from his father and mother being gone. A rage from dealing with racism. He raged. As angry as he had ever been.

Bunker Hill Community College, 2024,
where Charlestown State Prison once stood

Chapter 27
CAGED

The bars. The door of bars slammed in Malcolm's face that first time. All he could do was look out at them. Really see the bars. Really see where he was. Really see what the bars said about him. Bars caging him like he was a predator. When racism and poverty had preyed on him his whole life—and both remained free.

Bars became stapled into his memory for the rest of his life. Their cruelty. "Any person who claims to have a deep feeling for other human beings," Malcolm later said, "should think a long, long time before he votes to have other men kept behind bars—caged."

All the bars could do was anger Malcolm. As if he wasn't angry enough.

But the bars were only the beginning. Mice owned the place. Ran around everywhere. And the stench of the cellblock. It smelled horrible. Like feces! All the time. Because there wasn't plumbing. There was nowhere you could go to the bathroom and flush the feces away. Each incarcerated man had a covered pail. So people would go to the bathroom. And it would sit there. For hours. Only dumped once a day. Everyone smelled it. Even when they ate. Because they also ate meals in their cell. Just horrible.

There was nowhere for Malcolm to run away from the smell. His cell was likely seven feet long and three and a half feet wide. Malcolm lay on his thin mattress and could touch both walls. He felt cramped all the time.

• • •

On February 27, 1946, Malcolm walked into this prison. It was called Charlestown State Prison. On the other side of the Charles River in Charlestown, Boston's oldest neighborhood. Next to Cambridge, where MIT and Harvard are.

It was the oldest prison in the country still in use. Built in 1805. Back when Thomas Jefferson was president of the United States. Back when slavery was legal in the United States and President Jefferson enslaved hundreds of Black people. After the Civil War ended in 1865, the required number of states ratified the Thirteenth Amendment to the US Constitution. Abolishing slavery? Not totally. The Thirteenth Amendment reads, "Neither slavery nor involuntary servitude, *except as a punishment for crime whereof the party shall have been duly convicted*, shall exist within the United States, or any place subject to their jurisdiction." Check the added italics.

Slavery still exists in the United States. In prisons. Once convicted, Malcolm became enslaved to the state of Massachusetts. There are abolitionists today fighting to abolish prisons just as abolitionists fought to abolish slavery before the Civil War.

Slavery sought to transform human beings into things. That would pick cotton and make money for enslavers. Same with prison. Massachusetts forced a number on Malcolm like every other incarcerated person: 22843. His identity: a number. "You never heard your name, only your number," Malcolm recalled. "On all of your clothing, every item, was your number, stenciled. It grew stenciled on your brain."

The prison population in Massachusetts was about 91 percent White back when Malcolm entered Charlestown State Prison. Compared to now, not many people were being incarcerated. But powerful people remade prison as the new holding pen for Black

120

people in recent decades. After slavery. After Jim Crow segregation. Beginning in the 1960s, the government started providing more money to "fight crime." Which did not mean eliminating racism and poverty. Which did not mean ensuring everyone had a good-paying job, good schools, good health care. Which did not mean eliminating the root causes of harm and violence. No, it meant spending more money on police, on surveillance, on prisons, on punishment. Making sentences longer for everyone. Making it harder for convicted people to be free from slavery to the state. Not just for Black men dating White women. But everyone suspected of breaking any law. Especially Black men.

In 1946, when Malcolm first saw those bars, there were 140,079 people in state and federal prisons in the United States. That was an incarceration rate of 99 per 100,000 people at the time. In 2022, there were 1,230,100 people in state and federal prisons, and the incarceration rate had more than tripled, to 355 per 100,000 people. It was even higher for certain groups: 1,196 per 100,000 Black Americans, 1,042 per 100,000 Native Americans, and 603 per 100,000 Latino Americans, compared to 229 per 100,000 White Americans and 88 per 100,000 Asian Americans.

Charlestown State Prison no longer exists. It was so horrible that the state closed it in 1955 and demolished it. But something new is there. Where Malcolm should have been at twenty years old. A college. Bunker Hill Community College.

Back in 1946, Malcolm had to smell it all, see it all, feel it all. Not college. Prison.

Brother Philbert X in Malcolm's address book, circa 1958 to 1961

Chapter 28

SATAN

O h, the cruelty of being incarcerated. Malcolm used bootleg drugs in prison in an attempt to remove himself from this cruel reality. As drugs dangerously do for people. As drugs dangerously did for him in Roxbury and Harlem. But drugs are momentary. He had to face reality.

Reality angered him. He let everyone know. He shouted the filthiest words and names to everyone in his path.

His first letter came from his brother Philbert in Detroit. Philbert told Malcolm his church planned to pray for him. Malcolm replied with more curse words than those Christians had ever seen in a letter. He hated Christianity because he felt Christ had been nowhere to be found in his life. He believed Christ had not helped him. Had not saved him from all the pain he had experienced. From his father dying, to his mother being taken, to his family being split up, to all the poverty and all the close encounters with death. But most of all, Malcolm raged at Christ for not saving him from prison.

Oh, the prison psychiatrist got it bad! Thinking probably of his mother, Malcolm called him every bad name he could think of. And the prison chaplain, that man of God—well, he got it even worse.

Then Ella came. His first visitor. Her first sight: Malcolm's number on his faded clothes. She caught herself from showing sadness. She cracked a smile.

Malcolm did not curse her out. She was sending him money. And he hoped she was trying to get him out. But he might as well have cursed her out. Because he did something far worse. He did not talk much. When he did, he showed Ella that he did not care about all the worry of his brothers and sisters. Their worry about what had happened to his life. Malcolm told her he did not regret robbing houses. His only regret: getting caught.

Ella left that first visit upset. As upset as she had ever been with Malcolm. She seldom visited him again that first year.

Ella was also upset when Malcolm told her to stop bringing Aunt Sas and Aunt Gracie to visit him. Because whenever his father's sisters came to the prison or wrote letters to him, they pressured him to become Christian. He wanted no part of Christianity. He told Ella in a letter that Aunt Sas "can have her gospel. For the past month I've been praying like mad." He had been praying for the appeals court to reduce his sentence. "They refused to cut my sentence because of the racial mixture. Well if that's the Bible way of justice, it's not for me."

This letter is dated April 12, 1946. Two months into his incarceration. That time of his cursing. Cursing at prison workers. Fellow incarcerated men. Or even aloud when alone in his small cell. The favorite targets of his cursing: the Bible and God. His anti-Christian rants got so bad that in no time, fellow incarcerated men came up with a nickname for Malcolm.

Satan.

Maybe Malcolm's shouts against God were more than him sharing his anger. Or religious views. Maybe they were about getting attention and respect from everyone on his cellblock. After all, at this maximum-security prison, Malcolm was in there with some men who had killed people, raped people, robbed people. Not many of them were willing to curse God. Malcolm did.

But there was another way to gain attention and respect. One person showed him how. A teacher who became for Malcolm everything Mr. Kaminska could have been.

Chapter 29

JOHN

At 8:00 A.M. each morning, Malcolm was ordered out of his cell with the other incarcerated men. They returned empty food trays. They emptied the stinking toilet buckets. They reported to workshops. Remained there until 3:00 P.M. They received one hour of free time in the outdoor yard before returning to their cells with dinner trays by 4:30 P.M.

Malcolm worked in the license plate shop. Making plates for people in Massachusetts. Then and now, incarcerated people worked for little pay. Legal since they are enslaved to the state.

The incarcerated workers had to make a certain number of plates per day. Just like enslaved people had been expected to pick a certain amount of cotton per day. A quota. After the fifteen or so White and Black men finished their quota for the day, they always seemed to find themselves sitting around John. Playing some game, like dominoes. Listening as John talked, as he taught. On all sorts of topics. Even guards would come by and learn.

John looked like Malcolm. About his height. Light-skinned. Middle-aged. Freckles on his face. John was in for burglary like Malcolm. He did not respond to anyone's hip language, "What'cha know, Daddy?"

John's voice, all gruff. Almost hoarse. He gave it to people straight. He said what he meant and meant what he said.

John spoke about philosophers. Like Kant, Nietzsche, Thoreau. People Malcolm had never heard of. He spoke about religion.

Causing Malcolm to rethink his questions about the existence of God. Causing Malcolm to stop his curses against Christianity. Causing Malcolm to curse less. John never cursed.

John's favorite subject: history. He told stories from the past as if he was right there. The incarcerated men and guards would sit there. Riveted. Amazed. Shocked. Malcolm especially. "What fascinated me with him most of all," Malcolm said later, "was that he was the first man I had ever seen command total respect . . . with his words."

What Malcolm had chased after in the streets of Harlem and Roxbury. What Malcolm wanted to earn in the cells of prison.

Total respect.

But Malcolm soon learned the words weren't all. John could never have served up all those dishes of words if not for their ingredients: knowledge. A knowledge that did not come out of nowhere. A knowledge that came from reading books.

Charlestown State Prison had a small library. Nobody visited that prison library more, read more books there than John. He read more than anybody because he desired to know more than anybody. What made John smart was not all that he knew. It's all that he desired to know. Anyone can know a lot. But it takes a smart person to desire to know a lot. No matter what. No matter where they are. Even behind bars. That is an intellectual. Anyone, anywhere, can be an intellectual if they have a tremendous desire to know.

John noticed the potential of an intellectual in Malcolm before Malcolm noticed it in himself. He seldom said anything to Malcolm. And Malcolm seldom said anything to him. But Malcolm's eagerness to learn from John no doubt impressed him. Malcolm sensed that John liked him. He did.

One day, John upended Malcolm's world.

Chapter 30
BACK TO SCHOOL

They were sitting around. Out of nowhere, John told Malcolm he had some brains, if he'd use them.

The message his father had been saying to Malcolm when he brought Malcolm to Garvey meetings.

The message his mother had been saying to all her kids.

The message his brothers and sisters had been saying to him for years.

The message that his high grades had been saying to him in Mason.

The message Ella had been saying to Malcolm ever since he arrived in Boston.

The message all his relatives had been saying to him in visits and letters.

But Malcolm did not hear it. Or did not believe it. Until John, the smartest guy around the prison yard, said it. John had faith in Malcolm. At a time when his family's faith in him felt like it was slipping away.

Malcolm did not even think to curse at John. Or argue back. He just listened. And kept listening when John told him he should take books out of the library. He should take courses in prison. Basically, Malcolm should go back to school.

Twenty-one years old now, Malcolm had not been to a library or taken classes in seven years. Since eighth grade in Mason. Since that teacher shot down his dream of being a lawyer. The lack of schooling had affected his grammar, vocabulary, and writing. "I didn't know a verb from a house," he said.

Malcolm felt he had nothing but time on his hands. So Malcolm went back to school. To learning. School is anywhere you are learning. He took an English course. Listings of available books passed from cell to cell. Malcolm put his number next to titles that interested him.

It is hard to know why Malcolm went back to school. Was he just interested in getting total respect in the prison? Was he trying to get back in the good graces of his family? Did he think the learning would help him not get caught next time? Or was he truly serious about being an intellectual like John: learning and growing? Or did he change his behavior because he wanted to transfer out of the hell of Charlestown State Prison? Maybe some of the above? All the above?

Soon, Malcolm had read all the books that interested him. Probably read some of those books twice. Probably read some of the books that didn't interest him. His friend Jarvis had been transferred to Norfolk Prison Colony. There, the library was bigger and better.

By December 1946, Malcolm wrote "My Dear Sister," asking Ella to work her magic. Talk to authorities on getting "me transferred to Norfolk." He wrote, "My only reason for wanting to go is the library alone."

Weeks later, in January 1947, Malcolm had to be disappointed. Transferred not to Norfolk but to Concord Reformatory.

When Malcolm arrived there, his mood probably cheered up a bit. Concord Reformatory was slightly less of a hell than Charlestown State Prison. A bigger library. Malcolm made use of it. Cells had toilets that flushed instead of those stinking pails. Incarcerated men ate in a dining hall instead of their stinking cells. All the incarcerated men were around Malcolm's age.

Malcolm worked in the woodworking shop. Doing what his father had done. What he had no plans to do in eighth grade or even then at twenty-one years old: carpentry. He made furniture. He had raged before against his relatives, but now he was making them small jewelry boxes. He had stewed in hate, but now he had nothing but smiles when opening day came for Major League Baseball on April 15, 1947. Jackie Robinson made his debut for the Brooklyn Dodgers. Breaking the racist bar that kept Black players out of this league for nearly sixty years. News of it all created a sensation at Concord. No one more elated than Malcolm. He became a huge fan of Jackie Robinson. Whenever Jackie played, Malcolm's ears were "glued to the radio."

In time, Malcolm's eyes were glued to letters from his brothers. Those letters changed everything.

Tuesday morning
11-28-48

In the Name of "Allah", the Beneficent the Merciful, the Great
God of the Universe...and in the Name of His Holy Servant and
Apostle, the Horable Mr. Elijah Muhammad. All praise is due to
"Allah".

My Dear Brother Philbert,

As Salaam Alaikum. If you could only realize the blissful
happiness bestowed upon me by the arrival of your precious letter
you would write, to me continuously forever. All praise to Allah
for the moisture of your letter...moisture that cools the dust
from my thirsty soul...drops of Dew from that ever-flowing Spring.
Please, my Brother, accept my most humble thanks.

You've changed. I can see it just in the way you construct
your thoughts, the rhetoric style of your writing. You seem
completely contented and more sure of yourself...and certain of
ultimate goal. Five years ago you were the one that I thought
would never find happiness. I praise Allah for Blessing you, my
dear Brother.

They are beginning Bible classes in here starting tonight.
That is why this is being written this morning. I attend to let
their conversations familiarize my mind with biblical incidents
...but I shut out their conclusions. You know you break my heart
by mention of the literature you were "going" to send, and then
not send it. I'm a bug for reading matter, Phil, because I have
so much time on my hands...and anything you could send me to read
would be dearly appreciated. Just give it to Hilda and have her

**A letter from Malcolm to Philbert acknowledging
Philbert's interest in Islam, November 28, 1948**

Chapter 31
NATION OF ISLAM

Remember when Malcolm first arrived in prison? His older brother Philbert sent him a letter urging him to become a Christian. And Malcolm replied with all the curse words he could think of.

Well, Philbert was back at it again. This time writing to Malcolm at Concord Reformatory. Informing Malcolm of his new discovery. The "natural religion for the black man."

Not Christianity.

Philbert told Malcolm that he had joined an organization called the Nation of Islam. Malcolm did not think much of it. You know that person who is always doing something new? That was Philbert. Malcolm thought this was his newest thing.

Before, Philbert had urged Malcolm to pray to Jesus. Now Philbert urged Malcolm to "pray to Allah for deliverance."

Malcolm had been reading books left and right, small and large. But he had not read religious books. He did not really believe in any religion. Any God.

Malcolm wrote back to Philbert, attacking the Nation of Islam as angrily as he had attacked Philbert's church last time.

Sometime later, Malcolm received a letter from Reginald. The brother who came to Harlem and hung out with him. The less religious brother. Closer to Malcolm than any of his other siblings.

Reginald knew Malcolm the best. Reginald knew how to get Malcolm interested.

"Malcolm, don't eat any more pork, and don't smoke any more cigarettes. I'll show you how to get out of prison," Reginald wrote.

Malcolm's eyebrows probably lifted as he read these words. Reginald had him. Malcolm would do anything to get out of prison. The young man who smoked three packs *a day* when he fled Harlem for Roxbury finished his open pack of cigarettes.

Malcolm never smoked another cigarette again!

And he refused to eat pork the next time the prison served it. All the while, Malcolm kept wondering: What could it be? Did Reginald have a plan to get him out of prison? Was it as good as Malcolm's plan that got him out of being drafted into the army?

Malcolm never thought to associate the two letters from his two brothers. He could have never imagined that Reginald too had joined the Nation of Islam.

But he had. All Malcolm's brothers and sisters had.

● ● ●

In Christianity, in Islam, in all religions, there have been breakaway groups in the United States. For Christianity, there are Baptists, Pentecostals, Episcopalians, Mormons, African Methodist Episcopalians, members of the Church of God in Christ, Unitarians, Seventh Day Adventists, and on and on. All claiming their version of Christianity is the truest. Same with Islam. There are Sunni and Shiite Muslims. But the Nation of Islam hardly resembled the Islam practiced by most Sunni and Shiite Muslims around the world. But the Black members of the Nation of Islam didn't know this.

The story of the Nation of Islam begins long before this group came into being. Like really long.

The story starts in the nineteenth century, if not before. When White people were enslaving Black people in the United States. And defending slavery through . . . you guessed it: Christianity.

White ministers were preaching that the Bible said Black people were the cursed descendants of Ham. Cursed forever into slavery.

No, the Bible doesn't say that.

This was also when nations in Europe were at war with nations in Africa. When European nations won, they took over the African nations. Europeans took valuable diamonds and gold and minerals from Africa. They all grew Europe's wealth and Africa's poverty. But Europeans said their colonization was not about stealing Africa's wealth. They lied and said it was about civilizing African people and bringing them to Christ.

Yes, Africans were already civilized and practicing their own religions.

By the time Malcolm's parents were born, many Black Americans still practiced Christianity. Many antislavery and antiracist Americans were inspired by their Christianity. A Christianity that said God had sent Jesus to liberate the people from slavery and oppression. But some Black people had started turning away from Christianity for the same reason Malcolm did. They associated Christianity with racism. And they hated racism. So they hated Christianity. Cursed it like Malcolm did. Wanted a religion that uplifted Black people.

Black people started looking into other religions. One of those people was a young man from North Carolina. A go-getting man. A man who thought highly of himself. A man who was born four years before Earl Little.

Prophet Noble Drew Ali, founder of the
Moorish Science Temple, 1925

Chapter 32
MOORISH SCIENCE TEMPLE

The man's name: Timothy Drew.

Timothy migrated to Newark, New Jersey, where he came across Islam. He ignored the fact that Muslims in the Middle East had been enslaving African people and colonizing Africa like Christians in Europe. But many Black Americans did not know this. Did not know Islam. The lack of knowledge about Islam in the United States allowed Timothy to create a new brand of Islam geared to Black Americans. Kind of like when Mormon Church founder Joseph Smith created a new brand of Christianity geared to White Americans in 1830.

At twenty-seven years old, Timothy founded the Moorish Science Temple in Newark in 1913. He was very handsome. An inspiring speaker. He named himself Prophet Noble Drew Ali. He grew the temple into a religious form of Marcus Garvey's UNIA. Preaching Black pride. Good morals. The advancement of Black people. Doing it all through the most eye-catching and royal clothes and ceremonies.

Timothy differed from Marcus Garvey in one key respect. Marcus urged his followers in the United States to think of themselves as Africans. To see the continent of Africa as their homeland. To proclaim: "Africa for the Africans." At a time when they were constantly fed lies that Africans were backward savages.

Timothy urged his followers to think of themselves as Asians. As Asiatic. As Moors. Not Negro or Colored or Black or African. To see their homeland not as sub-Saharan Africa. But Morocco in North Africa. An area Muslims from the Middle East had controlled since the seventh century.

In Newark, Timothy attracted crowds of low-income Black people. These were people who either hated Christianity or loved Timothy. People who were looking to be delivered from poverty and racism. People who wanted a religion that told them they mattered. That they, as Moors, were somebody. Timothy spoke of great Moorish armies. Great Moorish empires.

By the year of Malcolm's birth in 1925, Timothy had established Moorish Science Temples in cities with large Black populations like Milwaukee, Cleveland, and Detroit. He moved his new headquarters to Chicago. Timothy's Moorish Science Temples claimed thirty thousand members in 1928. Timothy ordered members not to smoke cigarettes. Not to eat pork. Not to drink alcohol. Not to straighten their kinky hair.

One of the members Timothy attracted to the Temple in Detroit was a con man named Wallace Dodd. A con man gains the trust of people, gets them to believe something that is not true, and then takes advantage of them. Con men typically have many names. Wallace told people his name was W. D. Fard. He claimed he was an Arab man from the home of Islam: Mecca. There is a large Middle Eastern population in the Detroit area now. But back then, most Black Detroiters had never seen a person from the Middle East. So they believed Wallace. Even as he looked like a White man with his very sharp nose, very light skin, and very straight hair. Arab Americans were not legally considered White yet in the United States at this time. Not long after Wallace arrived in Detroit, a local judge there denied the citizenship petition of an Arab man from Yemen, writing, "Arabs as a class are not white and therefore not eligible for citizenship."

Around the neighborhood, Wallace went from house to house,

selling rugs, carpets, silks, raincoats. His sales pitch: These items were special because they were from a Moorish "homeland" abroad. When not selling, Wallace lectured the Black residents. Urging them to not eat pork. And attacking Christianity and the "White man."

In common cause, Wallace gravitated to the Moorish Science Temple in Detroit. And Timothy liked him. Especially since Wallace claimed he was an Arab man from the Middle East, where the Islamic practices of the Moors had originated.

As the membership grew, so did battles to control the Moorish Science Temples. And so did the police brutality against members. After Timothy reportedly killed a rival leader in 1929, the Chicago police arrested him and beat him up. Months after his release, Timothy was dead. Possibly murdered by a rival or the police.

Timothy's death left his members looking to a new leader. On July 4, 1930, Wallace set up his first mosque in Detroit. Wallace Fard renamed himself Wallace Fard Muhammad. He claimed to be "the spiritual reincarnation of Drew Ali." He claimed to be building the Nation of Islam. Wallace kept Timothy's strict diet and prayer practices and added some teachings of his own, such as the racist idea that the White man was a "blue-eyed devil." Wallace made up a story that a Black scientist named Yakub created White people as a "race of devils" six thousand years ago.

What Wallace's Black followers did not know was Wallace was not from the Middle East. He was . . . (record scratch)

. . . a White man!

COME TO PRAYER

COME and learn of our GOD ALLAH
and HIS ways
and be forever Blessed

COME TO SUCCESS

MUHAMMAD'S MOSQUE OF ISLAM
5333-35 Greenwood Avenue
Chicago 15, Illinois

4847 South Woodlawn Avenue
Chicago 15, Illinois 60615
September 2, 1963

As-Salaam-Alaikum

In the Holy Name of Almighty Allah, the Beneficent, the Merciful Saviour Who came in the Person of Master W. F. Muhammad to Whom I submit and seek refuge.

Dear Brothers and Sisters:

Your aid to me in the spread of Islam by your efforts and your charity, especially your charity to the Poor Treasure, is greatly appreciated. I wish it were possible for me to thank each of you personally for your charity; but I pray Allah you will accept my thanks through this medium of a letter.

My beloved brothers and sisters, because of the ever-increasing spread of Islam--of which we are so happy to see today--it has increased the expenses and has added more burden upon us (the Believers) to carry until the new believers see and understand the salvation in Islam as you and I.

Nineteen sixty-two and 1963 so far has been a tremendously expensive year on us. Remember the trial in Los Angeles, California involving the 14 brothers that is costing us around $100,000.00, and the other court cases of our Muslim brothers in New York and in Louisiana; the purchasing of our "Muhammad Speaks" newspaper office; the loaning of money to aid different Mosques such as No. 21, Jersey City, New Jersey, and we had to save Mosque No. 6, Baltimore, Maryland by taking over its mortgage notes? And various other Mosques and Muslims have been aided from the Poor, Saviour's Day, National Security and Central Point Treasures until now, I am compelled to ask you to increase your donation to the Saviour's Day gift to $150.00.

If you can possibly give this amount without burdening or taking away from yourself that which you cannot give without suffering, please do so. And you who can give more, please do so; for we are now taking on another step of advancement in Islam which we estimate to cost us around $250,000.00. But I am satisfied you are going to love this step, and we want to have made this step by February 26, 1964 for you. Sisters, you may give what you can; I cannot set a certain amount for you.

Thank you, may Allah bless you to help find converts like yourself to help finance this great burden of resurrecting the mentally dead of our people.

As-Salaam-Alaikum

Your brother,

Elijah Muhammad,
Messenger of Allah

EM:bb

Nation of Islam leader Elijah Muhammad asking
members for money, September 2, 1963

Chapter 33

ELIJAH

A White man teaching Black people that the White man is the devil? Yes, you heard that right. Wallace lied. All con men do. All producers of racist ideas do.

Wallace's Black followers had no idea they were being lied to. Wallace was a White man from New Zealand, not an Arab man from the Middle East. Wallace demanded their total loyalty. Total belief. No room for questioning.

Many of Wallace's followers were migrants from the South. They fled Klan violence only to find themselves facing the violence of White police officers in Detroit. They fled abusive White landowners only to face the abuse of White businessowners in Detroit. One of these migrants was a preacher's son, Elijah Poole. He migrated to Detroit from Sandersville, Georgia. A short drive from Reynolds, the hometown of Malcolm's father.

Twice Elijah saw Klansmen lynch Black people in Sandersville.

Twice these Klansmen claimed they were acting on behalf of Jesus Christ.

Elijah grew to hate White people and Christianity. The hate didn't relent when he arrived in Detroit. White racism during the Great Depression pushed his family into a hungry poverty. He watched White men get the few jobs available as his family ate out of garbage cans. Elijah tried to end his life. Lying across the railroad tracks. An unknown White man saved his life.

White people clearly were not devils. Just like Black people were not dangerous. But racist ideas have a way of cutting people off from reality.

In time, Elijah fell for Wallace's racist ideas. Elijah became Wallace's trusted servant. Elijah went out recruiting more members. Wallace remained hidden. Wallace didn't want any Black people to see him. He probably did not want them to see he was . . . White.

But Wallace could not remain hidden from the Detroit police. They kept harassing him and his members. Trying to destroy the Nation of Islam. In 1932, police arrested Wallace and banned him from Detroit.

Wallace bestowed the surname Muhammad on Elijah. He allowed Elijah Muhammad to take over the leadership of the Nation of Islam. Wallace came back to Detroit. Police arrested him again in 1933 "in connection with the cult activities" of the Detroit mosque, amid rumors of "human sacrifice." Sent him packing again.

Wallace gone, Elijah took over the Nation of Islam for good.

Now it was Elijah's turn to make up stories. Elijah told members that "Fard Muhammad directed himself back to the heavens." Elijah told members that Fard Muhammad was actually Allah himself. Elijah told members that he, Elijah Muhammad, was the "Messenger of Allah."

Elijah barely grew the membership of Nation of Islam over the next decade. Partly because he served three years in prison, jailed for telling members to not register for the draft or serve in the military. The Messenger, as he called himself, got out of prison in 1946, the year Malcolm went in.

Over the years, Elijah's followers had gathered a reputation in cities like Detroit. For not smoking. For not drinking. For challenging White supremacy. For encouraging Black people to do what was best for Black people.

Precisely how Malcolm's oldest brother, Wilfred, lived.

Wilfred worked at a furniture store in Detroit in 1946. He seemed to be always defending his Black coworkers before their White bosses. Like that time he saw the White manager being mean to a Black delivery truck driver. "Why don't you leave this man alone?" Wilfred said to the manager. "You know good and well that he deserves his raise. You're trying to intimidate him so he won't ask for it."

The White manager gave the Black delivery truck driver a raise. Thanks to Wilfred. The driver's name: David Farr.

"You're a Muslim, aren't you?" David asked Wilfred one day. Wilfred had never heard of the Nation of Islam. David told him all he knew. David went with Wilfred to his first meeting. Elijah's ideas resembled Marcus Garvey's ideas that Wilfred had learned from his parents.

That first meeting turned into a second. Which turned into Wilfred joining the Nation of Islam. Soon Wilfred brought in his brothers and sisters. Together again, with a spiritual father in Elijah. Malcolm's siblings probably felt some sense of home in Detroit. Elijah, a father figure, like Earl. But it did not feel complete. Not without Malcolm.

Elijah Muhammad, 1964

Chapter 34
DEVILS

The more Malcolm sobered up and educated himself, the more letters Ella wrote and the more calls she made to the prison officials. She worked hard to get Malcolm transferred to the prison of his choice: the Norfolk Prison Colony. It worked. Malcolm was led into Norfolk Prison Colony in March 1948.

He passed the five-thousand-foot-long, nineteen-foot-high wall topped by three inches of electrocuting barbed wire. He walked onto the thirty-five-acre property roughly twenty-three miles from Boston. About the size of one of the small liberal arts colleges dotting the New England landscape.

Though still not free, Malcolm was happy to remain far away from the stinking cellblocks of Charlestown State Prison. He now had his own room with a door and a window. He was now back hanging with his best friend, Malcolm Jarvis. Their cells were across the hall from each other. Jarvis had forgiven Malcolm for giving him up to the police.

Malcolm's first visitor, his closest sibling, the person he wanted to see: Reginald. Malcolm had been wondering for months how not eating pork and not smoking cigarettes would get him out of prison. But Reginald started out talking about family, about Detroit, about memories from their time together in Harlem. Finally, he got to the point.

"Malcolm, if a man knew every imaginable thing that there is to know, who would he be?"

"Well, he would have to be some kind of god," Malcolm replied.

"There's a *man* who knows everything."

Malcolm asked, "Who is that?

"God is a man," Reginald said. "His real name is Allah."

Malcolm sat there quiet, listening. Reginald went on. He said God had come to the United States. God had made himself known to a Black man named Elijah Muhammad. God let Elijah know the devil's "time was up."

Reginald said the devil is a man.

Malcolm stopped him. "What do you mean?"

Reginald looked around the visitors' room. He stared at the incarcerated White men.

"Them," he said. "The white man is the devil. All white people are devils."

"Without any exception?" Malcolm asked.

"Without any exception," Reginald responded.

Neither Malcolm nor Reginald knew that the person who taught Elijah this racist lie—Wallace Fard—was himself a White man.

Soon after, Reginald left. Malcolm returned to his cell.

A parade of White people flashed before Malcolm's eyes.

The White Klansmen in Omaha, Nebraska, who came to his home when his mother was pregnant with him, who demanded to see his father. Murder on their minds.

The White people who set fire to their home when they first got to Lansing, Michigan.

The White people he thought had killed his father.

The White officials who cheated his mother out of the insurance money.

The White people who refused to help when his family fell into poverty.

The White people who kept coming to the home to call his mother "crazy."

The White officials who took his mother away.

The White judge who broke up his brothers and sisters.

The Swerleins in Mason.

Everyone in Mason who treated him like a pet.

Mr. Kaminska, who said it was foolish for him to want to be a lawyer.

The "Whites only" dances at the Roseland State Ballroom.

The White railroad passengers who only liked him as a smiling servant.

The violent White police officers. In Lansing. In Boston. In Harlem.

The White jeweler who trapped him for the police.

His White girlfriend who betrayed him.

The White judge who gave him eight to ten years for messing with White women.

The White prison guards who enslaved him like an animal.

A few days later, Reginald came back. He could tell Malcolm's past had opened him to the teachings of the Nation of Islam. He poured them all in.

I pray Allah blesses and guides all

ry deepest love to all of my dear Broth

As-Salaam-Alaikum

Yo

I pray Allah blesses and guides all of you always. My
very deepest love to all of my dear Brothers and Sisters.

As-Salaam-Alaikum

Your Brother,

Malcolm X. (surprised?)

P.S. I have ulcers or something but I've had my "fill" of
hospitals since being in here. Ole man, I think I'm
actually falling apart physically. Nothing more physically
wrecks a man, than a steady prison diet...and I've had
four years of it now.   (grin, faintly)

Malcolm describing stomach ulcers he is
experiencing in prison to his brother

Chapter 35
FORGIVENESS

Reginald talked to Malcolm for two hours about "the devil white man" and "the brainwashed black man." Saying things like "You don't even know who you are. You don't even know, the white devil has hidden it from you, that you are a race of people of ancient civilizations, and riches in gold and kings . . . You have been cut off by the devil white man from all true knowledge of your own kind. You have been a victim of the evil of the devil white man ever since he murdered and raped and stole you from your native land."

Reginald probably called and told his sisters and brothers. He told them Malcolm's mind was open. Because Malcolm started receiving at least two letters a day from them! He learned they were all followers of "The Honorable Elijah Muhammad," also known as "The Messenger of Allah." They told Malcolm about Elijah Muhammad, or what Elijah Muhammad had told them. That he had migrated North from a Georgia farm. That he had met Wallace Fard, who claimed he was Allah in human form. That Wallace gave the Honorable Elijah Muhammad a message. That Black people were "the Lost-Found Nation of Islam here in this wilderness of North America." That Black people did not know they were lost. That the "devil white man" had cut Black people off from all knowledge of their own kind, own names, own language, own religion, own culture. That the "devil white man" taught Black people that they were inferior and White people were superior. So they would obey and worship White people. But the Honorable Elijah Muhammad taught that he had come to save Black people. That he wanted Black people and White people to be completely separated.

One after another, letter after letter, Malcolm's brothers and sisters urged him to "accept the teachings of The Honorable Elijah Muhammad."

For Malcolm, these letters hit like bricks. Knocked his mind over. Made him question everything. Like being told you lived on Mars when you had thought your whole life you lived on Earth.

Malcolm did not know what or whom to believe. He sat there for hours at a time. In his room. Staring at the wall. Deep in his thoughts. In the dining room, he could not eat. Everyone around him wondered what was going on.

Then . . . Hilda visited him. The sister who had been almost like a mother to him. She told Malcolm that whenever Elijah came to Detroit, he stayed with Wilfred. She told Malcolm that Elijah had been to prison, like him. She told Malcolm that Elijah lived in Chicago.

Hilda urged Malcolm to write to Elijah.

Malcolm did. All embarrassed by his poor spelling and grammar. His reading and classes had not improved his writing much.

Elijah sent a typewritten reply! Malcolm was so excited to read it and pleasantly surprised to see the five-dollar bill Elijah had enclosed with his letter.

Elijah told Malcolm to have courage. He urged Malcolm not to be ashamed of being incarcerated. Elijah stated that White society deprived Black men, kept them ignorant, refused to provide them decent jobs, causing them to break the law to survive.

But the last step in converting to the Nation of Islam was the hardest for Malcolm. He saw himself as evil, as Satan. It took him a long and hard week to humble himself. To get down. On his knees. To pray to the East. To admit all the hurt he had caused over the years. To ask Allah for forgiveness.

Once he did, he felt like a new man. His past life of harm slid away from him "like snow off a roof." It was as if someone else had lived that life.

Overnight, Malcolm became a hermit. He needed to be alone to read and write letters to his brothers and sisters. He needed to write to his old friends in Roxbury and Harlem about the teachings of the Honorable Elijah Muhammad.

Because as soon as he believed, he wanted others to believe. He had always been a man of action. When Malcolm felt passionate about something, he gave it his all. And he had never been more passionate about anything than the Nation of Islam.

Passion has limits. Malcolm could not articulate his thoughts in letters. Especially to Elijah. He got upset with himself when he couldn't fully understand certain passages in books. He had to skip words. Because he did not know what the words meant. He wanted to learn more words so he could write better, read better.

He requested a dictionary and some pencils and notebooks. For two days, he flipped through the dictionary. Amazed at all the words! Amazed at all the words he did not know. He wasn't sure where to start. So he started at the beginning.

BS100-27649

"January 9,1951

Indeed you are an excellent judge of character. Your experience in dealing with a great variety of personalities has quite evidently enabled you to understand the subconcious workings of a man's mind better than the man understands himself.

Why do I say this? Well, you once told me that I had a persecution complex. Quite naturally I refused to agree with you. The illusions by which I was at that time obsessed would not allow me to see how true your diagnosis was; and I was too beset with the idea that I know something to realize that I know absolutely nothing.

I was guided by hate, envy and the craving for revenge....deluded by my own vanity and self-esteem; I was blinded with my own ignorance and false-sense of reasoning. In my effort to justify my many self-inflicted wrongs I placed the blame upon everyone except the one who was mainly responsible for all of my troubles.....myself.

There is nothing that can now be said in my behalf; I offer no excuse, no deffense.

However, even though I greatly mis-led myself, you will admit that I was sincere. I thought that I was being motivated solely by the earnest desire to think, speak and act in the manner that all Muslims should. Well, I was wrong!

Most fortunately, during the recent holidays I received an enlightening visit from my family in Detroit, and my many past errors were then made known to me. I am not, and never shall be,

-8-

too proud to admit when I am wrong....and with great remorse I now think of the hate and revenge that I have been preaching in the past. But from here on in my words shall all be of Love and Justice.

I only pray that it is not too late to make amonds, and to take steps toward rectifying my many mistakes. I thought that I was doing right, and was sincere in all that I advocated. Now that the Way has been made clear to me my sole desire is to replace the seeds of hate and revenge, that I have sown into the hearts of others,with the Seed of Love and Justice....and to be Just in all that I think, speak and do.

This humble message is a note of thanks and sincere appreciation to you for the kind understanding and patience that you and your subordinates have so often exercised in my behalf, and it is also a humble apology for the unrest and mis-representation of the Truth for which I was responsible for fomenting while under your jurisdiction.

If my present sincerity is doubted, tell me of just one time that I have not always spoken from my heart just what I felt. You always spoke frankly to me, and treated me with squareness... so how could I ever be any other way except square and frank with you?

Very sincerely

/s/ Malcolm .. Little"

Muslims known to him either shave their hair or wear goatees.

According to records the Subject wears chin whiskers.

-9-

A prison letter to Elijah Muhammad, January 9, 1951

Chapter 36
A TO Z

A. Malcolm copied down everything on the first page of the dictionary. All the *A* words there, their meanings, the punctuation marks. Words like *aardvark*, a mammal in Africa that lives off termites. He read what he wrote down. Sounded it aloud. Again and again. Malcolm had an excellent memory. Once he wrote the words down and sounded them out, he remembered them.

It took him all day to copy down and sound aloud the first page of the dictionary. The following day, he did the next page of *A* words. The next day, the page after that. Until he had copied down and sounded aloud all the *A* words in the dictionary. He learned so much. Not just the words. But about people and places and things and historical events. The more he learned, the more he wanted to learn.

He went on to copying the *B*s. And the *C*s and the *D*s and the *E*s, until he finished all the words. *The entire dictionary.* It took him months. But nothing he had ever done for himself freed him as much. Oh, the power of learning. He could now fully articulate his thoughts in letters. He could now read books and fully *understand* them!

And Malcolm did read! Almost every available moment Malcolm spent reading. Nothing could pry him away from books. He felt the reading freed him from ignorance. "In fact, up to then, I never had been so truly free in my life," he said later.

The Norfolk Prison Colony's library was in its school building. Where professors from colleges like Boston University taught classes. But none of their students, whether incarcerated or not, were reading anywhere close to the number of books Malcolm was reading on his own. Malcolm read more than college professors.

• • •

Incarcerated men at Charlestown State Prison largely constructed Norfolk Prison Colony. They began building it in 1927. While other prisons were about punishment, Norfolk was founded to focus on rehabilitation. Not just punishment. So incarcerated people can grow before returning to society. In theory. But critics called the prison a "country club" for incarcerated people. They did not want the incarcerated people to heal and find and hone their talents. Critics wanted prisons to solely punish people.

In 1955, the Norfolk Prison Colony became MCI-Norfolk. By the 1980s, the prison had changed. Redemption through education and community is no longer the focus at Norfolk—just punishment. It is now the largest state prison in Massachusetts. And when an incarcerated person gets out and harms someone, the state only blames the former prisoner. And arrests and incarcerates them again. No resources for healing the victim of the harm. No resources for healing the person doing the harm. Just punishment, which doesn't stop the harm. And a disproportionate amount of people being punished in this way today are Black.

• • •

Elijah taught his followers that when White people write history, they leave Black people out. No other teaching hit Malcolm harder. It instantly sent him back to Mason. Back to his seventh-grade US history class. Back to the history textbook that covered Black people in one paragraph. Back to the White history teacher reading the

152

paragraph aloud. And laughing. And joking, "Negroes' feet are so big that when they walk, they leave a hole in the ground." Back to how bad he felt in that moment. That is how Black students still feel today when textbooks or teachers joke about Black history. Or don't teach it at all. That is how all students should feel when deprived of history.

But now, Malcolm felt so good reading about the glorious civilizations in Africa before European enslavers and colonizers arrived. He read about African American history from prominent scholars like W. E. B. Du Bois and Carter G. Woodson. He read about Mahatma Gandhi's struggle to push the British out of India. About China's resistance to Europeans. He read ancient and recent philosophers. But nothing shocked him more, interested him more than reading about the enslavement of Black people. "The world's most monstrous crime." Europeans enslaved and sold more than twelve million African people. Nothing excited him more than reading about Nat Turner. An enslaved preacher who launched a violent revolt in Virginia to free Black people from slavery in 1831. "I could spend the rest of my life reading," Malcolm said later.

Malcolm liked reading on his bed in his cell. He hated "lights out" every night around 10:00 P.M. That's when Malcolm jumped out of his bed. He went and sat on the hard floor where a light in the hall shined into a part of his room. And read. Until a guard approached. He jumped back into his bed. Acted like he was asleep. Until the guard left. Moved back onto the floor and read some more by that sliver of hall light. Until three or four in the morning. Night after night.

Only sleeping and eating and writing letters and the weekly debate club took Malcolm away from reading. The debate club was what Malcolm called his "baptism into public speaking." He developed his debating and speaking skills in matches against other supersmart incarcerated men and against some of the nation's best debate teams from MIT, Harvard, and Yale. It was in these jailhouse debates that Malcolm acquired the skills to one day become one of the greatest debaters and public speakers in the world.

But nothing prepared Malcolm to debate his own brother Reginald on Elijah Muhammad!

Chapter 37

FAITH

In late 1949, Reginald visited Malcolm in prison. Malcolm had been following Elijah for more than a year. But the brother who introduced him to Elijah attacked Elijah during that visit. Reginald said Elijah wasn't honorable after all. Reginald said Elijah wasn't the Messenger of Allah. Reginald called Elijah a hypocrite. The worst thing you could call someone in the Nation of Islam was a hypocrite.

It caught Malcolm off guard. Like the day Reginald first told him about the Nation. Malcolm had so much respect for Reginald and respect for Elijah. Didn't know what to believe, whom to believe. Malcolm trusted Reginald more than anyone in the world. And "Islam and Mr. Elijah Muhammad had changed my whole world," he said.

Reginald had a sexual relationship with the secretary of the New York City mosque of the Nation of Islam. They were not married. Making sex forbidden. Elijah was told. He suspended Reginald from the Nation. Angering Reginald. Because Reginald knew that Elijah had sexual relationships with *his* secretaries in Chicago. The hypocrisy: punishing someone for something you are doing. But Elijah denied the accusation.

Malcolm felt the need to defend his brother. He wrote to Elijah, explaining how much Reginald meant to him. Malcolm dropped the letter in the prison's mailbox. He spent the night praying to Allah. Praying for relief from the confusion he was feeling.

The next night, Malcolm was lying on his bed. Probably reading. All of a sudden, Malcolm said he saw a man sitting beside him in a chair. The man wore a dark suit. He wasn't Black or White. He looked Middle Eastern. The man had oily black hair.

Malcolm knew he wasn't dreaming. He didn't get scared. He looked right into the man's face. The man didn't speak. Malcolm didn't speak. As suddenly as he came, the man was gone.

Malcolm came to believe he saw Wallace Fard, the founder of the Nation of Islam, because Wallace had claimed he was Middle Eastern (when he was really White). Malcolm came to see this vision as his first step of clarity. The second was when Elijah replied to his letter. Elijah could tell Malcolm was having a crisis of faith.

"If you once believed in the truth," Elijah wrote, "and now you are beginning to doubt the truth, you didn't believe the truth in the first place. What could make you doubt the truth other than your own weak self?"

Malcolm did not know that Reginald was telling the truth. Malcolm believed whatever Elijah told him. Reading Elijah's letter removed the doubt and the confusion from Malcolm's mind. Watching Reginald's life fall apart in the aftermath of being expelled from the Nation kept the doubt and confusion out of Malcolm's mind.

Reginald kept visiting Malcolm. His once-nice clothes, now shabby. His once-clear words, now garbled. Malcolm had grown a beard. Reginald said each of Malcolm's hairs was a snake. And then Reginald started walking the streets of Roxbury telling people that he was the Messenger of Allah. Then that he was Allah. Then that he was greater than Allah. Reginald seemed to be growing more and more mentally unwell. Probably because all his brothers and sisters had rejected him for Elijah. Malcolm thought Reginald was being punished by Allah for not accepting "the truth." In time, officials picked him up. Put Reginald in a psychiatric institution, the same type of facility his mother resided in for all those years.

• • •

Sometimes a crisis in faith can strengthen one's faith. It did for Malcolm. Because he went from believing to getting even more people to believe. In time, no one brought more people into the Nation of Islam than Malcolm. Probably because he became a kind of lawyer after all: Black America's chief prosecutor of the United States. Charging the nation with racism. Charging the nation with violating the human rights of Black Americans. But that was years away.

He started by bringing together a small group of Black Muslims at Norfolk. Malcolm pressed for religious freedom in prison. A sacred right in the First Amendment to the US Constitution that believers of Islam, Judaism, Buddhism, traditional African religions, and other religions hardly had in 1950. Only Christians. Malcolm had to live off bread and cheese because cooks kept serving his food with utensils that had touched pork. But Malcolm fought for food without pork, cells that faced east for prayer, and more books by Black authors. He even wrote a letter to President Harry Truman, pledging his opposition to the Korean War.

All these fights led to punishment. In March 1950, Malcolm and his fellow incarcerated Muslims were transferred back to the hellhole of Charlestown State Prison.

Malcolm tried to make the most of it. By recruiting his fellow incarcerated Black men to the Nation of Islam. A lot of them attended Bible class. Malcolm went.

Leading the class one day was a tall, blond-haired, blue-eyed Harvard graduate student. After his lecture, the teacher encouraged the group to ask questions.

"What color was Paul?" Malcolm asked. "He had to be black . . . because he was a Hebrew . . . and the original Hebrews were black . . . weren't they?"

The White teacher's face became red. He answered, "Yes."

Malcolm was only getting started. "What color was Jesus . . . he was Hebrew, too . . . wasn't he?" Malcolm asked.

Now Malcolm had the attention of the incarcerated Black and White men in the room. They sat upright. All their lives Jesus had been pictured as White. The instructor walked around the room, thinking. He finally stopped. Probably looked at Malcolm. He said, "Jesus was brown."

Malcolm had gotten the Bible study instructor to admit that Jesus was not White!

Story of the exchange spread as only gossip can. Incarcerated Black men were the proudest. They kept coming up to Malcolm. Every chance Malcolm got, he'd reply, "My man! You ever heard about somebody named Mr. Elijah Muhammad?" Until that day he had been waiting for finally came.

Chapter 38

MEETING

On August 7, 1952, Malcolm finally departed Charlestown State Prison. He was twenty-seven years old. He received an early release. As a condition of his parole, he had to leave Massachusetts. And go to live with his eldest brother, Wilfred, in Detroit.

While on parole, Malcolm's life was still monitored like he was enslaved. Not by a prison guard. By a parole officer.

The first thing Malcolm did after leaving prison was take a bath. He scrubbed the filthy slavery of prison life off him.

The first things he bought he used more than anything else over the next thirteen years.

Eyeglasses. A suitcase. A watch.

His eyes had given out with all that reading late into the night with little light. He was about to spend most of his time traveling, suitcase in hand. Malcolm was about to live by his watch, ensuring that he made it everywhere on time.

Wilfred got Malcolm a job where he worked. At the White-owned furniture store. A store of exploitation. Meaning the customers often paid three or four times what the furniture cost the store. Some people call that making a profit, or capitalism. Malcolm called that "highway robbery."

Malcolm's first service at Mosque Number One in Detroit after he departed prison left him with mixed feelings. He loved the atmosphere. He loved being around Black people who loved Black people, in a society where Black people were taught to hate themselves.

Malcolm happily absorbed Minister Lemuel Hassan's speech about the teachings of Elijah Muhammad. But he could not help but look around. Every time he saw an empty seat, he got upset.

Malcolm complained afterward to his brother Wilfred. But the mosque had a passive approach. Wilfred thought Allah would bring the mosque more members. Malcolm believed members should go out into the streets. Bring people into the Nation. Wilfred told Malcolm to be patient. Malcolm tried. But he could not wait. And Malcolm could not wait to meet the Messenger.

• • •

It happened the Sunday before Labor Day.

August.

1952.

Chicago.

The headquarters of the Nation of Islam.

At Mosque Number Two.

Members of Mosque Number One in Detroit were in attendance. Ten cars had taken the four-hour drive west from Detroit to Chicago. They probably drove through Kalamazoo, where Malcolm's mother had been forcibly hospitalized for thirteen years. Aside from Reginald, all Malcolm's brothers and sisters rode in those cars. They probably saw the signs for Kalamazoo at the same time. They probably thought of their mother at the same time.

Or maybe not.

Maybe they only thought about how excited they were to see their new holy father. A man whose teachings reminded them of their mother. And father.

About two hundred or so Muslims were there. Seated. Happy. Eager. Waiting for the arrival of the Messenger of Allah.

He walked in from the back of the room. A small man. He looked even smaller surrounded by his large security guards.

Those well-trained men known as the Fruit of Islam. They wore dark suits, white shirts, and bow ties—the uniform of men in the Nation of Islam. Elijah wore a gold-embroidered fez. His brown face looked straight ahead. He walked toward the speaking platform. Everyone stared at him. No one more closely than the person who had studied Elijah's face in photographs for hours at a time in his jail cell. Who was seeing Elijah for the first time in person. Who was overcome with emotion. Whose body tingled.

Malcolm Little.

Messenger Elijah Muhammad Speaks
Concerning Duties of Laborers
Sunday, February 26, 1961

1. The Minister is the head of the Mosque and is under the direct authority of of The Messenger.

2. The Captain and the Secretary are under the authority of the Minister and must go in accord with his instructions so long as they are certain that he is following the instructions of The Messenger. They are not to follow the instructions of any Minister who wilfully and openly breaks the laws of The Messenger or seeks to change them without proper authorization.

3. The three of them (Minister, Captain, Secretary) must work together in perfect harmony and must NEVER show disagreement in front of the believers. They should all carry themselves in such a manner so that they can be approached by anyone who may be over them or under them.

4. The Minister is not to use his authority (pulling rank) on the Captain and Secretary unless it is absolutely necessary. In short, a Minister should seek to be and act in the same way to his laborers (Capt. and Secy.) as The Messenger acts towards his Ministers and laborers.

5. "As laborers we should be willing to take instructions and advice from anyone. Be intelligent enough to take the good and leave the bad". The Messenger stated he himself has listened to much advice from his followers and used the good and discarded the bad without hurting anyone's feeling and making them feel as though they could not tell him anything (even though they couldn't).

6. We must strive for peace and harmony among the believers and never turn anyone against us by being overly harsh. Harshness makes enemies. If we, as laborers, happen to get into some difficulty; then those whom we have wronged or hurt will be the first to say, "good enough for him. He never wants anyone to tell him anything".

7. In dealing with the believers, we must instill in them the desire to "want to do" rather than force them to do.

8. Keep Mosque affairs out of reach of the ordinary believers. Be discreet in handling Mosque affairs. Never let any Muslim know that there is any disagreement among the officials regardless to the circumstances.

9. The Minister is in complete charge of the Mosque and is therefore free to come to any meeting held in the Mosque. Whenever he comes into them, his authority must be recognized. If he attends the FOI and he observes that the Captain isn't doing his job properly, then the Minister is within his authority to instruct the Captain or even take charge of the meeting and do it himself. He may also teach any of the classes in the FOI meeting that he wants to or have the ability to perform.

10. The Minister's job is to deliver the message and oversee the Mosque. The Captain's duty is to implement the Minister's plans for the Mosque. The Secretary must keep the records and work in conjunction with the Captain to put the program over. Actually, the three of them should be working together so hard until they should not have time to see or worry about who is the boss. If everyone does his job, then they would not have time for such.

—more—

Elijah Muhammad on the duties of mosque leaders, February 26, 1961

Chapter 39
BELIEF

Malcolm sat forward as the Honorable Elijah Muhammad spoke before him for the first time. Elijah spoke of how in the wilderness of North America the "white man" had brainwashed the "so-called Negro." Elijah spoke of the "white man" kidnapping Black people from their homeland. Stripping them of their language, culture, and names. Until they did not know who they were.

That is why Elijah renamed his followers. Malcolm's last name, Little, was not just his father's name. Little was the name of the people who had enslaved Malcolm's ancestors. White enslavers forced their last names onto the Black people they enslaved. Forced the name Little onto Malcolm's ancestors.

So Elijah renamed him Malcolm X. The X symbolized that Malcolm did not know the original name of his ancestors in West Africa. Elijah gave almost everyone in the Nation of Islam an X for a last name. But no one named X became more prominent than Malcolm X.

Elijah spoke on. About how Black people are "mentally, morally and spiritually dead." He said when Black people gained a true knowledge of themselves in the Nation of Islam, they would rise from the dead at the bottom of society and rise to the top, where they had begun.

Elijah said he had not stopped speaking this truth "for the past twenty-one years." He spoke of efforts to stop him from speaking "the truth." He spoke of being sent to prison for four and a half years "for teaching this truth."

Elijah ended his speech. He paused for a breath.

He called Malcolm's name.

The sound of his name coming from the Messenger's voice hit Malcolm like a lightning bolt. Elijah asked Malcolm to stand. Malcolm shot up like a lightning bolt returning to the sky.

Elijah told the crowd that Malcolm had just got out of prison. He had been strong in prison. "Every day," Elijah said, "for years, Brother Malcolm has written a letter from prison to me. And I have written to him as often as I could."

Elijah shared a parable. A parable is a story that teaches a lesson. God bragged about how faithful Job was to him, Elijah began. The devil said Job was only faithful because God protected Job. He was only using God. The devil said remove the protection and Job won't be faithful.

Elijah said the devil could claim that Malcolm had just used Islam to get out of prison. That now out of prison, he would return to drinking, smoking, drugs, and breaking the law. "We will see how he does," Elijah said. "I believe that he is going to remain faithful."

Malcolm felt pleased. A fatherly figure believed in him. What he had been searching for since the day his father died. Since the day his hope for his future died. Since the day his eighth-grade teacher did not believe in him.

After the service, Elijah invited Malcolm's entire family to dinner at his home. Elijah's family had just moved into a mansion on South Woodlawn Avenue, on a tree-lined street in the Kenwood neighborhood of Chicago. A mansion made of brown bricks with multiple levels. It had twelve thousand square feet. (Most newly built houses in the United States today are about two thousand square feet.) It had twenty-three rooms. Elijah would live in this home for the next twenty years, until 1972.

The house sat vacant for twenty years. Except for a large family of raccoons. But the raccoons are gone today.

Businesswoman Wendy Muhammad bought the property. She has people fixing it up, making it into a house museum. Where people can learn about Elijah Muhammad and his economic program of Black-owned businesses that by 1975 generated about $30 million in annual revenue and employed more than 11,000 people.

The first floor is being restored to look like it did when Elijah lived there, when Malcolm first saw the home in 1952. On that first floor: the dining room with a large table where Elijah ate dinner. There, Elijah had conversations with the Reverend Martin Luther King Jr., James Baldwin, Muhammad Ali, and many other influential African Americans. These conversations were taped. As museum visitors tour the dining room, they will hear three-minute recordings of these conversations. History lives.

Probably the most important conversation Elijah ever had at his dining room table was that first one with Malcolm and his family.

ones who are in the thick of the battle, they sit back (in their idleness) thinking of things to say that will kill the spirit of the one who is trying to DO.

I have always enjoyed hearing from you and Sister Martha, because your letters from the start always filled me with inspiration to Help our Leader and Teacher. I have never ceased in my love and respect for both of you. As my duties increased I have been unable to write as before, when I was doing nothing, but that did not mean I had stopped thinking of both of you. I just can't write as before, and also it isn't too wise for me to be writing too much. I received a letter from Sister Shirley today, which was open when it arrived. The contents of the letter was tearing me apart, and I imagine that if the "man" is the one who opened it, he has some good material to use against me. Letters nowadays should always be well sealed with extra musalege. The devil is never at rest when it comes to looking for somthing which he can use to harm us.

Most of these young Sisters should just throw me out of their minds, and go out and bring in the DEAD. We are rewarded according to our DEEDS. If we serve ALLAH HE will bless us with the fulfillment of our greatest desires. I don't worry about any particular Sister, because I know that ALLAH will bless me with WHOM HE WILLS when HE SEES FIT, as long as I serve HIM and obey His Holy Apostle. I'm thinking about spreading Islam, not about marriage. The restrict- ive LAW is our success.

With the Help of Allah, we plan to have Temples spread from Boston to Florida before this year ends. And we can't do this by sitting around finding fault with those who are "at least trying". Let us always try to ENCOURAGE the laborers, not discourage them. It is JOB enough to labor, without all the added burdens. I owe much to you, and want you to know this. The only time you may see me clam up around you is when one of your sons who is not in the Temple come on the scene. I have patience with lostfounds, but don't care to socialize with anyone who is not in the Temple. This especially includes my own blood. This also may be the reason why they are saying I'm be- coming self-righteous, but it is AGAINST OUR LAW, THE LAW GIVEN US BY ALLAH HIMSELF, for any of us to socialize, sypathize, or even trust in any way, someone who is not in good standing with our Nation. After seeing the chastisment ALLAH put on my Brother, Reginald, I have been very careful of never being around or trusting him or anyone else who was once in the Temple and is now out. I do greatly fear the chastisment of ALLAH and His Messenger. The beginning of wisdom is the fear of ALLAH.

So be patient with me, and please try to understand. I always look foward hearing from you and Sister Martha, and also any other Sister WHO IS TRYING TO HELP IN THE SPREAD OF ISLAM. Please give the greeting to all the Muslims there, and tell all to Work hard, as we are now nearing the FINAL CHAPTER of this wicked world. There is no more time for sport and play, nor for idle chatter and foolish conjecture. Tell Brother Clarence that I hope when I next hear from him he will have Temples set up in Harrisberg, Pa and Richmond.

As-Salaam-Alaikum:

Bro Malcolm X

Special greetings to Sis Martha,

Malcolm writing about the Nation of Islam and Reginald's departure from it in a letter to a member, March 5, 1955

Chapter 40
THOUSANDS

Malcolm never forgot that first dinner. He sat there at Elijah's dining room table wanting to hear Elijah's wisdom. But Elijah encouraged Malcolm's family to talk. His brothers and sisters did. Malcolm remained silent. Silent in thought. Thinking about all the Black people Elijah's teachings could save in the way they had saved him. Thinking about all the empty seats at the Detroit mosque.

The talking slowed. Malcolm found his voice. Asked Elijah how many Black people should be attending Mosque Number One in Detroit.

"There are supposed to be thousands," Elijah said, probably knowing there were not even one hundred.

"Yes, sir," Malcolm said. "Sir, what is your opinion of the best way of getting thousands there?"

"Go after the young people," Elijah said. "Once you get them, the older ones will follow through shame."

• • •

Malcolm returned to Detroit as a man possessed. Possessed with a mission.

He went fishing for himself—for who he was before he was incarcerated and joined the Nation of Islam. Malcolm knew exactly where to find himself: his old conked hair and zoot suits and hip talk. On the corners. In the bars. In the poolrooms. He went to these places every evening. Right after finishing work at the furniture store. "My man, let me pull your coat to something—"

The rejections were constant. "Aw, man, get out of my face!"

The rejections hurt Malcolm. Hardly anyone let him pull their coat. Hardly anyone wanted to learn about the teachings of Elijah Muhammad. Hardly anyone agreed to visit Mosque Number One for their next meeting. But the hurt did not stop him. He kept trying.

Elijah saw a future minister in Malcolm. Malcolm did not see a future minister in himself. He had no problem serving Elijah in the lowliest capacity. Fishing for people. Out of the spotlight. Then again, he had never shied away from the spotlight.

The minister of the Detroit mosque asked Malcolm to speak one day. The squealing of pigs from the slaughterhouse nearby could be heard. But all Malcolm could hear was the excitement running through his body. In ten years, Malcolm would become one of the most sought-after speakers in the world. One everybody wanted to hear. He would go on to speak before thousands of people in an auditorium or millions of people through television screens. But no speech ever compared to the first one in 1953. When he spoke before about a hundred people. When he felt confident speaking about Christianity and the horrors of slavery. A confidence born of all his reading on those topics in prison. The greatest speakers are the greatest readers.

"My brothers and sisters, our white slavemaster's Christian religion has taught us black people here in the wilderness of North America that we will sprout wings when we die and fly up into the sky where God will have for us a special place called heaven. This is white man's Christian religion used to *brainwash* us black people!" Malcolm shouted. "And while we are doing all of that, for himself, [the white man] has *twisted* his Christianity, to keep his *foot* on our backs . . . to keep our eyes fixed on the pie in the sky and heaven in the hereafter . . . while *he* enjoys *his* heaven right *here* . . . on *this earth* . . . in *this life.*"

The people loved it! In no time, Malcolm became the assistant minister of Mosque Number One in Detroit. He quit his furniture job for this one. Malcolm started driving to Chicago by himself, passing his mother in Kalamazoo, to visit Elijah Muhammad. He no longer had to ask his parole officer because he had finished his parole on May 4, 1953. He was free to travel. Even back to Boston if he wanted to.

At his home in Chicago, Elijah treated Malcolm like one of his sons. After eating, they would talk at the dinner table for hours. Or Malcolm rode with Elijah on his daily rounds to one of the stores the Nation owned. Wherever there were mosques, members were striving to own and operate Black businesses. To finance the Nation of Islam. To show Black people that they could rely on themselves "and thus quit being exploited by the white man."

One day, at one of the stores, there was a dirty glass on the counter. Elijah put a clean glass beside it. He turned to Malcolm. "You want to know how to spread my teachings?" Elijah said. "Don't condemn if you see a person has a dirty glass of water. Just show them the clean glass of water that you have. When they inspect it, you won't have to say that yours is better."

The lesson stuck with Malcolm. But it was hard for Malcolm to put into practice. He loved to tell Black people certain glasses were dirty. Dirtied by racism.

He kept going out into the community to fish. A handful of new people showed up at the mosque each week. A few became members. Only a few. But that few plus a few, plus a few, week after week after week, started to add up. Big-time. Within two or three months, Mosque Number One had tripled its membership! Pleasing the Honorable Elijah Muhammad.

Elijah's flock was growing. And he knew—everyone at the Detroit mosque knew—it was because of the tireless work of Malcolm X.

Good work invites praise. Good work also invites jealousy. People don't like you because you are doing a better job than them. They want the praise you are getting.

And many people don't like change. Some of the Detroit members liked how things were before Malcolm arrived. Before he started bringing in all these new members. In not liking the change, they didn't like Malcolm.

They started complaining to Elijah. Spreading rumors about Malcolm that were not true. It all caused Elijah to sit Malcolm down for a meeting at the end of 1953. Probably at Elijah's home in Chicago.

Elijah likely told Malcolm about the first six mosques of the Nation of Islam. The ones he founded in the 1930s and early 1940s.

Mosque Number One. In Detroit.

Mosque Number Two. In Chicago.

Mosque Number Three. In Milwaukee.

Mosque Number Four. In Washington, DC.

Mosque Number Five. In Cincinnati.

Mosque Number Six. In Baltimore.

Elijah probably shared with Malcolm that these founding mosques had many of the original members of the Nation of Islam. These original members were older like Elijah. The Messenger in 1953 turned fifty-six years old. These members were not really open to young ministers half their age. Malcolm in 1953 turned twenty-eight years old.

They were not really open to growing the mosques with new

members. They felt they were already well run. In many ways, they were. Even without many members.

There were seven East Coast mosques that remained not only small but disorganized. With bad leadership. Elijah told Malcolm he wanted him to leave the Detroit mosque. Head back east.

Elijah sent Malcolm back to his old stomping ground. Boston.

It was there that Malcolm heard about the murder of a Black boy that changed the country.

Emmett Till, 1954

Chapter 41

EMMETT TILL

Remember when Malcolm was around fourteen years old? Hanging out with his friend and two White girls in downtown Lansing? Back in 1939 in Michigan? Remember when a White police officer walked up to Malcolm? Pulled out his gun. Pointed it at Malcolm's head. All because this racist cop did not want Black boys and White girls to be boyfriends and girlfriends. Remember that?

Something similar happened to a fourteen-year-old Black boy in 1955. But far worse. Emmett Till was from the Midwest like Malcolm. Chicago, to be exact. Malcolm's father, Earl, had been from Georgia. After living other places, Lansing became Earl's home. Emmett's mother, Mamie, had been from Mississippi. After Mamie lived other places, Chicago became her home. Earl and Mamie both traveled from the South to the North in the Great Migration.

Many Northern families sent their children back down South to live with their grandparents and aunts and uncles and cousins during summer breaks. To connect with their family members and relieve their parents of childcare. Earl didn't. Maybe Malcolm wished he'd gone to Georgia. Maybe not. Maybe he feared the Georgia Klan.

In 1955, Mamie's uncle came to visit her family in Chicago and attend a funeral. Moses Wright was sixty-four years old. He told Emmett stories about living near Money, Mississippi.

After the funeral, Moses planned to take Emmett's cousin Wheeler to visit relatives in Mississippi for the summer. Emmett asked his mother Mamie if he could go too. He wanted to hang out with Wheeler and his other cousins in Mississippi.

Mamie said no. She wanted to take Emmett on a road trip to Detroit and Omaha (where Malcolm was born).

Emmett begged his mother to let him go. Mamie said yes. The night before Emmett left for Mississippi, Mamie gave him his father's ring. He decided to take it to Mississippi. The ring had the initials "L. T."

Emmett's father was named Louis Till. Louis and Mamie married in 1940. They were both eighteen years old. On July 25, 1941, Emmett was born—his parents' only child. Mamie and Louis had a violent relationship. Mamie obtained a restraining order. That is when a judge orders someone—in this case, Louis—to stay away from someone else—in this case, Mamie—or go to jail. Louis kept disobeying the order. He wouldn't stay away from Mamie. He wouldn't stop harming her. In 1943, a judge gave Louis two options: jail or the army.

When this happened, Louis and Malcolm were around the same age. Remember Malcolm had gotten out of fighting in World War II by acting like a wild man when army doctors examined him? Louis wasn't so lucky. He entered the US Army and was sent to Italy.

One day, an Italian woman was killed and two other Italian women were forced to have sex against their will in a town near Rome, Italy. A soldier accused Louis and another Black solider named Fred A. McMurray. Two Black men accused of these violent acts against White women? They had no chance of proving their innocence. The US Army was segregated abroad, like Mississippi was segregated at home.

The US Army arrested Louis and Fred. Found them guilty. Hanged them on July 2, 1945. Emmett's father died at twenty-three years of age for acts he likely did not commit, according to a recent review of Louis's case. Racism may have killed Emmett's father, L. T. Just as Malcolm thought racism had killed his father.

A year before Emmett boarded a train to Mississippi, Malcolm boarded a train to Boston. Malcolm was not as eager to go as Emmett.

5 Wellington Street in Boston, where Malcolm
lived with Lloyd X, pictured in 2024

Chapter 42

GROWING

Elijah wanted Malcolm to establish or grow mosques across the northeastern United States. Boston first.

There was at least one member of the Nation of Islam who already lived in Boston. Not Malcolm's big sister Ella. She still lived in Boston but had not joined Elijah's Nation. Malcolm had not tried to convert her either. Too hard. "I wouldn't have expected anyone short of Allah Himself to have been able to convert Ella," Malcolm said back then.

Malcolm lived with Lloyd X at 5 Wellington Street, a brownstone. Malcolm's new home was a two-minute walk to the famous intersection of Massachusetts and Columbus Avenues. Remember that's where all the jazz clubs were back then? Remember that's where Malcolm saved a Black woman from police harassment? Remember that's where Wally's Café Jazz Club still lives on today? Wally's is across the street from where Malcolm remembered it, but still here at this intersection. Near the intersection is a newer jazz club serving soul food Malcolm would have liked (save the pork). It is named Darryl's Corner Bar & Kitchen.

Go to the intersection now. You won't see as many Black people as Malcolm saw when he arrived back in Boston before Christmas in 1953. But back then, Malcolm could not have picked a better living spot to recruit Black people.

It would not be easy, starting a mosque. After putting together a core group, Malcolm had to rent a meeting hall. He had to assemble about fifty male and female members. Only then would Elijah Muhammad assign a permanent minister. The minister would secure regular offerings from the members. And send most of that money to Nation of Islam headquarters in Chicago. With money coming in regularly, Elijah Muhammad would establish the new mosque and assign a number. More members meant more money for Elijah and his family because every member was ordered to give 10 percent of their annual income. Many gave more.

Word traveled fast that Malcolm was back in town on some "religious kick." When he approached people he had known before prison, Malcolm could see their discomfort. He said hello like them, "What you know, Daddy?" putting them at ease. Malcolm found his old best friend, Jarvis, who went to prison with him for robbing houses and dating White women. Jarvis had a little band. Probably played sometimes at Wally's. Still ate pork and dated White women.

Malcolm never mentioned the Nation or Elijah Muhammad to most of his old friends. "I knew, from what I had been when I was with them, how brainwashed they were," Malcolm remembered. Meaning: He knew how much they wanted to be White and hated being Black. But Malcolm had success recruiting other people to Lloyd's living room each Sunday night. Malcolm would speak about Elijah Muhammad. Maybe on some nights he had flashbacks to watching his father in living rooms speaking about Marcus Garvey. Maybe he smiled to himself. Thought his father would be proud. Elijah, his new father, proud.

Malcolm's favorite subject in these living room speeches before ten or so Black people was the violence of White Christians. "I know you don't realize the enormity, the horrors, of the so-called *Christian* white man's crime," Malcolm would begin. He would describe the horrors. Especially during slavery. All the violence it took for White Christians to enslave Black people. Malcolm would declare that the Honorable Elijah Muhammad had come to save Black people from the violence—and begin their own Nation of Islam.

At the end of his living room speeches, Malcolm asked: "Will all stand who *believe* what you have heard?" Everyone almost always stood. Malcolm's speeches were that electrifying! The people gradually sat back down. When everyone was seated again, Malcolm asked: "How many of you want to *follow* the Honorable Elijah Muhammad?" Far fewer people would stand. But in three months, enough people stood that Elijah established Mosque Number Eleven in Boston with Malcolm as the minister.

By March 1954, Elijah had moved Malcolm again, this time to Philadelphia. He rented a small apartment at 1522 North 26th Street. If you go to this street today, you will see a red-painted townhome at 1520 and another home at 1524 with squares of different browns. But there's no home at 1522. Just an empty lot with a fence and garbage cans. The home where Malcolm lived was demolished at some point. On the concrete sidewalk in front of the empty lot is a large tree. An old tree. A large old tree that saw Malcolm every day when he came out of his apartment to fish for new recruits to Elijah's Nation in Philadelphia.

Within three months, again, Malcolm had grown the local membership. Rented a meeting hall. Sent money from members to Chicago. So Elijah established Mosque Number Twelve in Philadelphia. And now today, Philadelphia has one of the largest Black Muslim populations in the United States.

The establishment of this new Philadelphia mosque came in May 1954. The same month the US Supreme Court ruled it was unconstitutional for Black and White schoolchildren in Mississippi and around the United States to be sent to different schools. This was the famous *Brown v. Board of Education* decision that outlawed Jim Crow segregation in public education.

Racist White Southerners were angry at the *Brown* decision. Angry at the Supreme Court. Angry at civil rights activists. Angry at anyone pushing for equality. Angry at anyone pushing for White people and Black people to go to school together, be together, live together, work together, love together. All this anger led to massive resistance in Mississippi and around the United States.

Three days after he arrived in Mississippi, Emmett Till got a bitter taste of all the massive resistance.

Chapter 43
MASSIVE RESISTANCE

Racist White Southerners did not want anything changed. They did not want to end the hard Mississippi life for most Black people—and poor White people—that made life for rich White people easier. Especially all that picking cotton.

A lot of clothes back then—as well as today—were made of cotton. For as long as Black people could remember, they had been forced to pick cotton on fields usually owned by rich White people. During slavery, Black people were forced against their will to pick cotton. They did not get paid. Even after slavery ended, Black people received very little money. Because former enslavers used written and unwritten racist rules to trap Black people on the same plantations they labored on during slavery.

Racist White landowners created the system of sharecropping. Black families paid White landowners to live on and grow crops on their land. Black families usually paid the White landowners a share of the crop. But Black families rarely made much money on their own share of the crop. Because they also had to pay the White landowner for necessities like farm tools, household goods, and food. White landowners typically set the prices for these goods much higher than they were worth to make as much money as they could off Black families. Many Black families fell into debt to landowners. Racist laws and sheriffs barred indebted Black families from leaving White landowners. This semi-slavery is known as debt servitude.

The Klan attacked Black sharecroppers trying to move for better opportunities. When Black families refused to work under debt servitude, racist laws allowed authorities to arrest and fine unemployed Black people. Black Southerners were typically too poor to pay the fines. Since people convicted of crimes are enslaved to the state, governments in states such as Mississippi, Alabama, and Georgia then "sold" these human beings to racist White landowners and companies who paid off their fines and court costs. So they could acquire these enslaved people. So racist White landowners could force Black people to work against their will. The human trade all over again. Slavery all over again.

Some Black people were able to escape the trap of sharecropping or incarceration. These Black people were able to work for wages. But racist White businesses' refusal to pay Black workers equal wages with White workers for the same work outlived the laws passed in the decades immediately following emancipation. Under all these conditions, generations of Black people were unable to rise out of poverty.

The Klan and other racist terrorists beat up or killed people who rose out of poverty or tried to change their situation. People who tried to be antiracist. And end all the poverty. Malcolm had learned all about this racism and resistance while reading in prison.

After a long day of sitting at home while the others picked cotton in the summer sun, Emmett begged his cousins, including Simeon and Wheeler, and friends from the neighborhood to go into town with him when they returned from the fields. They went to Bryant's Grocery and Meat Market to buy some candy and soda. Emmett purchased some bubble gum from the store clerk, a twenty-one-year-old White woman named Carolyn Bryant. Seconds after Emmett left the store, Carolyn came outside and walked toward her car. Emmett let out a wolf whistle at Carolyn.

Emmett loved to laugh. He loved to make other people laugh. He lived with joy. Wanted to bring joy to others. It did not matter the situation. Emmett was going to find joy. Perhaps that's why Emmett wolf whistled at Carolyn. That signal to someone that you like them.

If he did. A joke?

But Carolyn did not like it. Didn't see a fourteen-year-old boy joking with his cousins. A Black teenage boy signaling he liked a young White woman? Just like Malcolm's dating a White woman in Boston and talking to a White teenager in public in Michigan, Emmett's whistle was a no-no among racist White people. Especially in rural Mississippi. Especially after the *Brown* decision the year before.

Simeon and Wheeler got scared when Emmett wolf whistled on August 24, 1955. They knew all about racist violence. The cousins left the area quickly. Emmett asked his cousins to not tell his great-uncle Moses. Emmett was staying with them at Moses's house. He probably did not want to get in trouble with people who loved him. Emmett had no idea he was already in trouble with people who hated him.

Yes, people who did not know Emmett hated Emmett. Hated him because they hated Black people—as if they knew all Black people, including Emmett; his mother, Mamie; his uncle and aunt and cousins. How can people hate a fourteen-year-old Black teenager they do not know? How can people hate a Middle Eastern or White or Latino or Native or Asian person they do not know? A major problem in 1955. A major problem today.

Carolyn's White husband was out of town. When Roy Bryant returned, he found out about Emmett's wolf whistle. He got so angry. Roy told his half brother, J. W. Milam. They drove to Moses's home. Kidnapped Emmett in the middle of the night. Emmett was so scared. His family was so scared.

Roy and J. W. drove Emmett to a barn in Drew, Mississippi. They beat up Emmett very bad. Then they shot him in the head. No one could recognize Emmett anymore.

Roy and J. W. tied Emmett's body to a metal fan. So the body would sink to the bottom of the Tallahatchie River. So no one would find it. It was as if they had done this before. Many Black people had been lynched in those parts of Mississippi. Their bodies never seen again.

• • •

Moses told the local sheriff about the kidnapping. On August 29, 1955, the sheriff arrested Roy and J. W. Days later, authorities found a body. Pulled it from the river. Face gone; no one could identify it.

Moses came to see the water-soaked body. Couldn't tell who the body was. Until he looked at the fingers. Saw the ring with the initials L. T. It was L. T.'s son, Emmett Till.

Mamie, Emmett's mother, had the body shipped back to Chicago. When she opened the box holding his body, she did not see her son's face. It had been beaten away. Mamie saw the face of racism. In her sadness, she wanted to "let the people see what they did to my boy." So no one could deny racism's existence. So the world could be moved to join the movement against racism in 1955.

When Mamie had Emmett's funeral at Roberts Temple Church of God in Christ, she opened Emmett's casket. She invited everyone from the community to come. And see what was left of Emmett's face.

Over four days, more than one hundred thousand people came through that church in Chicago and laid their eyes on the face of racism. Perhaps Elijah Muhammad came. Perhaps other members of the Nation of Islam came. Photographers from *Jet* magazine and the *Chicago Defender* came—the largest Black-owned magazine and newspaper in the United States. The cameras and the people saw. Most people couldn't look long. Too scary. Millions more people saw Emmett's body in pictures in newspapers. Including Malcolm X.

Everybody followed the murder trial of Roy and J. W. that started on September 19, 1955. Everybody including Malcolm X. Racist and sexist practices did not allow Black people or women to serve on the jury. So the jury was all White men. They listened to Carolyn lie about what happened at the store. She said Emmett touched her hand and grabbed her by the waist.

The evidence was everywhere that Roy and J. W. murdered Emmett Till. But the White men on the jury ignored all the evidence and found the men *not* guilty. The same thing happens today when it is obvious that White police officers murdered a Black person. Juries still say not guilty. Just as they are today, many people back then were outraged. Including Malcolm X.

5743 DREXEL AVENUE

January 14th, 1964

ZELIC FREEDMAN, M.D.
NS' FUND RESEARCH PROFESSOR

THE UNIVERSITY OF CHICAGO

CHICAGO 37, ILLINOIS

DEPARTMENT OF PSYCHIATRY
PSYCHIATRIC RESEARCH UNIT
5743 DREXEL AVENUE

January 14th, 1964

LAWRENCE ZELIC FREEDMAN, M.D.
FOUNDATIONS' FUND RESEARCH PROFESSOR

Mr. Malcolm X
Muslim Mosque Number Seven
New York City, New York

Dear Sir:

In the New York Times, January 10th, 1964, I read an article concerning the extraordinary success which you and your associates have had in rehabilitating narcotics addicts and alcoholics. This is a problem which has engaged my concern for many years.

I would be very grateful to you if you could provide me with any information concerning the cure and rehabilitation of narcotics addicts.

If you are unable to devote the time necessary to responding to my inquiry, I would like very much to be able to talk with someone here in Chicago whom you might wish to recommend.

Yours truly,

Lawrence Zelic Freedman, M.D.

LZF:jac

A letter from a forensic psychiatrist asking Malcolm for
guidance on treating addiction, January 14, 1964

Chapter 44
MOSQUE NUMBER SEVEN

Ever since he started recruiting in Detroit, Malcolm had talked about White violence against Black people. In Boston. In Philadelphia.

And then Elijah gave Malcolm the opportunity he had been waiting for. The opportunity to lead Mosque Number Seven in the place he still loved more than any other: Harlem.

In Harlem, Malcolm talked about White violence against Black people, with an emphasis on the thousands of Black people who had been lynched in the United States since the late nineteenth century. And the racist terrorists almost always got away with the lynchings. Which Malcolm said was why Black people needed to practice self-defense. And why Malcolm said Black people needed to separate from White people and form Elijah's Nation.

After he heard about the lynching of Emmett Till, Malcolm made sure everyone knew about it. After Emmett's killers were set free, more than ten thousand people came together at Williams Institutional Church in Harlem. They demanded that President Dwight D. Eisenhower convene a special session of Congress and recommend the immediate passage of a federal anti-lynching bill. President Eisenhower refused. Black lives apparently did not matter to President Eisenhower. Congress did not pass an anti-lynching bill until 2022. It was named the Emmett Till Anti-Lynching Act.

But Black people—and all Americans—are still being killed. By the police. About one thousand Americans a year now. Americans who are disproportionately Pacific Islander or Black or Brown or Native American. And many White people too. The police are still walking free. An old problem. A problem Malcolm would have to deal with.

• • •

Expanding the membership in Harlem ended up being much harder than in Detroit, Boston, and Philadelphia. In Harlem, all those Black migrants coming from the South, all those longtime New York residents—together they probably had more political power than any other group of Black residents in the United States.

The National Association for the Advancement of Colored People (NAACP), which fights for the civil rights of African Americans, had its offices there in Harlem. Harlem resident Hulan Jack had become the first Black president of the borough of Manhattan the year before Malcolm came back to Harlem. Adam Clayton Powell Jr., the pastor of Harlem's Abyssinian Baptist Church, had represented Harlem in Congress for about a decade at that point.

It seems as if each Black political organization had a street speaker. Each of these street speakers brought their stepladder to the corner of 125th Street and 7th Avenue—the heart of Harlem. They typically spoke outside the House of Common Sense and Home of Proper Propaganda. The front of this Black-owned bookstore displayed a huge sign that declared WORLD HISTORY BOOK OUTLET ON 2,000,000,000 (TWO BILLION) AFRICANS AND NON-WHITE PEOPLES. People saw pictures of influential Black leaders, including Marcus Garvey. People in the community usually called the Black-owned bookstore Michaux's, pronounced "Mi-shows," after its owner Lewis Michaux. When it closed in 1974, the store had two hundred thousand books written by or about Black people.

Public rallies to speak out against racism happened all the time near this bookstore. Protests against racism were common. And yet Elijah Muhammad was against his followers voting and protesting.

This made no sense to many Black people in Harlem.

Many people did not like the very strict moral code in Elijah's Nation. No drugs. No pork. No cigarettes. No sports. No dancing. No gambling. No attending movies. No breaking of laws. No sex before marriage. No disrespecting of women. No lying. No long vacations from work. No alcohol. No eating more than one meal a day. No to all the things Malcolm enjoyed doing before joining the Nation of Islam.

No minister in the Nation of Islam policed these rules more than Malcolm X. He was so demanding of his members. Because he was so demanding of himself. He expected the members to never break the rules. Because he never broke the rules. He was probably the only minister who never broke the rules. Malcolm was more devoted to Elijah's rules than Elijah was. Even Elijah—and his family members—broke the rules a lot. As Malcolm would find out later.

Despite its lack of political action, despite its strict moral code—or in some cases because of it—Malcolm steadily grew the small Mosque Number Seven. How?

NAME AND ADDRESS | PHONE

Temple #1
5401 John C. Lodge
Detroit, Mich.   Temple 18029

Temple #1
5401 John C. Lodge
Detroit, Mich.

Temple 18029

Temple 406
Youngs

NAME AND ADDRESS	PHONE
Temple #1 5401 John C. Lodge Detroit, Mich.	Temple 18029
Temple #2 5335 So. Greenwood (at 54th) Chicago, Illinois	Mu 48693
Temple #3 1316 N. 9th Street Milwaukee, Wis	Broadway 20701
Temple #4 1325 Vermont Ave (Nw) Washington, DC	
Temple #5 407 W. Court St 2nd floor Cincinnati, Ohio	
Temple #6 1000 Pennsylvania Ave Baltimore, Md	Vernon 75771
Temple #7 102 W. 116th St NYC 3rd floor	University 4-9838
Temple #8 3102 Clay Ave San Diego, Cal	

NAME AND ADDRESS	PHONE
Temple #9 406 Elk St Youngstown, Ohio	Princessle 4 46
Temple #10 Atlantic City, N.J.	
Temple #11 552 Columbus Ave Boston, Mass.	
Temple #12 1643 N. Bailey Phila 21, Pa	Epler 3 4526
Temple #13 684 Dwight (at Congress) Springfield, Mass	
Temple of Islam #14 1097 Main St Hartford, Conn	
Temple #15 150 Auburn St NE Atlanta, Ga	
Temple of Islam (West?) 244 W. 63rd St Los Angeles, California	Pleasant 96628
Temple #18 7209 Quincy Ave (Rear) 1100s Albany Cleveland, Ohio	

Nation of Islam mosques in Malcolm's
address book, circa 1958 to 1961

Temple #5
3102 Clay Ave
San Diego, Cal

Temple
244 W.
Los Ange
Temple
7209
Clevelan

Chapter 45

LOUIS

Malcolm went to meetings of Black political organizations to recruit people already interested in advancing Black people in Harlem. "Come to hear us, too, brother," Malcolm said, stuffing a flyer on Elijah's Nation into hands. "The Honorable Elijah Muhammad teaches us how to cure the black man's spiritual, mental, moral, economic, and political sicknesses."

But Malcolm got the most recruits on Sundays. Around 1:00 P.M., he and other recruiters would go to the small storefront churches where low-income Black people worshipped. When services finished and the people came out, they would see Malcolm and the others. "Come to hear us, brother, sister."

With anyone curious, Malcolm shared where Mosque Number Seven was. Shared that their service started at 2:00 P.M. Some people walked straight over. Or went home first. Or got some lunch first. And came to hear Malcolm. To listen to him speak about "what this white man's religion that we call Christianity has *done* to us." About the "special religion for the black man."

After the service, most people stood saying they believed his message. Only a few stood to follow Elijah. But the membership grew. Too slowly for Malcolm. Maybe it would have grown faster if Malcolm did not have to leave all the time to start or grow mosques in other cities. He was growing mosques all over the East in towns like Hartford, Connecticut; Springfield, Massachusetts; and Camden, New Jersey.

Malcolm got up every day at 5:00 A.M. to say his prayers. He hated being late for a meeting. Almost never was. He ate one meal a day after sundown. His favorite dish: lamb shanks. He drank a whole quart of milk with his daily meal. For dessert, he loved banana splits. He fasted three days per month—not eating anything. For exercise, he walked around Harlem—to recruit. He walked very, very fast.

Malcolm wore dark suits, white button-down shirts, and ties like a uniform. Always cleaned. Always ironed. Pants with perfect creases. Tie always neat. Shoes shined.

When Malcolm wasn't at the mosque, or out of town, or fishing for new recruits, he was usually at home. He had moved into the home of a Black couple in Queens. The home was in East Elmhurst. When coming home, Malcolm could probably hear planes from nearby LaGuardia Airport.

At home, Malcolm would analyze his recorded speeches. To get better. Or he read books. He'd stay up past midnight almost every day. He slept only about four hours per night. Extremely unhealthy—as adults need at least seven hours of sleep a night. Teens and kids need even more. But Malcolm was so devoted to the Nation. He worked sixteen to eighteen hours a day, month after month.

In February 1955, Malcolm traveled to Chicago, where all Elijah's followers came together for the Saviour's Day convention. He did not travel alone. He had personally recruited hundreds of people there. Malcolm did not know the Nation's most important ever recruit—after Malcolm—was there.

His name, Louis Eugene Walcott. A twenty-one-year-old calypso singer, Louis was already a celebrity. He was performing in Chicago when a friend invited him and his wife, Khadijah, to the Saviour's Day convention. Someone told Elijah they were there and where they were sitting. At one point during Elijah's speech, he turned to Louis. Started speaking to him. Urging him to join the Nation. Louis did, that night. So did Khadijah.

But Louis's first exposure to the Nation had been through Malcolm. Khadijah and Louis lived in Boston. They actually lived close to Malcolm, near that famous intersection of Massachusetts and Columbus Avenues. Louis performed at one of the jazz clubs there.

Louis and Khadijah lived in a small apartment on Massachusetts Avenue, a few doors down from where Wally's Café Jazz Club is now. You know who also lived on that block at that same time? A few doors down from Louis lived Martin Luther King Jr. and his wife, Coretta Scott King. At 397 Massachusetts Avenue—where there is an official plaque today. King was finishing his PhD at Boston University. Coretta Scott King was on scholarship studying at the nearby New England Conservatory of Music.

Do you know what this means? Five of the most influential African American leaders in history all lived within minutes of each other in Boston in 1954. Because after Elijah died in 1975, Louis Farrakhan—as he is now known—took over the Nation of Islam. Khadijah became the First Lady of the Nation of Islam. Louis and Khadijah have led the Nation to this day.

Louis and Malcolm first met at Chicken Lane in 1954, before Malcolm left to go to Philadelphia. Chicken Lane was a popular food spot near the jazz clubs at the intersection of Massachusetts and Columbus Avenues. Malcolm had on all brown: hat, coat, suit, and gloves. Louis heard Malcolm talk bad about White people. So he got scared for Malcolm. Louis knew all about racist violence. The kind of violence that killed Emmett Till.

Yes, Louis ended up being the most important recruit to the Nation of Islam after Malcolm. But to Malcolm personally, another recruit was even more important.

Betty (right) holding Qubilah, 1960

Chapter 46
BETTY

Since leaving prison, Malcolm had not really dated any women. He found it hard to trust them. He should not have thought all women were like those who had hurt and betrayed him. But humans often do. If you have a bad experience with a member of a group, you are only having a bad experience with that individual. Not the whole group. Yes, people may look the same. Have the same gender. But all individuals are different.

Maybe Malcolm did not date anyone because he did not find anyone he liked. That is, until he started to get to know a smart, confident, and attractive brown-skinned woman. He liked her sparkling smile.

Her name, Betty Sanders.

Betty joined Malcolm's mosque in Harlem in 1956.

Elijah considered Black women to be valuable. As birthers of Black children. As supporters of Black husbands. As caretakers of Black households. Women of all skin colors can do so much more, and some women did not want to birth children, marry men, or take care of homes. Women did not need to be controlled by men as if they were children. But sexist ideas confined Black women in Elijah's Nation to the traditional station as mothers and wives and caretakers. Still, Elijah's Nation attracted Black women. In a world where they were spoken badly about and harmed, Black women were attracted to Elijah's offer of respect and protection and stability, regardless of its gendered limitations.

Betty seemed familiar to Malcolm. Maybe because she was from Michigan too.

Betty was a nursing student. Also, a good teacher. She led classes on basic medical facts for women on Thursday evenings at the mosque. Malcolm stopped by the classes sometimes. One day, Malcolm struck up the nerve to ask Betty out on a date. He didn't call it a date. He asked her to go with him to the American Museum of Natural History. Betty said yes.

Then Malcolm got nervous. Called Betty to cancel. "Well, you sure waited long enough to tell me, Brother Minister," she said. "I was just ready to walk out of the door."

Malcolm felt embarrassed. He agreed to go.

From Harlem, they ventured down Manhattan to Central Park. Inside the museum, they probably had a lot to talk about. If they wanted to talk about racism. Because many of things they saw were racist. Like the *Hall of the Age of Man*, which had opened in 1911. It had a *Family Tree of Man* displaying people from Europe, Asia, and Africa as if they were different species. Like dogs and cats are different species. This is a racist idea—to think humans of different colors are not the same. Are created unequal. Are not equals. This racist exhibit presented Europeans as not only a different species. But the most superior species. And Africans as the most inferior species, more like apes than Europeans.

Even before they entered the museum, Malcolm and Betty had something to talk about. As they walked up the steps to the museum's entrance, they probably noticed a statue of the twenty-sixth president of the United States. Theodore Roosevelt. On horseback. On one side of the horse was a Native American man—on the other side, an African man. This statue symbolized the racist ideas that White people are above Native American and African peoples. And that Native American and African peoples are more like animals.

President Roosevelt believed these racist ideas. The museum did not remove this statue from the entrance until 2020.

You read that year right: 2020.

Malcolm asked Betty all sorts of questions. To really understand how she thought. Betty impressed him. Malcolm impressed Betty.

They had a nice first date. More nice dates and conversations afterward. But Malcolm was not really looking to get married. In any case, Elijah liked Betty. Urged Malcolm to marry her. And they did. Got married in 1958. And Betty gave birth to their first of six daughters together. They named her Attallah.

• • •

Malcolm attracted many people to Elijah's Nation around the Northeast. Like Betty and Louis. But he had done so privately.

Outside the Nation of Islam, very few people had heard of Malcolm X. Even where he ministered in Harlem. There were many leaders of small religious groups around town. Malcolm was just one of them. A minister in a crowd of ministers. And not many people in Harlem had heard of Elijah's Nation of Islam.

Everything changed for Malcolm, for Elijah's Nation on the afternoon of April 26, 1957.

My throat + my ankle have been giving me a fit. Miami Sunday and Jacksonville Monday are my two remaining major hurdles —

I will be doing some more college lecturing in Atlanta Tues + Wed, and then should see you by Thurs.

Meantime, kiss Stillah and her mother (smile) for me. I didn't say too much to you on the phone because some people were sitting there.

Your loving husband
As Salaam Alaikum

A note from Malcolm to Betty about his tour
through Southern cities, circa 1960

Chapter 47
POLICE BRUTALITY

Remember how Malcolm's father hit his mother sometimes? Remember how Emmett Till's father hit his mother, Mamie? Domestic violence is wrong. Most times it happens in homes. Sometimes in streets. On April 26, 1957, a Black man named Reese hit an unnamed woman at the corner of 125th Street and Lenox Avenue in Harlem.

Officer Ralph Plaisance was probably nearby when Reese started hitting the woman. The officer came over. Reese was angry. Officer Plaisance tried to arrest Reese. Reese resisted, angering Officer Plaisance. He pulled out his nightstick. He started beating on Reese. Another officer came and started beating Reese with his nightstick too.

The woman Reese had hit snuck away. She probably did not want to get hit by the officers too.

It was in the afternoon when those officers were beating on Reese in 1957. The intersection was packed with Black shoppers. There were many stores around this corner, then and now. The stores are different today. Starbucks. CVS. Raymour & Flanigan furniture store. Cohen's Fashion Optical.

Lenox Avenue also has another name today: Malcolm X Boulevard. Because no other incident was more important to people in Harlem first hearing the name Malcolm X.

Many people stopped to look. All witnessing these two White officers beat Reese. Many observers got angry. Because even as they knew what Reese had done was wrong, they saw what the police were doing was wrong too.

No one watching this grew angrier than three members of Malcolm's mosque: Johnson X, Lpyssi X, and Frankie Lee X. They had heard Malcolm preach many times about being peaceful. About never harming anyone. But "if someone puts his hand on you," then defend yourself!

Malcolm preached for Black people to practice self-defense. Many of the martial arts preach self-defense. Learning those skills *not* to harm people. But to prevent violent people from harming you and others. Malcolm had observed all these racist White people harming Black people like Emmett Till. Malcolm did not teach his members to walk away from racist terrorists or violent White police officers. And so, when the White police officers harming Reese ordered the gathering crowd of Black people to leave, you know what the Black Muslims did? Johnson, Lpyssi, and Frankie Lee refused. It was probably Johnson who shouted, "You're not in Alabama—this is New York."

Officer Mike Dolan had just arrived on the scene. Heard what Johnson likely said. Didn't like it. Officer Dolan charged at Johnson, swinging his nightstick. Beat Johnson hard on his head. Really hard. So hard, Officer Dolan bruised Johnson's brain. It started bleeding. Blood in someone's brain can kill them.

Soon, the officers arrested the badly beaten Johnson along with the others. Pushed them into the police car. Rode a few blocks to the police station.

A woman who saw it all ran up the block to a restaurant owned by Elijah's Nation. She burst in. She told Elijah's followers the police had badly beaten one of their own. And took him to the police station instead of the hospital.

By the time the sun had set, Malcolm had been informed. He assembled the Fruit of Islam—about fifty Black male members of his mosque. The Fruit of Islam was trained in martial arts. Trained in self-defense. These Black men in suits went to the police station. Lined up in military formation outside. Behind them gathered more and more angry Black people who had their own experiences being beaten by the police.

Malcolm had so many experiences with police violence. He didn't yet know that one of the worst would happen a year later. After marrying, he and Betty moved into a duplex house in East Elmhurst, Queens. Malcolm and Betty shared the upstairs home with a family from his mosque. Other mosque families lived downstairs.

Two White police officers showed up looking to arrest someone. At the bottom-floor home, they were met at the door by Yvonne. She said she would not let them into the home without a search warrant. The law states that police need a search warrant to enter private homes. But the lawmen did not care about the law. They tried to push past her. Other women came. They managed to get the officers out and shut the door.

But the police came back later that night. Tried to push themselves into the home again without a warrant. By now, Yvonne's husband, John, had come home. John tried to hold the officers off outside the door. But they shattered the glass door to open the lock to break into the house. Someone hurled a bottle at an officer from an upstairs window. It hit him. The officer pulled out his gun and shot through the door.

The residents now scattered. The police broke into the house. Searched it. Didn't find the person they were looking for. Arrested everyone, including Malcolm's pregnant wife, Betty.

Malcolm heard what had happened. He returned to New York a man on fire. He organized a picket line outside the police station where Betty and his members were taken. He went straight to the newspapers to complain about "the gestapo tactics of white police."

The gestapo were Adolf Hitler's secret state police who terrorized Jews and others identified as political enemies in Nazi Germany. "Where else and under what circumstances could you find situations where police can freely invade private homes, break up furniture, break down doors, threaten to beat pregnant women, and even try to shoot a 13-year-old girl," he asked, "but right here in American Negro neighborhoods."

How could Malcolm not think the same thing the year before? After the police beat up Johnson X.

Chapter 48
MARCH ON HARLEM

Malcolm went into the police station. He asked to see Johnson. The police said they weren't holding Johnson. Malcolm didn't believe them.

The crowd outside got larger. Some five hundred raging people. Malcolm said he wasn't leaving—and the crowd wasn't leaving—until the police let him see Johnson. The growing crowd changed the minds of the police. They allowed Malcolm to meet with his fellow Muslim.

When he saw Johnson, Malcolm could barely contain himself. He saw blood and bruises on Johnson's head, face, and shoulders. Johnson was barely awake. He appeared to be dying inside a dirty jail cell.

Johnson told Malcolm the pain was bad when he arrived at the police station. So bad he fell to his knees to pray. The lieutenant in charge pulled out his nightstick and struck Johnson in the mouth and on his legs. He couldn't even pray without the police beating him.

"That man belongs in the hospital," Malcolm told the lieutenant in charge. Probably the same officer who had struck Johnson.

The police called an ambulance, worried about the crowd. Took Johnson off to Harlem Hospital at 135th Street.

Outside now, Malcolm looked at the line of Muslims. He gave the order to march. Behind Malcolm, who was behind the ambulance.

They marched up Lenox Avenue—now conamed Malcolm X

Boulevard—the busiest street in Harlem. Behind the Muslims marched the Black people of Harlem.

By now, it seemed as if everyone knew about the police beating. Because it seemed as if everyone knew what was happening—or learned what was happening as they saw the March on Harlem. People coming out of stores and restaurants and bars on Lenox Avenue joined the march. Or stood and watched Malcolm lead fifty Black Muslims to Harlem Hospital. Those Black Muslims were a sight to see marching those thirteen blocks. Like soldiers. Lined up straight. Heads high. All in dark suits. White shirts. Serious looking. Like the tall, light-skinned, red-haired man leading them, Malcolm X.

Chapter 49
THAT MUCH POWER

O utside the hospital now, the crowd had grown to two thousand people. "Harlem's black people were long since sick and tired of police brutality," Malcolm remembered. The New York Police Department called "all available cops." Maybe because they knew what was about to happen?

Out of nowhere, the police took the badly hurt Johnson out of the hospital. The medical staff had stopped much of his bleeding. But his skull and brain remained seriously injured. He needed surgery.

But the police took him back to the 28th Precinct. Placed him again in a cell.

Everyone marched back down to the police station. Angrier than ever. More people than ever. At least four thousand strong.

But the police were most worried about the fifty members of Elijah's Nation. Lined up again a half a block long in front of the station. Disciplined. Still. Not saying a word. Awaiting orders from Malcolm X.

Malcolm entered the station again, this time with his lawyer, Charles J. Beavers. Charles told the police that Johnson should be returned to the hospital. Johnson could not stand on his own. Police refused to take him back, saying he had already been to the hospital. They claimed he had to remain in jail before seeing a judge in the morning.

When Charles asked the police to give Johnson a pillow, they said no. But they did allow Johnson to use his coat as a pillow. With that, the cell door closed on Johnson. It was 2:30 A.M. Malcolm and Charles left the police station. Hoping Johnson survived. Angry that his life did not matter to the police.

Malcolm looked out at the angry crowd. He could have unleashed them on the police—on all the White-owned stores nearby with owners who mistreated Black people. But Malcolm did not preach violence. He preached self-defense. He felt he had done all he could to defend Johnson that night.

Malcolm stepped in front of his line of Black men. He gave a hand signal. The Fruit of Islam quietly marched away. The angry crowd left too. An amazed White policeman said to a reporter, "No one man should have that much power."

Many White men had that much power. That White patrolman who beat Johnson for one. The racist men who led attacks on Malcolm's childhood homes. The European and US authorities directing operations against efforts for freedom in Africa, Asia, and Latin America.

What that White policeman really meant? No *Black* man should have that much power. But that is precisely what Malcolm wanted for Black people: power.

The next morning, the Muslims came back. Bailed Johnson out. Took him to the hospital. Barely saved his life. Hundreds of stitches held his head together. Surgeons inserted a metal plate in his skull that Johnson had to live with for the rest of his days. The Muslims helped Johnson sue the city for police brutality. A jury awarded him $75,000. The largest police brutality judgment the city ever had to pay out up till then.

But just like the White men who brutalized Emmett Till, the White officers who brutalized Johnson did not go to jail. The whole affair received front-page coverage in Harlem's *Amsterdam News*.

It seemed as if everyone in Harlem was joining Elijah's Nation or talking about "those Muslims." After this case in 1957. After the police broke into "those Muslims'" home in 1958.

These experiences showed Malcolm how he could best bring in more members. By publicly confronting racism. By joining the emerging civil rights movement. By recruiting people to Elijah's Nation through the media.

Letter to Malcolm from a Nigerian government official, celebrating Nigeria's independence from British colonial rule, October 4, 1960

Chapter 50
HATE THAT HATE

Maybe it was this March on Harlem that first exposed the Nation of Islam to a young Black journalist named Louis Lomax. Or maybe he liked the Nation's pride in Black people. Its refusal to rely on White people. Its commitment to relying on themselves. Especially through self-defense and opening Black-owned businesses.

This young Black journalist worked as a producer on a show hosted by Mike Wallace on the local television station WNTA, Channel 13. Wallace was a familiar face to New Yorkers who watched television in the late 1950s. Ever heard of the show *60 Minutes*? Your teachers and parents have probably heard of it. The show still airs today on Sunday evenings on CBS. It is one of the oldest news shows on TV. And the most famous. Mike Wallace was one of the first journalists on *60 Minutes*. Became a legend because of it.

But back in 1959, Wallace was trying to make a name for himself. Lomax too. What boosts the names of television journalists, then and now? Ratings. Many people watching. Today, and back then, a lot of people like watching the controversial. The dramatic. The unbelievable. Things that make them very angry or very sad or very happy. Things people will argue about. Lomax thought he found all that in Malcolm and Elijah's Nation.

Lomax pitched Wallace on doing a series. Wallace agreed. Lomax did the filming and interviewing. Wallace did the narration. They created five half-hour shows. Named the documentary *The Hate That Hate Produced*.

The five shows aired on television in New York City each night from July 13 to July 17, 1959. Malcolm was not in town. He was traveling out of the United States for the first time. Traveling in the Middle East and Africa. To prepare for Elijah's same trip later. He visited Egypt, Saudi Arabia, Sudan, Israel, Nigeria, and Ghana. Visiting the African nations recommitted him to Marcus Garvey's belief that Black people worldwide needed to unite. Visiting the Muslim nations caused him to see just how little he knew about Islam. Elijah's ideas and rituals were so different from the way most Muslims thought and practiced their religion around the world. Malcolm learned that racial categories in the United States—like Black or White or Asian—did not operate in the same way in other countries. Because Malcolm was so light-skinned, some people abroad did not view him as Black. Maybe he started questioning the idea that all White people were devils. If he did, then he did not say so publicly.

Malcolm came back and showed Elijah's followers pictures and films from the trip. They loved the images of overseas. The same cannot be said of *The Hate That Hate Produced*.

The shows were designed to shock White viewers. Viewers saw Elijah describe Black people as godly—and White people as devils. And Malcolm agreed. With this, Wallace called members of the Nation of Islam "Black supremacists." But the title did not fit. Elijah's followers were not the same as White supremacists, like the Klansmen who terrorized Malcolm's family. Yes, Elijah's followers hated White people, just as White supremacists hated Black people. Yes, Elijah's followers and White supremacists opposed Black and White people marrying each other, living next to each other, going to school together. Both this hate and this advocacy of separation were racist. But Elijah's followers did not push for Black *supremacy*. Meaning Elijah's followers did not push for Black people to *rule* White people.

Nonviolent White people had nothing to fear from the Fruit of Islam. Elijah taught his followers to never attack White people, to only defend themselves when attacked. And Elijah's followers were not like White supremacists when it came to what mattered the most: money and politics. White supremacists wanted *Black people* to . . .

buy from White-owned businesses

work for very low pay at White-owned businesses

pick cotton on White-owned land

and be ruled by White politicians.

White supremacists lynched Black people who didn't allow all this White supremacy. They lynched those Black people who ran successful businesses, who pushed for higher pay, who tried to vote Black politicians into office, who owned their own land.

In the documentary, Malcolm attacked civil rights leaders pushing for integration. This came as a shock to many White people who thought all Black people wanted to live next to them. They had never heard of a Black person like Elijah preaching complete separation of the races. He sounded like Klansmen. Except that he was not. Elijah wanted Black people buying from Black-owned businesses (and White people buying from White-owned businesses). Elijah wanted Black people working at Black-owned businesses (and White people working at White-owned business). Elijah wanted Black people working Black-owned land (and White people working White-owned land). All in separate nations. Elijah was a Black *separatist*, not a Black *supremacist*. Elijah preached Black separation from White people. Not Black supremacy over White people.

But that is not what the viewers of this documentary were shown. Louis Lomax asked Elijah several questions about a coming race war. The show pictured the Fruit of Islam training in karate. Making it seem as if Elijah and his followers, like Malcolm, were preparing to kill White people or rule over White people. Not leaders who wanted to separate from White people because White people refused to allow Black people to be equals in the society that already existed. Racist ideas had long taught White people to be scared of Black people.

A lot of the shocked White people became very scared. A lot of that fear turned to anger. A lot of their anger was unleashed on the Nation of Islam. White critics came at Elijah's Nation left and right. Called Elijah's followers "hate-messengers" . . . "black segregationists" . . . "hate-teachers" . . . "violence-seekers" . . . "black racists" . . . "anti-Christian" . . . "possibly Communist-inspired." Even some Black leaders who worshipped White people or who wanted to integrate with them took every opportunity to attack Elijah's Nation. "By no means do these Muslims represent the Negro masses," they liked to say. Which was not necessarily true.

Members of the Nation of Islam were not ready for all this attention. Malcolm was. He answered calls nonstop from White reporters.

White reporters asked: Why does the Nation push for separation? "The guilty, two-faced white man can't decide *what* he wants," Malcolm would respond. He would go on to say that for years White people have been killing Black people who were trying to integrate. "Now, when Mr. Muhammad speaks of 'separation,' the white man calls us 'hate-teachers'!"

White reporters asked: Why do Black Muslims hate White people? "Why, when all of my ancestors are snake-bitten," Malcolm said, "and I'm snake-bitten, and I warn my children to avoid snakes, what does that *snake* sound like accusing *me* of hate-teaching?"

Some of Elijah's followers did not like all the hostile questions from reporters. Many followers did not like all the attacks. Some didn't just blame the attackers. They blamed Malcolm X.

The growing dislike of Malcolm did not surprise Elijah. He had already met privately with Malcolm. Elijah told Malcolm that he wanted Malcolm to become well-known. "Because if you are well known, it will make *me* better known," Elijah said. "But, Brother Malcolm, there is something you need to know. You will grow to be hated when you become well known. Because usually people get jealous of public figures."

Ministers and members of Elijah's Nation complained about the negative publicity. Some of these ministers were actually jealous of the attention Malcolm was getting. Wallace had introduced Malcolm on TV as "a remarkable man."

But even with bad publicity, Malcolm knew it could be good. Black people were used to television shows calling them inferior. They saw Elijah's followers calling Black people superior, almost godlike. They were used to shows worshipping White people as superior. They saw Black Muslims criticizing White people. It made some Black viewers feel better about themselves. Just as the regular programming of White superiority made White viewers feel better about themselves. Like the Western *Gunsmoke*, the top TV show that year, with all those stories about White men that made them feel better about themselves. Why can't we all just feel better about our equality? That no racial group is superior.

Some Black people shared Malcolm's criticism of civil rights leaders who preached nonviolence. Who taught Black people *not* to defend themselves when hit. Malcolm would be outraged in the spring of 1960. When he saw Black college students sitting in at "Whites only" businesses in Southern cities. When he saw White mobs attacking them. When he saw the college students not defending themselves. But those sit-ins were successful. They desegregated many businesses.

And these nonviolent protests were successful in alienating some Black people from the civil rights movement. Why should Black people have to allow themselves to get beaten to be served equally at White-owned businesses? Why couldn't Black people own their own businesses? Many of the Black people asking these questions started gravitating to Malcolm and Elijah's Nation.

Some of those new recruits were readers of Black newspapers. Malcolm started writing a series of pieces for Harlem's *Amsterdam News* called "God's Angry Men." Elijah took over the series. So Malcolm's writings appeared in another Black newspaper, the *Herald-Dispatch* in Los Angeles. Which was good timing. Because Elijah sent Malcolm to start a new mosque in Los Angeles in 1957. While in town, Malcolm visited the offices of the *Herald-Dispatch*. Watched how the staff put the newspaper together. Because he wanted to create a newspaper for Elijah's Nation. The negative publicity over the television show taught Malcolm that Elijah needed his own voice in the media. So he created a newspaper. Named it *Muhammad Speaks*.

But he didn't stop there. Malcolm wanted to share Elijah's teachings with as many people as possible. He wanted to share what was happening in Elijah's Nation. He started speaking a lot on television and radio.

And on college campuses.

Chapter 51

HOWARD

Malcolm X appeared in the doorway. He saw the Black college students inside the room. They were seated around a few tables. Eating. Talking. Laughing.

Silverware clanged on plates. Until it stopped . . . when all their heads turned to the doorway. They saw the man they had invited to Howard University. About two miles from the US Capitol and the White House in Washington, DC.

Howard was the nation's most famous historically Black university. In the 1800s, White people did not allow any or many Black people to attend their historically White universities. So Black people did what Malcolm was urging them to do in his time. Black people founded their own colleges. Generations of Black leaders have attended Black colleges. Martin Luther King Jr. Oprah Winfrey. Kamala Harris. The author of this book.

• • •

Malcolm gave most of his college speeches at historically White colleges. He boldly preached to nearly all-White crowds about the history of White people. Often talking about their role in enslaving Black people. At one college in New England, he rocked a White student to her core. Because a few days after the speech, she followed Malcolm to New York City. She seemed to come from a rich Southern family. Her accent. Her clothes. The way she carried herself.

She burst into the Muslim restaurant in Harlem. The same one that Black woman burst into when the police were beating up the Muslims. Malcolm happened to be there. Seated. Probably eating. She walked right up to his table.

"Don't you believe there are any *good* white people?"

Malcolm didn't want to hurt her feelings. So he said, "People's *deeds* I believe in, Miss—not their words."

"What can I *do*?" she asked.

"Nothing," Malcolm said.

She burst into tears. Ran out of the restaurant. Malcolm came to regret telling her—and other White people—*nothing*. They could fight anti-Black racism too. But he wanted Black people to lead that fight.

• • •

Malcolm stood tall in the doorway. Howard students noticed his slender body. His glasses as clear as his eyes. His presence. When Malcolm appeared, people noticed.

He walked into the room. "As-Salaam-Alaikum, brothers and sisters," Malcolm said. A traditional Muslim greeting meaning "Peace be upon you."

Malcolm sat down to speak with the students. He declined to eat. He told the students about how in his religion he ate only one meal a day. He had no problem drinking coffee. No sugar. No cream. Black. Strong with caffeine.

He drank cup after cup of coffee. Drinking away his tiredness. He rarely slept. Because he was almost always on the road. And because he was probably hurting.

Because Elijah Muhammad was hurting. Elijah had long battled asthma. The disease that produces extra mucus that blocks inflamed airways. Making it difficult to breathe. Bringing on coughing. Chest pain.

All this got worse in 1961, the year Malcolm sat down with these Howard students. Malcolm had just visited Elijah in Chicago. They were talking. Elijah started coughing. Harder and harder. His small body jerking in pain from the coughs. Painful for Malcolm to watch. Elijah couldn't talk anymore. He went back to his bed.

Inhalers for asthma had recently been invented. But doctors recommended a drier climate than Chicago. Elijah found a home in Phoenix.

The seriousness of Elijah's condition spread quickly through the Nation of Islam. The pain spread. "To us, the Nation of Islam was Mr. Muhammad," Malcolm recalled. Ministers and members identified as followers of the Honorable Elijah Muhammad. If Elijah died, whom would they follow? Who would lead the Nation?

People started thinking about Malcolm. Some people wanted Malcolm to take over.

Some did not. They spread false rumors that "Minister Malcolm is trying to take over the Nation." Or that "Malcolm X is making a pile of money." All the money made from speaking at colleges and other events, Malcolm sent to Elijah. Malcolm's wife, Betty, grew upset. She urged him to save money for their growing family. They now had two daughters, Attallah and Qubilah. Qubilah was born on Christmas Day in 1960. And by the end of 1961, Betty was pregnant with their third daughter, Ilyasah, who arrived on July 22, 1962.

But Malcolm refused to keep some of the money and save it. Betty persisted. Finally, Malcolm convinced Betty that if he died, the Nation of Islam would take care of his family. Another decision he regretted. Betty was right.

Because the leaders around Elijah were becoming Malcolm's enemies. Because they were not following the Nation's moral rules. They were secretly using the Nation's money to buy expensive stuff. They knew if Malcolm took over, all that would stop.

The leaders also knew what Malcolm would start. How he would use the money. He was tired of people saying, "Those Muslims *talk* tough, but they never *do* anything, unless somebody bothers Muslims." Muslims would start doing under Malcolm. Wherever Black people organized against racism, Muslims would be there. Like they were there outside the police station in Harlem. Like they were there when they marched to the hospital. Not just for Muslims anymore. All Black people. Disciplined. "For all the world to see, and respect, and discuss," Malcolm said. Just as all the world was seeing and respecting and discussing Martin Luther King Jr. and civil rights organizations like the NAACP, the Student Nonviolent Coordinating Committee, and the Congress of Racial Equality.

After Emmett Till's murder in 1955, the civil rights movement kicked into overdrive with Malcolm and Elijah's followers watching from the sidelines. Rosa Parks stepped forward one hundred days after Emmett's murder to help take down "Whites only" signs in the front rows of public buses in Montgomery in 1956. "Whites only" practices that persisted in public education in defiance of the *Brown* decision were challenged at a public high school in Little Rock, Arkansas, in 1957. Protesters were forcing down "Whites only" signs. At lunch counters and restaurants in 1960. At bus stations and in bathrooms in 1961. And many of those protesters were students at Black colleges like Howard.

Chapter 52

DEBATE

Malcolm's first time speaking at a Black college almost did not happen. Howard students invited him to speak in February 1961. But Howard leaders canceled it. They opposed Malcolm's view on separating the races, even as they led a Black college. Finally, Malcolm was allowed to speak if he debated someone who advocated integration.

Malcolm faced Bayard Rustin. He is most known for organizing the March on Washington where Martin Luther King Jr. gave his "I Have a Dream" speech in 1963. But Malcolm knew Bayard as one of the best debaters in the country. Bayard had already beaten Malcolm in a radio debate the previous year by exposing the essential weakness of the Nation of Islam. For all its rules concerning self-improvement, for all its talk of improving the lives of Black people, Bayard argued in the earlier debate, the Nation of Islam did nothing to improve the conditions Black people faced. Because Elijah's followers did not directly attack racism. The racism that kept too many Black people in low-paying jobs, in unpleasant housing, in poor schools, in poor health, in toxic neighborhoods—in police stations, dying, after being beaten by racist officers or terrorists. And Malcolm knew Bayard had been right in that earlier debate.

Now Malcolm had another opportunity to debate Bayard. After dinner, the students escorted Malcolm to Howard's new Cramton Auditorium. Every one of the 1,500 seats was taken. Five hundred people were not happy, standing outside, wanting to see the debate.

It was Malcolm's turn to speak. He opened by saying he was speaking not as "a Republican, Democrat, Christian or Jew, and certainly not as an American." But as a "BLACK MAN!"

The crowd of students went wild!

The Nation of Islam, Malcolm said, represents the masses of Black people without good jobs. Without good places to live. Without much money.

The Nation of Islam, Malcolm said, represents the masses of Black people who are angry about their treatment at the hands of White people.

The Nation of Islam, Malcolm said, represents the masses of Black people dealing with prison sentences. Dealing with police violence. Dealing with drug addiction.

• • •

There was a lot of truth to Malcolm's framing of the Nation of Islam. Perhaps no organization in the United States had done a better job getting incarcerated people back on their feet than the Nation of Islam. Perhaps no organization in the country did a better job working with people addicted to drugs.

Elijah's followers had a six-step process.

Step 1. Admit that they were addicted to drugs.

Step 2. Learn *why* they used the drugs.

Step 3. Be shown the way to stop the addiction.

Step 4. Gain the self-esteem to realize they could end the addiction.

Step 5. Stop using any drugs.

Step 6. Once cured of the addiction, find friends who were addicted to drugs and who could start these six steps.

Elijah's Nation had become a haven for the formerly incarcerated and addicted to make something of their lives. Malcolm, the prime example. Malcolm reflected on this during his other most important speech at a college campus in 1961. Speaking at Harvard University forced him to come to grips with how far he had come since those days when he was robbing houses in the Boston area. At one point at Harvard, he looked out a window. He was looking in the direction of the apartment where his old gang hid out after robbing houses. "It rocked me like a tidal wave," Malcolm explained. "Scenes from my once depraved life lashed through my mind."

Malcolm became overcome with awareness. Aware how deep in the mud he had been. How deep Elijah had had to go to lift him out. How Elijah had saved his life. The more he thought about it all, the more grateful he became. The more grateful he became, the more loyal he felt to Elijah. "I believed so strongly in Mr. Muhammad that I would have hurled myself between him and an assassin."

In front of the Howard students, Malcolm spoke about a different kind of loyalty and disloyalty.

HOWARD UNIVERSITY
WASHINGTON 1, D. C.

STUDENT COUNCIL OFFICE
COLLEGE OF LIBERAL ARTS

October 19, 1961

Mr. Malcolm X
Temple No. 7
116th Street and Lenox Avenue
New York, New York

Dear Mr. X:

The Liberal Arts Student Council of Howard University was very pleased to learn through Mr. Bayard Rustin of your willingness to participate with him in a discussion entitled "Separation or Integration" on October 30th in Cramton Auditorium.

As you may know, this discussion will be the first in a series presented by the Liberal Arts Student Council in an effort to stimulate student interest in major controversial issues. We are confident that your acceptance of our invitation will contribute significantly to that end.

The meeting will begin at 7:30 p.m., but we should be particularly happy if you could arrange to have supper with a small group of students and faculty members at 6:00 p.m. in the Mahogany Room of Frazier Hall. After the meeting in Cramton Auditorium, we are planning a reception at which you and Mr. Rustin will have the opportunity to answer informal questions and relax with refreshments.

If you would like to remain in Washington for the evening, or arrive a day in advance, we should be happy to prepare comfortable accommodations for you. Please let me know as soon as possible when your flight will arrive and what accommodations you will require.

Mr. Rustin has informed us that you will be flying in from California. As a student organization, our funds are quite limited, but we are in a position to offer you the equivalent of first-class fare from New York to Washington and return. I wish we could do more, but I hope you will understand our situation.

On behalf of the Student Council, I want to thank you for accepting our invitation to speak at the University. I am looking forward to meeting you.

Sincerely,

Michael Winston

Michael Winston,
President

A letter from the Howard University liberal arts student council president confirming details for Malcolm's debate with Bayard Rustin, October 19, 1961

Chapter 53

PLANTING SEEDS

Too many Black leaders do not represent the masses of Black people, Malcolm said to the Howard students. Too many Black leaders survive and sometimes thrive "off of gifts from white people," Malcolm said. Too many Black leaders are "dependent upon the white man" to whom they give "false information about the masses of black people."

Too many Black leaders are forcing integration these days, Malcolm said. But "the black man in America will never be equal to the white man as long as he attempts to force himself into his house." Black people need to stop trying to be with White people, stop trying to be like White people, stop trying to be loved by White people.

Malcolm said Black people must be with themselves. Like themselves. Love themselves.

Plus, the White house is burning, the ship of America is sinking, Malcolm said. Black people need to abandon the ship!

Bayard Rustin had a powerful reply.

"You say America constituted is a sinking ship, and Negroes should abandon this ship, for another called 'Separation' or another state. If this ship sinks, what possible chance do you think your 'separate' state would have?"

The crowd cheered. Malcolm came back. He came back the way he had been coming for the last year. He had joined with civil rights leaders to speak at the Harlem Freedom Rally on May

28, 1960. About four thousand Black people at 125th Street and 7th Avenue stood for five hours to hear several speakers. Malcolm appealed to Black people to unite against White supremacists in the United States. Malcolm had also appealed to people of color to unite in their common fight against White supremacy worldwide. People like Cuban revolutionary Fidel Castro, whom Malcolm met when he spoke at the United Nations in September 1960. But Elijah was growing concerned about Malcolm's political efforts at united fronts. And Elijah criticized Malcolm for meeting with Castro, whom the United States was striving to remove from power. Months before Malcolm's debate at Howard in 1961, the United States organized a failed invasion of Castro's Cuba.

• • •

"My stand is really the same as that of twenty-two million so-called Negroes," Malcolm said at Howard. "It is not a stand for integration. The stand is that our people want complete freedom, justice, and equality.

"Some think that integration will bring this about. There are others who think separation will bring it about," he said. We have the same objective: freedom and respect as human beings.

The crowd erupted.

Howard students were standing and applauding and shouting. Challenged to their very core. Proud to their very core. Proud to be Black in a nation that constantly told them they should want to be White. Proud to challenge racism in a nation that constantly told them they, Black people, were the problem. A Howard professor noticed all this. "Howard will never be the same," the professor told a reporter that night. "I feel a reluctance to face my class tomorrow."

Malcolm planted a seed in students at Howard that night. Namely Stokely Carmichael, Michael Thelwell, and Courtland

Cox. In a few years, the seed sprouted. These students would help change the civil rights movement for desegregation. Into the Black Power movement for liberation and respect. A Black Power movement that inspired Black people to gain control of their own communities. A Black Power movement that inspired Black people to say "Black is beautiful."

As much as the Howard speech planted a seed in the students, the students and Bayard encouraged a passion to bloom in Malcolm. He wanted to talk more about politics, about challenging racist power.

But Elijah kept saying no.

It got so bad that Elijah wrote Malcolm a stern letter weeks after the Howard speech. "When you go to these Colleges and Universities to represent Teachings that Allah has revealed to me for our people, do not go too much into the details of the political side," Elijah wrote to Malcolm on February 15, 1962. But Malcolm did not stop. The more Malcolm talked about the racism harming Black people, the more racist White officials attacked the Nation of Islam. Elijah saw the damage: White officials lurking around his mosques. Making their lives harder.

In August 1962, Elijah ordered Malcolm to cancel his upcoming speeches at colleges. Few people in the United States were being requested to speak more at colleges than Malcolm. Malcolm was devastated. But his attention had shifted elsewhere. To something that devastated him in Los Angeles.

[11/26/62]

Los Angeles, Cal
Monday, morning

As Salaam Alaikum

In the Holy Name of Allah, whom we thank
for His Last Messenger, the Honorable Elijah
Muhammad.

Dear Betty,

I pray Allah that you and the
children are well and happy. I think
of all of you quite often, and would
write more, but you know the hectic
pace I keep and the tremendous
pressures under which I live,
especially when I'm here in Los
Angeles.

These preliminary trial hearings
seem to be going quite well. Allah
is manifesting the devils as real
liars. I was on TV here for

Malcolm telling Betty about the preliminary trial
hearings for Los Angeles mosque members following
the police raid there, November 26, 1962

Chapter 54

INVASION

Elijah's male followers were known around the United States as well-dressed. Not just Malcolm. Even police departments trained their officers to spot Black Muslims by their dress. A training manual for San Diego police read: "The 'clean cut' Negro, well-dressed and groomed, is the most likely member of the organization; male members of the inner circle wear dark suits, white shirts, and maroon ties."

San Diego did not have many followers of Elijah Muhammad in 1962. But Los Angeles did up the road in California. Los Angeles police probably advised San Diego police. Because Malcolm organized Mosque Number Twenty-Seven in Los Angeles back in 1957. Elijah still did not allow his followers to break the law or use weapons. But Los Angeles police considered the Black Muslims—really all Black people—to be armed and dangerous. Referring to the Nation of Islam in 1962, Los Angeles Police chief William H. Parker said, "We have been watching it with concern for a long time."

Sometime after this, two of Parker's White officers were near Mosque Number Twenty-Seven. Probably ordered there to watch the Black Muslims. It was very dark. Getting close to midnight.

Malcolm had been to this mosque several times. Seen the Glick Brothers hardware store to the left of it. Seen the beauty salon to the right of it. Looked up and saw the huge sign: MUHAMMAD'S MOSQUE NO. 27. Between the second-floor windows. Below the star and crescent. That widely used symbol of Islam.

The mosque was located on South Broadway in South Los Angeles, where many Black people lived in 1962. Today, mostly Latino people live in that neighborhood. The mosque is now RTLA Church "that exists to REACH an unchurched generation." Lively services with Latino Americans worshipping Jesus.

Today, RTLA Church has a parking lot to the right of the building. At some point, the beauty salon was torn down. Because back in 1962, the mosque did not have a parking lot. The Black Muslims had to park their cars down the street.

Midnight passed. Two White officers may have watched the car park on April 27, 1962. The officers likely watched two Black Muslims unload clothes from the car. They unloaded dry-cleaned clothes. With all their suits, Elijah's followers spent quite a bit of money on dry cleaning.

There had been robberies of clothing stores in the area. So the officers suspected these Muslims. Or maybe they were ordered to harass Elijah's followers that night. Or maybe they decided to do so on their own.

The officers approached the car. The two Muslims were in no mood to be arrested for something they did not do. No mood to be harassed.

A violent struggle occurred. Between the two Black Muslims and two White officers. People inside Mosque Number Twenty-Seven down the street heard the noise. Started coming out of the mosque. The officers called for backup. One officer pulled out his gun. Threatened to shoot the growing crowd. Someone grabbed his gun to disarm him. The gun went off. Did the officer shoot his partner in the elbow?

Backup arrived. About seventy officers. They did not come to the scene of the struggle down the street. They went straight to the mosque. Invaded it like an army. Shot and beat unarmed Muslims. Shot and beat their way inside. The shooting and beating lasted fifteen minutes. The officers trashed the holy mosque. One yelled, "Let's tear those pretty suits off those [N-words]." The officers ripped off clothes, claiming they were searching for weapons. No one had any weapons.

At one point, an officer shot William X in the back. Paralyzed him for life. Officers also shot William's brother Robert and Roosevelt, Arthur, Clarence, and Monroe. Ronald X came outside to help carry the injured Roosevelt to a car. Ronald was the secretary of Mosque Number Twenty-Seven, a close friend of Malcolm's. He raised his hands in the air and pleaded with the officers to stop shooting. Officer Donald Weese shot Ronald. Killed him. Left him lying there in his own blood.

This happened to eighteen-year-old Michael Brown in 2014. After shooting him and killing him, police left Michael lying in his own blood. For hours in Ferguson, Missouri. Inspiring the Black Lives Matter movement.

Back in 1962, several Muslims lay wounded or dying in their own blood on the sidewalk outside the mosque in Los Angeles. Their Black lives did not seem to matter. It took an hour for ambulances to come. Healthy White officers received medical attention first. Three of the injured Muslims were brought to jail and held there for two days. Without medical treatment! Like Johnson in Harlem!

None of the officers were charged with crimes. A number of Muslims—who were beaten and shot—were charged with crimes.

Remember when police officers invaded Malcolm's house in Queens? Arrested his pregnant wife, Betty! Remember, he came back from Boston a man on fire.

Well, when Malcolm heard about the killing of his friend Ronald.

When he heard about the police paralyzing William.

When he heard five other Muslims were shot, all of whom Malcolm probably knew well.

When he heard the police ransacked the holy mosque. (Imagine the police ransacking your church? Your synagogue? Your home?)

When he heard about the police tearing off suits.

When he heard the police left his brothers on the street in their own blood, without medical attention.

When Malcolm heard it all, he wept. Hard. He wept a pool of tears on the streets of Harlem. Tears dropped from his life. A life harmed again and again by racism.

Malcolm did not cry long. His tears turned to anger.

Chapter 55

RESPONSE

In his anger, Malcolm desired a response. He wanted Black Muslims to harm the Los Angeles police officers who had harmed Black Muslims.

For years, Malcolm had been attacking civil rights leaders for not practicing self-defense—for allowing segregationists to beat and kill nonviolent protesters. For years, Malcolm had been saying that "the Honorable Elijah Muhammad teaches us" that Black Muslims are peaceful. But when attacked, we defend ourselves.

But in this instance, Malcolm left self-defense behind. He wanted to attack back. He wanted an "eye for an eye" and "a head for a head, and a life for a life." The problem is, as the old saying goes, "an eye for an eye makes the whole world blind."

Elijah shot down the plan of attacking the Los Angeles Police Department. Disappointing Malcolm. Bitterly. Completely.

Elijah wasn't about peace. He wasn't worried about continuing the cycle of violence. No, it was about money for Elijah. That's why Elijah didn't want the Nation of Islam to go to war against the police. A lot of his followers would be killed or arrested. Fewer followers, less money coming to Elijah.

Malcolm never saw Elijah the same way again. He no longer saw Elijah as a protector of Black people. Or even of Black Muslims. Malcolm saw Elijah as interested in protecting his riches. Malcolm saw all the riches flowing into Elijah's hands from mosques and members around the country. And Elijah and his family members and his officials in Chicago wanted even more money. Not war with the police.

Every member had to send a portion of their wages to Elijah. Many donated extra funds. After Ronald's death, every Muslim was ordered to obtain two new subscriptions to *Muhammad Speaks* per day.

EVERY. SINGLE. DAY.

Those who refused to do so were kicked out of the Nation of Islam. This order caused great difficulty among members. It was like a second job. But Elijah did not care. He wanted more money from more people buying his newspaper.

Malcolm carried on. He flew out to Los Angeles. He felt encouraged by civil rights leaders and their outrage at the police killing of Ronald X. Leaders like NAACP leader Roy Wilkins.

Malcolm presided over Ronald's funeral with the minister of Mosque Number Twenty-Seven. More than one thousand people came out to attend the service or join the funeral procession. It was Malcolm's turn to speak.

"In the name of Allah, the Beneficent, the Merciful. To whom all praise is due, whom we forever thank for giving us the Honorable Elijah Muhammad as our leader, teacher, and guide," Malcolm said. "I . . . open up like that because I am a representative of the Honorable Elijah Muhammad. And were it not for him, you and I wouldn't be here today."

Malcolm remained grateful to Elijah. But he could not speak *for* Elijah in that moment. At that funeral. He had to speak for himself. To this room of Black people. From this point forward, he started speaking for himself more and more. Saying "the Honorable Elijah Muhammad teaches us" less and less.

And after Ronald's death, he did not feel right attacking civil rights leaders. Malcolm started the speech congratulating and praising civil rights leaders and organizations. He wanted to join with them in Los Angeles to fight racism. He wanted all Black people to unite against police brutality.

"Let us remember that we are not brutalized because we're Baptists," Malcolm said. "We're not brutalized because we're Methodists. We're not brutalized because we're Muslims. We're not brutalized because we're Catholics. We're brutalized because we are black people in America."

But Black people don't know this, Malcolm said. Because Black people in America don't even know who they are. "Twenty million black people don't even know their own language. Why? Because [the white man] took it away from you," Malcolm said. "Twenty million black people who don't even know the history of their ancestors. Why? Because he took it away from you." He went on.

"Who taught you to hate the texture of your hair?" Malcolm asked.

"Who taught you to hate the color of your skin?" Malcolm asked. "To such extent that you bleach, to get like the white man. Who taught you to hate the shape of your nose and the shape of your lips?

"Who taught you to hate yourself, from the top of your head to the soles of your feet?" Malcolm asked. "Who taught you to hate the race that you belong to, so much so that you don't want to be around each other?"

Malcolm knew the answer. The crowd of Black people knew the answer. Racist White people taught Black people to hate themselves.

And racist White people taught *White people* to hate Black people. Not just Black men. Black women too. "The most disrespected person in America is the black woman. The most un-protected person in America is the black woman," Malcolm said. "The most neglected person in America is the black woman. And as Muslims, the Honorable Elijah Muhammad teaches us to respect our women, and to protect our women."

Malcolm now realized that Elijah's vision of a separate Black nation was nowhere in sight. He had to stop police violence here and now to protect Black women and men. Stop racism here and now. Where Black people lived. And Malcolm realized that Black Muslims could not do it alone. That is why Malcolm wanted Black people to unite. That is why in the days after Ronald's funeral, Malcolm worked hard to unite Black organizations against police violence in Los Angeles. To get some sort of justice for Ronald X.

But again, Elijah told Malcolm to stand down. Not to work with civil rights leaders. Not to organize protests with them against police violence in Los Angeles. Let Allah fight. Malcolm did as Elijah ordered.

Soon, civil rights leaders did not want to work with Malcolm.

Chapter 56

BARRED

O n June 3, 1962, 121 White people from Atlanta were killed in an airplane crash in Paris. Malcolm called this unspeakable tragedy "a very beautiful thing." Evidence that his prayers had been answered. NAACP leader Roy Wilkins and Martin Luther King Jr. both commented on Malcolm's words, claiming that his "hatred" and "glad feelings over death" did not represent the feelings of most Black people. Malcolm realized he had gone too far. Avoided speaking to the media. Civil rights organizations avoided him. Did not want to work with him.

Civil rights leaders not working with him did not shatter Malcolm. What really shattered him was Elijah barring Malcolm from organizing and protesting against racism—with or without civil rights leaders. Malcolm felt imprisoned again. Barred from joining and redirecting the civil rights movement at its height in 1963.

Malcolm had to simply stand by as Black people were harmed by racism in 1963.

The spring. Police blasted fire hoses on Black children marching against segregation in Birmingham, Alabama.

The summer. A Klansman assassinated Mississippi NAACP head Medgar Evers outside his home on June 12, 1963.

The fall. White supremacists bombed a Black church in Birmingham, killing four Black girls ages eleven to fourteen.

Malcolm had to stand by as other leaders protested against racism. Hundreds of thousands of people marched on Washington in 1963.

Dr. Martin Luther King Jr. gave his "I Have a Dream" speech on the National Mall. Malcolm went. He stood under a tree. Watching the march pass him by just as he watched the civil rights movement pass him by. All Malcolm could do was attack King and other civil rights leaders. Because he thought these civil rights leaders sold out on the March on Washington. Allowed the US government to control the march. Control when activists arrived in the nation's capital, when they had to leave. Control the march route and what posters marchers could use. Controlled who spoke and who did not speak. Malcolm did not speak at what he called the "Farce on Washington." Maybe he was a little envious of Martin, who gave the second greatest speech of his career. (The first would be when Martin came out against the US war in Vietnam in 1967.) The greatest speeches of Malcolm's career were still to come.

Chapter 57

GRASS ROOTS

Malcolm's second greatest speech of his career happened on November 10, 1963. Back home, in Michigan. In Detroit. Not far from where Malcolm lived after he got out of prison. Not far from where Rosa Parks had settled. Not far from where Motown Records had been founded a few years earlier, eventually launching the careers of singers like Michael Jackson.

The event was organized by someone who thought like Malcolm. Reverend Albert Cleage. At his church, Reverend Cleage was about to have a massive painting put on the wall behind the pulpit. A painting of Jesus as a Black baby being held by his mother, the Black Madonna. Malcolm would have loved the painting. But it wasn't up yet in 1963. And Reverend Cleage held the conference at another church that could seat thousands: King Solomon Baptist Church.

Malcolm stood before two thousand Black people. To give his "Message to the Grass Roots." A speech recorded and heard by millions of people ever since.

Being Black in America was like catching hell, Malcolm declared.

"You don't catch hell," he said, "because you're a Methodist or Baptist, you don't catch hell because you're a Democrat or a Republican, you don't catch hell because you're a Mason or an Elk, and you sure don't catch hell because you're an American; because if you were an American, you wouldn't catch hell. You catch hell because you're a black man. You catch hell, all of us catch hell, for the same reason."

And the hell included the United States drafting Black men to fight and die in the war in Vietnam. Telling Black people to violently defend the United States abroad. Telling those same Black people to be nonviolent at home. To not defend themselves from all the hell. Malcolm called out this hypocrisy.

"If violence is wrong in America, violence is wrong abroad. If it is wrong to be violent defending black women and black children and black babies and black men, then it is wrong for America to draft us and make us violent abroad in defense of her. And if it is right for America to draft us, and teach us how to be violent in defense of her, then it is right for you and me to do whatever is necessary to defend our own people right here in this country."

Malcolm called for revolutionaries. He did not believe civil rights leaders pushing for desegregation were revolutionaries. "The only revolution in which the goal is loving your enemy is the Negro revolution. It's the only revolution in which the goal is a desegregated lunch counter, a desegregated theater, a desegregated park, and a desegregated public toilet; you can sit down next to white folks—on the toilet. That's no revolution."

Some of these Black people, Malcolm declared, don't want to be free. Some of these Black people want to be White.

"To understand this, you have to go back to . . . the house Negro and the field Negro back during slavery. There were two kinds of slaves . . . The house Negroes—they lived in the house with master, they dressed pretty good, they ate good because they ate his food— what he left . . . and they loved the master more than the master loved himself. They would give their life to save the master's house—quicker than the master would . . . If the master got sick, the house Negro would say, 'What's the matter, boss, *we* sick?' *We* sick! He identified himself with his master . . . And if you came to the house Negro and said, 'Let's run away, let's escape, let's separate,' the house Negro would look at you and say, 'Man, you crazy.'"

Malcolm said there were still such people "running around" in 1963. "This modern house Negro loves his master. He wants to live near him. He'll pay three times as much as the house is worth just to live near his master, and then brag about 'I'm the only Negro out here,'" Malcolm said. "And if someone comes to you right now and says, 'Let's separate,' you say the same thing that the house Negro said on the plantation. 'What you mean, separate? From America, this good white man?'"

Malcolm returned to history. "On that same plantation, there was the field Negro," Malcolm said. "There were always more Negroes in the field than there were Negroes in the house. The Negro in the field caught hell . . . The field Negro was beaten from morning to night; he lived in a shack, in a hut; he wore old, castoff clothes. He hated his master . . . That house Negro loved his master, but that field Negro . . . they hated the master . . . When the master got sick, the field Negro prayed that he'd die. If someone came to the field Negro and said, 'Let's separate, let's run' . . . he'd say, 'Any place is better than here.' You've got field Negroes in America today.

"I'm a field Negro," Malcolm announced. "The masses are the field Negroes."

Malcolm had started to question whether Elijah was a field Negro. He had started to question whether the other Nation of Islam leaders around Elijah were field Negroes too.

July 24, 1964

As-Salaam-Alaikum:

In the Name of Almighty Allah, The Most Merciful Saviour; Our De
Master of the Day of Judgment. To Allah alone do I submit and se

4847 South Woodlawn Avenue
Chicago, Illinois 60615
July 24, 1964

As-Salaam-Alaikum:

In the Name of Almighty Allah, The Most Merciful Saviour; Our Deliverer.
Master of the Day of Judgment. To Allah alone do I submit and seek refuge.

My Son:

I am very busy today with mail, articles, and an hour tape which has
to be made for Chicago this afternoon. So, I do not have time to sit and talk with
you. Here are the conditions on which you may return and be recognized as a true
Muslim Believer in Allah Who came in the Person of Master Fard Muhammad and
follow me, His Messenger to His people.

You will continue to see the failure of any opposition that is directed at me. This
is Allah's protection which He has granted to me, and as the Holy Qur-an teaches you
and others, that all opposition aimed at the destruction of the Apostle and his message will
be to no avail (would not prosper).

Allah comes to hypocrites from whence they do not expect and strikes terror
in their hearts, and He excites them. To read your disbelief in the paper and from what
others heard from your mouth after all the proof that I have given to you from your
cradle that I have met with Almighty Allah, was absolutely shocking to me.

Condition No. 1--That you go now and tell the people every where, where you
already stated your disbelief and opposition of my mission, that you now repent that you would say such things and that you are asking me to forgive you
and hope that the public will forgive you for speaking such evil things against
your father without a cause, aiding and abetting others who are known the
world over to be his enemies. This you will ask the public to forgive you and
to strike it out of their minds what you have said. And go around our businesses
and tell all of my followers there the same. Make yourself submissive to
Allah Who came in the Person of Master Fard Muhammad and submit and follow me, His own recognized and established Messenger in America to the
Lost and Found Nation of Islam. When you do this, then you come back to
me, then I will present you to the people.

Condition No. 2--You will also have to tell your wife the same because of her
ugly talk against me in the way of disbelief that I have heard. I will not forgive you or her for even living with a person like that, if you wish to sincerely
return and follow me, if they will not repent themselves, I still could not
accept you.

As-Salaam-Alaikum

Your father, Elijah Muhammad
Messenger of Allah.

**Letter from Elijah Muhammad to his son Wallace, outlining
the conditions for reentry into the Nation, July 24, 1964**

Chapter 58

HURT

Back in February 1963, Malcolm had lived in Chicago for a few weeks. He noticed how many of Elijah's leaders and relatives were acting immorally and buying expensive items with money from members. One of these leaders likely worked for the FBI. To take down Malcolm.

Why? J. Edgar Hoover led the FBI. A man as racist as they came. A man working to take down all antiracist leaders from Martin Luther King Jr. to Malcolm X.

Malcolm noticed that one of the few leaders *not* trying to take him down, not acting immorally, was Elijah's son, Wallace. Malcolm went to talk to Wallace about the Nation of Islam. He knew Wallace well. Wallace had been the minister of the Philadelphia mosque that Malcolm started in 1954. In Philadelphia, Wallace started learning the Sunni Islam practiced by most Muslims around the world. There is nothing more valuable than learning. We learn from seeking out evidence and facts and, in the case of religion, different perspectives.

In 1961, Wallace had gone to jail for refusing to be drafted into the US Army. In prison, he studied the Quran, Islam's holy book, as closely as Malcolm had studied the dictionary.

Wallace came out a different Muslim in 1963, weeks before his long conversation with Malcolm. Wallace told Malcolm:

Elijah's beliefs were not Islam.

Elijah was not a messenger of Allah.

Fard, the (White) founder of the Nation of Islam, was not Allah.

Did Malcolm think to himself: If Fard was not Allah, then that meant Fard's idea that White people were devils was not true? And if White people were not devils, then Black people did not need to separate from them? The problem Black people faced was not evil White people. The problem was racism. Did Malcolm start to realize this truth as he spoke to Wallace?

What is certain: Wallace rocked Malcolm's faith in the teachings of the Nation of Islam that Malcolm had taught to millions since leaving prison. Malcolm did not know what to believe.

More than the Nation of Islam, Malcolm believed in Elijah Muhammad. That is, until Wallace told Malcolm that Elijah was not honorable. One of Elijah's strictest rules for married people was to only have sex with their husband or wife. Wallace told Malcolm that his married father had been having sex with his young secretaries for years. Even fathered children with some of them.

Malcolm had heard the rumors for years. Remember, his brother Reginald had tried to tell him even before Malcolm left prison. But Malcolm had refused to believe it. Malcolm had only believed what Elijah told him. "I don't think I could say anything which better testifies to my depth of faith in Mr. Muhammad than that I totally and absolutely rejected my own intelligence," Malcolm explained later.

After speaking to Wallace, Malcolm had to see for himself. He met with three former secretaries of Elijah. Each confirmed what Wallace had told him.

And each told Malcolm what Elijah had told them: Malcolm was his best follower. But one day, Malcolm would turn on him.

This really hurt Malcolm. He trusted Elijah, but Elijah did not trust him.

Malcolm flew out to Phoenix to see Elijah in April 1963. Elijah took Malcolm into his backyard. As they walked, Malcolm walked with all his emotions. He thought of Elijah as "the man who had given me wings—to go places, to do things I otherwise never would have dreamed of."

They sat down. Water calmly flowed from the pool. Not calming the flow of Malcolm's emotions.

"Well, son," said Elijah, "what is on your mind?"

Malcolm told Elijah what he knew about the secretaries and the children. Elijah did not deny it. He said it was the fulfillment of prophecy. Malcolm sat there shocked. Elijah likened himself to holy figures in the Bible who had committed immoral acts like David and Noah and Lot.

Malcolm left Elijah's home hurt. It was as if his father had died all over again. Then again, this father lived. And Malcolm X was not ready to leave the father who had raised him. Malcolm felt the need to protect Elijah.

Malcolm went back to Harlem. He believed leaders of mosques would soon find out. Malcolm thought it would be better for Elijah if they found out from Malcolm. Or at least that's what he told himself.

Malcolm informed the leaders about what Elijah had done. Malcolm gave them the explanation Elijah had given him.

The Nation of Islam leaders who did not like Malcolm found out that Malcolm was talking about Elijah's out-of-marriage children. Probably told Elijah that Malcolm was sharing the information to hurt Elijah, to take over the Nation of Islam. And the FBI made it worse. Had its agents and informants inside the Nation telling Elijah that Malcolm wanted to take over. Had false letters planted. Had Malcolm writing that he wanted to take over. Made sure Elijah saw the false letters.

Elijah's immoral leaders retaliated against Malcolm. To stop him from taking over. To stop him before he stopped their moneymaking. They rolled back coverage of Malcolm in *Muhammad Speaks*. Probably started urging Elijah to silence Malcolm. Elijah probably did not need much urging.

2118 East Violet Drive
Phoenix 40, Arizona
February 15, 1962

2118 East Violet Drive
Phoenix 40, Arizona
February 15, 1962

Mr. Malcolm Shabazz
4847 South Woodlawn Avenue
Chicago 15, Illinois

As-Salaam-Alaikum

In the Holy Name of Almighty Allah, the Beneficent, the Most Merciful Saviour, Sole

Master of the Day of Judgment. To Him alone do I submit and seek refuge.

Dear Brother Minister:

Sequel to our telephone conversation yesterday, I intended to mention to you that when you go to these Colleges and Universities to represent the Teachings that Allah has revealed to me for our people, do not go too much into details on the political side; nor into the subject of a separate state here for us. Speak only what you know they have heard me say or that which you yourself have heard me say.

Stay away from such subjects, for they are very ticklish subjects to handle by those who do not know as yet what the Teacher has in back on his mind for even mentioning such things. Make the public to seek me for the answers. Do not you see how I eject the devils on such subjects, by telling them I will say WHERE when the Government shows interest? There are two other Ministers who have already gone too far on this subject.

Best wishes for success and may the peace and blessings of Allah forever be upon you.

As-Salaam-Alaikum

Your brother,

Elijah Muhammad,
Messenger of Allah

EM:bc

A letter from Elijah Muhammad cautioning Malcolm
not to discuss politics publicly, February 15, 1962

Chapter 59

ROOST

The Manhattan Center sits between skyscrapers. Standing outside it, you can look down 34th Street and see the famous Empire State Building. Or you can walk in the same direction to Madison Square Garden. The New York Knicks and the Rangers play there. The New York Liberty used to play there.

Madison Square Garden is known as the World's Most Famous Arena. Maybe the best event venue in the world. What the Manhattan Center has always wanted to be. If Madison Square Garden holds some of the best events with twenty thousand people, then the Manhattan Center holds some of the best events with around one thousand or two thousand people. The Grateful Dead and Bob Marley have performed at the Manhattan Center. NBC's *America's Got Talent* has taped episodes there. *WWF Monday Night Raw* had its first episode there at the Grand Ballroom in 1993. This wrestling event happened thirty years after Malcolm X gave his last speech in the Nation of Islam. In that very same Grand Ballroom.

Malcolm almost did not give that speech at the Manhattan Center on December 1, 1963. Elijah was supposed to give it. But Elijah had to cancel at the last minute. He selected Malcolm to speak in his place.

Elijah called Malcolm before the speech. He ordered Malcolm not to speak about the recent tragedy that had shocked people worldwide. President John F. Kennedy had been assassinated days before. The nation was mourning, including many Black Americans who adored President Kennedy. Five months before his death, Kennedy had called on Congress to pass civil rights legislation. Elijah told all his ministers not to speak about the assassination. Not to criticize President Kennedy. Not to invite more attacks on his Nation.

Elijah sent his secretary, John Ali, to the Manhattan Center to ensure that Malcolm obeyed orders. John liked the assignment. Elijah did not know that John was working for the FBI. He was leading the charge to ruin the relationship between Elijah and Malcolm.

Malcolm saw Elijah's order and the presence of John at the Manhattan Center as another bar. Another attempt to imprison him. But Malcolm tried to obey. During his long speech, he did not say anything about President Kennedy or the assassination.

But then, after his speech ended, Malcolm took questions from the audience.

Of course, someone asked what was on everyone's mind: Malcolm's thoughts on the assassination of President Kennedy. Malcolm said President Kennedy had not even been buried before White reporters began asking the Nation of Islam to comment on his death. White reporters tried to trap the Nation into making, in Malcolm's words, a "fanatic, inflexibly dogmatic" statement. A statement like "Hooray, hooray! I'm glad he got it!"

A roar of laughter and claps rose up. Engulfing Malcolm. It fired him up. He probably wanted to stop there. Had been ordered to. But Malcolm could not. He could never be stopped from saying what he believed was right.

President Kennedy had been "twiddling his thumbs" when the president of South Vietnam had been murdered, Malcolm said. President Kennedy had been twiddling his thumbs when the prime minister of the Congo, Patrice Lumumba, had been murdered, Malcolm said. President Kennedy had been twiddling his thumbs when Klansmen murdered NAACP leader Medgar Evers in Mississippi and four young Black girls in a church bombing in Birmingham, Alabama. The United States—and its president—had allowed so much death, Malcolm said.

There's a saying: chickens coming home to roost. It means when someone does bad things, those bad things will come back to harm them.

Malcolm said he "never foresaw that the chickens would come home to roost so soon" for President Kennedy. "Being an old farm boy myself, chickens coming home to roost never did make me sad; they've always made me glad."

The crowd erupted in laughter, louder than before. Clapped even harder. As they watched Malcolm's huge grin.

Hardly any of the Black Muslims thought much of the joke. Except seeing it as funny. Malcolm added humor to something weighing heavily on people.

Assassinations are no joking matter. Malcolm had walked into the trap set by the media, and John Ali eagerly watched it unfold. John finally had his hook to kill Malcolm's relationship with Elijah. To do his job for the FBI. To ensure that Malcolm never took over the Nation of Islam—nor got rid of John and the leaders living large.

John Ali called Elijah after the speech. He told Elijah that Malcolm had defied his order to not speak about President Kennedy. He probably advised Elijah to punish Malcolm. Expel Malcolm. Or suspend Malcolm.

The next day, Malcolm flew out to Chicago for his regular monthly visit with Elijah.

23-11 97th Street
East Elmhurst 69, N. Y.
March 21, 1964

Mr. Elijah Muhammad
2118 East Violet Drive
Phoenix 40, Arizona

As - Salaam - Alaikum

In the name of Allah the Beneficent the Merciful to
whom we forever give praise and thanks for the
Honorable Elijah Muhammad as our Leader, Teacher and
Guide.

Dear Holy Apostle:

I am still a believer in Master W. F. Muhammad as our
Saviour Allah. I am still your number one follower.
You know well that I would never leave you of my own
free will. In fact, when you were in Philadelphia, you
told that vast audience yourself that I would follow
you until I died or that they would have to kill me to
keep me from following you. This is more true today
than was then.

I have always been a realist all my life. During the
twelve years that I was a registered Muslim in the
Nation of Islam, I encountered more opposition inside
than I ever did from either devils or from lost-founds.
I have reached the conclusion that I can spread your
message among our people in this country much more
successfully if I never again place myself under the
restraining influence of what I consider to be very
narrow-minded officials in Chicago. If I am properly
motivated, Allah will bless me with success. If I am
not properly motivated, no one else has to oppose me for
Allah Himself will make me fail.

I believe in your analysis and your solution. But, I
see nothing being done by those around you to help you
make your program materialize. Everyone seems interested
only in self. Some very bad lies have been spread and
are still being spread about me among the Muslims by the
officials. They succeeded only in creating confusion.
I open my mouth only to the degree that they force me
in order to defend myself.

Malcolm swearing his continued devotion to
Elijah Muhammad, March 21, 1964

Chapter 60

BETRAYAL

Elijah and Malcolm embraced. They walked into Elijah's living room. Malcolm could sense Elijah was upset about something. But Elijah talked about other things. Then, suddenly:

"Did you see the papers this morning?" Elijah asked. Malcolm probably thought about the headline in the *New York Times*: "Malcolm X Scores U.S. and Kennedy: Likens Slaying to 'Chickens Coming Home to Roost.'"

"Yes, sir, I did."

"That was a very bad statement," Elijah said. "The country loved this man. The whole country is in mourning. A statement like that can make it hard on Muslims in general."

Almost every time Malcolm visited, he learned there was something he did or said that Elijah did not like. For years, he had been pushing past Elijah's rules on political activism. For years, Elijah had been trying to remind Malcolm of his rules. But Malcolm never could have foreseen what Elijah would say next.

"I'll have to silence you for the next ninety days—so that the Muslims everywhere can be disassociated from the blunder."

Malcolm went numb. He could not speak publicly, to the media or in speeches! He could not even preach at his mosque! It was as if someone told him a loved one died. He gathered himself. As much as he disagreed with Elijah, following Elijah was all he knew. "Sir, I agree with you," Malcolm said, "and I submit, one hundred per cent."

• • •

On his flight back to Harlem, Malcolm prepared himself to tell his assistants at Mosque Number Seven. But when he got home, they already knew. All the New York City newspapers and radio shows and television stations already knew. John Ali had already shared the news.

John had an announcement go out to every member of the Nation of Islam. Malcolm was silenced. He would be reinstated in ninety days *"if he submits."*

But Malcolm had already submitted to Elijah. So the announcement made Malcolm suspicious. He got more suspicious when days later he received word that one of his assistants told a member: "If you knew what the Minister did, you'd go out and kill him yourself."

Wait, what? Malcolm was not the hypocrite. He was not preaching against sex outside marriage and then having babies with young secretaries. That was Elijah. Malcolm was not taking money from members and buying expensive stuff. That was Elijah, John Ali, Elijah's greedy children—except Wallace—and other leaders in Chicago. Malcolm still fumed over that time his members worked long and hard to raise tens of thousands of dollars to build a new mosque in Harlem. When he phoned John about it, he told Malcolm the money had been used on something else. Malcolm told an assistant that John probably used the money to dress up his wife in diamonds and a fur coat and take her out on the town.

John needed Malcolm out before Elijah died. Because if Malcolm was still in the Nation when Elijah died, John believed that Malcolm would take over. And all the money being stolen from members would end. All the rich lifestyles and corruption of leaders would end. And John's time in the Nation would end.

Elijah feared a scandal over his misdeeds. He allowed John to publicly humiliate Malcolm to ensure no minister talked about his extramarital children. No other minister wanted to be silenced like Malcolm.

Within days of speaking to Elijah, Malcolm realized what was happening. His enemies like John Ali had unleashed a three-step plan to get him out. A plan Elijah had approved.

Step 1. Make it seem as if he had defied Elijah.

Step 2. Suspend him forever.

Step 3. Provoke a Muslim to kill him for Elijah.

Hearing the death talk did not anger Malcolm the most. For the last twelve years, he had been ready each day to die for Elijah, to die for the Nation of Islam. "The thing to me worse than death was the betrayal," Malcolm recalled. "I could conceive death. I couldn't conceive betrayal—not of the loyalty which I had given to the Nation of Islam, and to Mr. Muhammad."

More than anyone else, Malcolm had made Elijah Muhammad a household name. Malcolm had withstood years of attacks. He had traveled countless miles, given countless speeches, growing the Nation of Islam from Harlem to Los Angeles. From hundreds of members and a handful of mosques. To thousands of members and mosques all over the United States. And now, this. He was silenced. His second father cast him out of his house—that Malcolm spent years building. Betrayal can be worse than death.

The pain must have been unbearable to Malcolm. Maybe Malcolm started wanting to die. To escape the pain. A horrible choice. Because all the people who loved him would be in pain.

Maybe there was another way. Leaving prison, a second time. Escaping Elijah's bars.

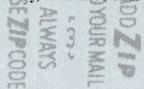

Note from Malcolm to Alex Haley, circa 1963 or 1964

Chapter 61

SILENT

For twelve years, since leaving prison, Malcolm was driving or flying somewhere. Walking fast in Harlem somewhere. Traveling somewhere to speak on behalf of the Nation of Islam. Now that Elijah had silenced him for ninety days, he had time to himself, for himself. So he answered letters. He met with journalist Alex Haley to work on his autobiography.

Malcolm spent time worrying about something he had never worried about: money. He had always believed the Nation of Islam would provide for him and his family. Maybe because he had provided so much for the Nation. He had provided dues from the thousands of new members he recruited. He had sent Elijah all the money he received from speaking at colleges. Malcolm probably made millions for the Nation of Islam. Leaders in Chicago used the money to buy various businesses and properties. Like 1,600 acres of farmland in Indiana. And large houses in Chicago and Phoenix.

Malcolm only received a salary of about $150 per month. Barely enough to cover expenses for his growing family. Now that he was suspended, he risked losing that income. Malcolm owned his car. But the Nation of Islam owned the house where Malcolm and his family lived. Now the Nation was talking about kicking them out. Malcolm did not make enough money to save up—in case Elijah fired him.

Malcolm tried to tell himself all would be okay with money. Elijah would reinstate him. So Malcolm spent most of his time trying to get back in Elijah's good graces. Initially, he thought the people around Elijah were the main problem. People like John. So Malcolm made direct pleas—calls and letters—to Elijah to end his suspension. Malcolm said he was being lied about. He said the people around Elijah were jealous and intent on driving a wedge between them. But Elijah ignored these calls and letters. He kept Malcolm silenced. Elijah was not interested in organizing and protesting against racism. He was not interested in radicalizing the civil rights movement. Elijah silenced Malcolm to keep his Nation out of the movement, to keep his extramarital affairs off the lips of his ministers.

The more silence Malcolm received from Elijah, the more he realized the problem was not just the moneymakers around Elijah, the problem *was* Elijah. But you know what really opened Malcolm's eyes? That fateful day, in February 1964.

A member of Malcolm's mosque told him that he had been ordered to kill Malcolm. He had been ordered to put a bomb under Malcolm's car that would go off when Malcolm turned the car on. Word of this got out. It angered Malcolm's followers. Many left Mosque Number Seven. They all knew, as Malcolm knew, an order to kill a member of the Nation of Islam could only come down from one person: Elijah Muhammad.

Malcolm suffered from Elijah's betrayal. The worst betrayal of a life of betrayals. And yet another betrayal was coming.

Chapter 62
BETRAYAL AGAIN

For about two years, Malcolm had been ministering to a big-talking young boxer from Louisville named Cassius Clay. When he wasn't in the ring, Cassius had become a frequent visitor to Nation of Islam mosques, businesses, and events. Inside the ring, Cassius kept winning. And now, he had a shot at the heavyweight championship.

The fight was set for February 25, 1964. Cassius invited Malcolm to come to his training camp in Miami in January. Silenced by Elijah, without anything else to do, Malcolm agreed. He brought along Betty and their girls. All were happy to escape the New York winter. Their first family vacation ever.

Malcolm hoped Cassius won. He hoped Cassius became the heavyweight boxing champion of the world. He hoped Cassius became a major celebrity. Because Cassius could then demand Malcolm's reinstatement. With his fame and power and money, Elijah would want to satisfy Cassius. Or Cassius could remain with Malcolm and help him start a new organization.

But Elijah Muhammad, John Ali, and their circle had other thoughts. They did not pay Cassius any mind or attention. They believed Cassius was going to lose to Sonny Liston—just as most people did.

Cassius shocked most people and beat Sonny Liston. Then he betrayed Malcolm. Cassius publicly sided with Elijah. In siding with Elijah, Cassius ended his relationship with Malcolm. Elijah publicly renamed Cassius, Muhammad Ali, on March 6, 1964. Muhammad Ali would go on to become the greatest boxer of all time. He broke many hearts with his gloves in the ring. But Muhammad Ali left Malcolm the most heartbroken of all.

Malcolm's last play to be reinstated, to end his silence, had failed. Only one option remained.

Chapter 63

READY

Malcolm knocked on the front door two days later, on March 8, 1964. Meyer S. Handler answered the door. Or maybe his wife, Helen, did. Whoever answered the door, they could tell Malcolm needed to say something important. It was nighttime. But Malcolm could not wait until the morning.

Meyer was known as "Mike" to his friends. He was a reporter for the *New York Times*. He had written stories on Malcolm over the last year. But in many ways, they were becoming friends. Which is saying a lot. Because Malcolm disliked almost all the White journalists he encountered. He thought they did not do their jobs. He thought they did not report the truth about racism or him. He thought they were constantly making him out to be a demon. Like the *New York Times* reporter who wrote the story on his "chickens coming home to roost" comment that got him suspended. That reporter was not Mike.

Malcolm had grown to respect Mike as a journalist and as a person. Had come to trust that Mike would report his views exactly. Malcolm recognized Mike's power. "The press is so powerful in its image-making role, it can make a criminal look like he's the victim and make the victim look like he's the criminal." But Mike used his power to make the innocent *innocent* and the guilty *guilty*. As any good journalist would. And in all Mike's stories, in all their conversations that could run for hours, Malcolm had seen that Mike did not hold the usual racist ideas that White journalists held about Black people.

Mike's most-read piece on Malcolm X did not appear in the *New York Times* but in *The Autobiography of Malcolm X*. Mike wrote the introduction. "No man," he said, "in our time aroused fear and hatred in the white man as did Malcolm, because in him the white man sensed an implacable foe who could not be had for any price—a man unreservedly committed to the cause of liberating the black man in American society rather than integrating the black man into that society."

Mike treated Malcolm—and Black people—with respect. As equals. Which probably surprised Malcolm. With all the pain Malcolm had experienced at the hands of White people. With the Nation of Islam teaching Malcolm—and Malcolm teaching others—that White people were devils. Malcolm saw that Mike was not a devil. Just as Malcolm saw the eagerness and openness of White youth at colleges. As Malcolm spoke at more colleges, as Malcolm got closer to Mike, he could not help but rethink whether his ideas about White people were true. He could trust this White man at the same time he lost all trust for men like Elijah Muhammad, who was Black. Maybe he started to think individuals could do evil. Not races.

• • •

Mike and Malcolm had first met a year before Malcolm knocked on Mike and Helen's door. Malcolm had Mike meet him at Malcolm's favorite meeting spot. The Mosque Number Seven Restaurant in Harlem. Mike arrived first in March 1963. He found a table and sat down. He felt uneasy being the only White person there. Uneasy because there was silence in the restaurant. Likely because Mike was there.

Malcolm arrived. Mike saw a tall and slender man. Malcolm saw a large man. Mike stood to greet him. Held out his hand. Malcolm looked at it. Slowly lifted his hand to shake the White man's hand. Malcolm asked if he could take the seat facing the door. Mike had heard similar requests from leaders in European capitals. These leaders lived in danger. They feared being assassinated, like President John F. Kennedy would be later that year.

The two men sat down. They talked for more than three hours. Mike was devastated by Malcolm's views about White people. But Mike noticed something: "At no time did he transgress against my own personality and make me feel that I, as an individual, shared in the guilt." And the more Mike watched Malcolm's public appearances, the more he understood what Malcolm was really doing: expressing the despairs and hopes of the most oppressed Black people. He was not "giving hell" to White people for the sake of it. He was giving hell to White people because he knew Black people were catching hell. This endeared Malcolm to millions of Black people longing to escape the hell of racism. They knew Malcolm would be there every step of the way. "Malcolm will never betray us," a Black artist once told Mike. "We have suffered too much from betrayals in the past."

• • •

Elijah Muhammad betrayed him. Muhammad Ali betrayed him. But somehow, in that moment, Malcolm did not believe that Mike would betray him. Despite their difference in age. Mike, fifty-eight years old. Malcolm, thirty-eight years old. Despite being identified as different races.

Their similarities probably helped Malcolm trust Mike. Mike grew up in the Midwest, like Malcolm. Chicago. And like Malcolm, Mike had the air of a great teacher. Wise. Seemingly all-knowing. Combined with the energy of a great student. Constantly observing. Constantly reading. Constantly questioning. Hungry to know more. Mike and Malcolm, two intellectuals, cut from different cloth. Malcolm studied philosophy and history in prison. Mike studied philosophy and history at some of the best universities in the Western world: the University of Chicago, Harvard, and the Sorbonne in Paris. No one could probably tell who, between them, was educated at college or in prison.

They were both well traveled by 1964. Malcolm had traveled to nearly every town up and down the East Coast and across the Midwest. He seemed to have traveled to every major town with Black people outside the Southern United States. Malcolm had learned to speak the language of Black people wherever he went. He learned their struggles. So he could recruit them to the Nation of Islam.

From 1933 to 1962, Mike had traveled to Paris, London, Berlin, Belgrade, Moscow—to major capitals across Europe. Writing stories on European wars and political struggles for the *New York Times*. He spoke French, German, Russian, Italian, Bulgarian, and Serbo-Croatian. Learned to understand and respect difference—while seeing a shared humanity across human differences. Both important to being antiracist.

Carrying trust, Malcolm walked into Mike's house.

Chapter 64

SPEAK

Malcolm and Mike sat down in the living room. Mike's wife, Helen, was there. She had been looking forward to meeting Malcolm. As much as her husband talked about him, as many stories her husband had written on him.

Helen served cakes and coffee. She may have sat down next to her husband to hear Malcolm out. Or maybe she listened in as she moved between the living room and the kitchen.

Mike could see Malcolm was there in his living room. But then again, Malcolm was not fully there. Malcolm was at a crossroads somewhere. He had come to Mike's home because he was ready to make a decision. Malcolm knew once he spoke, there would be no going back. Mike would write about what he said. The story would likely appear the next day in the *New York Times*. On its front page. Which is exactly what happened.

But Malcolm probably felt he had no choice. Muhammad Ali had betrayed him days before. Malcolm had just received a letter from Elijah telling him he was suspended indefinitely. Which meant he was silenced permanently. Silenced as Black Americans fought racism. He could no longer remain silent. Not now.

Malcolm told Mike that he was leaving the Nation of Islam. "I have reached the conclusion that I can best spread Mr. Muhammad's message by staying out of the Nation of Islam and continuing to work on my own among America's 22 million non-Muslim Negroes," Malcolm said.

"Are you still a Muslim?" Mike probably asked.

"I remain a Muslim."

What Malcolm did not say to Mike was that he had been secretly attending Friday prayers at the Islamic Cultural Center in New York City. The director, Dr. Mahmoud Youssef Shawarbi, started teaching Malcolm about Islam. Dr. Shawarbi had been telling Malcolm that Elijah's theology was not Islam. Malcolm had heard this many times before. Now he believed it.

Malcolm got around to answering the most important question: Why was he leaving the Nation of Islam?

Elijah had stopped him from participating in antiracist struggles. "It is going to be different now," Malcolm said. "I'm going to join in the fight wherever Negroes ask for my help."

Malcolm said he would be forming his own "black nationalist party." It would actively unite Black people. Actively defend Black people from White supremacists across the United States. Not fight for integration into White society. But liberation from racism. For Black people to control their own lives.

Malcolm would actually form, in the coming days, a religious organization: the Muslim Mosque, Inc. For his followers who had left the Nation of Islam and needed a spiritual home. But he urged Elijah's followers to not follow him. They did anyway. Reducing the money the Nation collected from its members. Angering Elijah. Angering John Ali. Increasing the death talk. Increasing the attacks on Malcolm in *Muhammad Speaks*.

Malcolm told Mike he would support Black people in their efforts for "good education; housing and jobs." But these efforts "cannot solve the main Negro problem." There must be a revolution against racism "and it is nonsense to describe the civil rights movement in America as a revolution."

Malcolm told Mike that he was willing to accept "all important speaking engagements at colleges and universities because I find that most white students are more attuned to the times than their parents and realize that something is fundamentally wrong in this country." It was his popularity as a college speaker that brought upon jealousy from other ministers and Elijah's family. "Envy blinds men and makes it impossible for them to think clearly," Malcolm told Mike.

Malcolm soon left. Mike and Helen turned to each other to discuss the conversation they had just had with Malcolm. But Mike had no words. Just sat there, thinking.

"You know, it was like having tea with a black panther," Helen said.

Mike thought the description fit Malcolm. He saw the black panther as royal, as a natural leader. "He is beautiful. He is dangerous." Just like Malcolm. And now, outside the Nation of Islam, Malcolm became the most beautiful to Black people and the most dangerous opponent of racism he had ever been. Perhaps activists Bobby Seale and Huey P. Newton had the same thoughts about the black panther when they named their new Black Power political organization the Black Panther Party in 1966. Earlier that same year, perhaps Stan Lee and Jack Kirby had similar ideas when they created the Black Panther character—the leader of Wakanda—in a Marvel comic book, which became a popular blockbuster film in 2018.

When Elijah heard the news of Malcolm's departure from the Nation, he was shocked. He cried. He had not foreseen Malcolm leaving.

Malcolm at Martin Luther King Jr.'s press conference on
the day of their first and only meeting, March 26, 1964

Chapter 65

MLK

It was around 9:00 A.M. in Washington, DC. Where Malcolm had just taken his seat in the US Capitol. In the Senate gallery: four rows of seats that look like a balcony.

Seated, Malcolm looked down on a huge room. The chamber of the US Senate held one hundred old wooden desks. One hundred wooden chairs. Arranged like a crescent moon. Facing an American flag and two long, elevated desks.

There are one hundred US senators. Two elected from each state. Malcolm looked down and saw fifteen empty desks. Eighty-five Senators were present on March 26, 1964. All but four were White men. These White men made laws that affected every single American. More than half of those Americans were women. About 12 percent of those Americans were people of color in 1964. Sexism kept women out of those powerful seats. Racism kept people of color out of those powerful seats.

Racism kept Black people from voting and electing politicians to represent them. Racism kept Black people out of places that served the public, like hotels, restaurants, and theaters. Racism kept Black people out of public facilities, like bathrooms, libraries, schools, and colleges. Racism kept Black people out of good-paying jobs. Racism kept Black people out of programs and institutions paid for by federal dollars raised by taxes on Americans of all races.

Or if they were not kept out, Black people had to ride in the back of buses, get take-out food at the back of restaurants, take the lowest-paid jobs, or go to school in the oldest buildings with the oldest books. Antiracist Americans had been fighting against all this racism for years. Malcolm had wanted to join this fight.

Barred no more by Elijah, Malcolm was free. And with that freedom, he was there. Seated. In the Senate chamber.

Why?

Well, back in June 1963, President Kennedy had proposed a new civil rights act to make forms of racism illegal. This came in response to all the racist violence against Black people that year. And all the efforts of the United States to do business in Latin America and newly decolonized nations in Africa and Asia. Many Senators started lining up behind the civil rights act. After President Kennedy was assassinated, Lyndon B. Johnson became president. Days before Malcolm talked about the chickens coming home to roost, President Johnson gave his first address to Congress in the US Capitol. "No memorial oration or eulogy could more eloquently honor President Kennedy's memory than the earliest possible passage of the civil rights bill," he said.

On February 17, 1964, the US Senate received the civil rights bill that had recently passed the US House of Representatives. On March 9, the day Americans learned that Malcolm had left the Nation of Islam, Americans also learned that racist senators refused to allow the consideration of the civil rights bill. What they did is called a filibuster. A filibuster is like taking a time-out in sports. Everything stops. And the racist senators stopped everything. By giving speeches. Day after day. So that a debate could not even be started on the civil rights bill.

Malcolm probably expected to hear more speeches when he took his seat. Probably also expected to see a familiar face he had never met. Far across the gallery, Malcolm saw Martin Luther King Jr. There to urge the passage of the civil rights bill too. Martin no doubt saw Malcolm X as well.

• • •

At some point, Martin and Malcolm left their seats. Malcolm and his assistant, James 67X, walked to a nearby conference room. They sat on a sofa in the back. Malcolm leaned his elbow onto the armrest. His right hand, on his head. His left hand, clutching his overcoat. At one point, smiled big as they waited. About two dozen reporters sat around two long tables in the middle of the room. They all looked up as Martin entered. As he went up to the podium.

Martin faced the reporters. Started taking questions about the civil rights bill. Saw Malcolm listening intently to the answers.

Martin's press conference ended. Malcolm and Martin left through different doors. Neither man sought out the other. But James 67X guided Malcolm around a marble column. And Malcolm and Martin ran into each other. They were both surprised. They stood face-to-face.

"Well, Malcolm, good to see you," Martin said, holding out his hand.

"Good to see you," Malcolm said, shaking Martin's hand.

They walked together. Photographers taking pictures.

Flashbulbs went off. They shook hands again.

Malcolm wisecracked: "Now you're going to get investigated."

Both men smiled widely. They said their goodbyes. It was the only time they ever met.

Sometime that morning, Malcolm and Martin watched as racist senators voted to allow the civil rights bill to be considered. Racist senators had finally stopped their speeches. After two weeks. The first filibuster had ended. The victory, short-lived. Because the racist senators planned to filibuster it again—the longest filibuster with multiple speakers in US history.

The second filibuster lasted sixty days. The US Senate did not pass the Civil Rights Act until June 19, 1964. It was the sixth civil rights act in US history. Congress had passed Civil Rights Acts in 1866, 1871, 1875, 1957, and 1960. But the previous civil rights acts had not ended racism, and Malcolm did not think the Civil Rights Act of 1964 would be any different. Because its rules barring forms of racism had to be enforced. If the government could not even enforce the Supreme Court's ruling in *Brown v. Board of Education*, Malcolm reasoned, "how can anyone be so naive as to think all the additional laws brought into being by the civil-rights bill will be enforced?"

Freeing himself of Elijah's thoughts, Malcolm had embarked on a journey of his own thoughts. His thoughts about racism. His thoughts about Black people. Malcolm shared his new thoughts in the best way he knew how—in a speech.

Chapter 66
HUMAN RIGHTS

On April 12, 1964, Malcolm gave a speech in his home state, Michigan. Back in Detroit. He spoke again at King Solomon Baptist Church, where he had given his "Message to the Grass Roots."

Two thousand people showed up to hear Malcolm give the speech known as "The Ballot or the Bullet." He had given a similar speech days earlier in Cleveland. But there was something about his home state of Michigan. Something about this church that brought out the very best of Malcolm. Because he never gave a greater speech. One of the greatest speeches in US history.

"This afternoon we want to talk about the ballot or the bullet," Malcolm opened. "But before we get into it, I would like to clarify some things that refer to me personally . . .

"So today, though Islam is my religious philosophy, my political, economic and social philosophy is black nationalism . . .

"The political philosophy of black nationalism only means that the black man should control the politics and the politicians in his own community," Malcolm said. Not White people. Not Black puppets of White people. But Black people.

"The economic philosophy of black nationalism only means that we should own and operate and control the economy of our community." White people don't allow non-White people to control their housing, control their jobs, control their business. "But you will let anybody come in and control the economy of your community," Malcolm said.

When you control the economy of your community, you control the jobs. When you control the jobs, you can create jobs "for the people in the community," Malcolm said. When you can create jobs for the people in the community, you won't have to demand jobs from racist White business owners.

"Anytime you have to rely upon your enemy for a job, you're in bad shape."

The line hit the crowd like a lightning bolt. The applause boomed like a bomb.

"He is your enemy. You wouldn't be in this country if some enemy hadn't kidnapped you and brought you here." Another lightning bolt of applause. "On the other hand, some of you think you came here on the *Mayflower*."

Malcolm could hear the people laughing at his joke. About the ship that had carried the English pilgrims to what is now Massachusetts in 1620.

"How you gonna tell me you're a second-class citizen? They don't have second-class citizenship in any other government on this Earth," Malcolm continued. "They just have slaves and people who are free! Well, this country is a hypocrite! They try and make you think they set you free by calling you a second-class citizen. No, you're nothing but a 20th century slave . . .

"I'm not a Republican, nor a Democrat, nor an American— and got sense enough to know it," Malcolm shouted, as people shouted back at him through their claps. "I'm one of the 22 million black victims of the Democrats. One of the 22 million black victims of the Republicans and one of the 22 million black victims of Americanism."

Malcolm paused during the ovation. He started back.

"And when I speak, I don't speak as a Democrat or a Republican, nor an American. I speak as a victim of America's so-called democracy. You and I have never seen democracy—all we've seen is hypocrisy."

Everyone seemed to clap in agreement.

But times are changing. "Twenty-two million black victims of Americanism are waking up and they are gaining a new political consciousness." Because Black people are angry. You are waking up, Malcolm told the Black audience. You are seeing trends in recent elections. You see that White Americans are evenly divided between Republicans and Democrats. So, you see, if we stick together, we can decide elections, Malcolm said.

Malcolm had changed. Elijah kept his followers from voting. Now Malcolm saw Black people voting together as power. But voting wasn't enough.

"You're the one who has that power," Malcolm shouted, looking out at that sea of Black faces.

You sent the Democrats into the White House, Malcolm said. But they've been down there for four years. And now, after everything else, they are working on the Civil Rights Act. "You put them first and they put you last. Because you're a chump! . . .

"You been misled. You been had. You been took," Malcolm said.

• • •

"It's the ballot or the bullet. Today, our people can see that we're faced with a government conspiracy," Malcolm continued. "This government has failed us. The senators who are filibustering concerning your and my rights, that's the government . . .

"As long as you fight it on the level of civil rights," Malcolm said, you have to deal with the White American government that has failed you. "You're going to his court expecting him to correct the problem. He created the problem. He's the criminal! You don't take your case to the criminal, you take your criminal to court."

Malcolm stopped as the church shook from the mighty applause.

The "court" he was talking about? The United Nations. It was formed after World War II to maintain international peace and defend the human rights of people everywhere. These human rights were outlined in the Universal Declaration of Human Rights, adopted in 1948, while Malcolm was in prison.

"When the government of South Africa began to trample upon the human rights of the people of South Africa," Malcolm continued, "they were taken to the U.N. When the government of Portugal began to trample upon the rights of our brothers and sisters in Angola, it was taken before the U.N. . . .

"Now you tell me"—Malcolm's voice was rising—"how can the plight of everybody on this Earth reach the halls of the United Nations and you have twenty-two million Afro-Americans whose churches are being bombed, whose little girls are being murdered, whose leaders are being shot down in broad daylight? Now you tell me why the leaders of this struggle have never taken" the treatment of African Americans before the United Nations?

"Uncle Sam is guilty of violating the human rights of twenty-two million Afro-Americans right down to the year of 1964 and still has the audacity or the nerve to stand up and represent himself as the leader of the free world? Not only is he a crook, he's a hypocrite," Malcolm said. "Here he is standing up in front of other people," pointing his finger at other countries, "with the blood of your and mine mothers and fathers on his hands. With the blood dripping down his jaws like a bloody-jawed wolf."

With the blood . . .

With the blood . . .

With the blood . . .

• • •

To stop the bloodshed, Malcolm felt he needed to leave the United States. And appeal to the world. Through the United Nations.

He didn't know it at the time. But this was to be his final campaign. Before he embarked, Malcolm wanted to prepare himself. He needed to get his "spiritual self strengthened." He left the United States the next day.

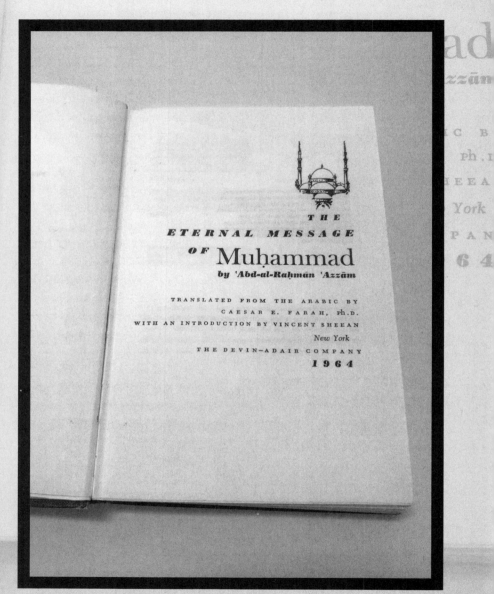

Title page of the first English edition of *The Eternal Message of Muhammad* by Abd al-Rahman Azzam, published in 1964

Chapter 67

DEPARTURE

Leaving Elijah's Nation sent Malcolm on a search to finally learn and practice Islam in the way most Muslims did around the world. Dr. Shawarbi, who had been ministering to Malcolm about Islam, urged him to go to Mecca. Every Muslim who is able, who has the money, is supposed to visit Mecca. That holy city in Saudi Arabia.

This is called the hajj.

When Malcolm got to the airport the day after his speech, he probably felt a sense of relief. Probably felt a sense of freedom. Free of battles over the Civil Rights Act. Free of Elijah's followers who hated him, who were trying to harm him. Free of the difficulty of starting a new organization, the Muslim Mosque, Inc.

A pregnant Betty, a five-year-old Attallah, a three-year-old Qubilah, and a nearly two-year-old Ilyasah—their three daughters—and a few associates came with Malcolm to see him off. At John F. Kennedy International Airport, renamed after the president assassinated months earlier.

Malcolm boarded a Lufthansa plane headed to the first stop: Frankfurt, Germany. His last stop: Mecca, Saudi Arabia.

The plane took off. In his hands, a book. *The Eternal Message of Muhammad* by Abd al-Rahman Azzam. Muhammad is to Islam what Jesus is to Christianity. Messengers of their Gods.

The author, Abd al-Rahman, was a citizen of Saudi Arabia, where Malcolm was headed. Abd al-Rahman was close to Prince

Faisal, the ruler of Saudi Arabia. Abd al-Rahman had given Dr. Shawarbi his book to give to Malcolm. "He has followed you in the press very closely," Dr. Shawarbi told Malcolm one day. The author's son, Omar Azzam, lived in Jeddah, the last stop before Mecca. Dr. Shawarbi gave Malcolm Omar's phone number.

Book in hand, plane cutting through the clouds, Malcolm introduced himself to the two men sitting next to him. They were both Muslims. Delighting Malcolm. He felt it was a sign that Allah was with him on his journey that began on April 13, 1964.

Chapter 68

EQUAL

Malcolm arrived in Frankfurt, Germany. He did some sight-seeing.

He then flew from Germany to Cairo, Egypt. Entering Egypt was entering the Muslim world. In the United States and Europe, most people practiced Christianity. In Egypt, most people practiced Islam.

Malcolm did more sightseeing in Cairo. But nothing prepared him for the sights he would see when he returned to the airport, where he was surrounded by Muslims going on their own hajj. To fly to Jeddah. When he boarded the plane to Jeddah. When he reached Jeddah. That city on the Red Sea in Saudi Arabia. An hour drive away from Mecca.

Malcolm recorded his sights of being swept up in all these Muslims embarking on the hajj in a diary. The most amazing sight was how "people white, black, brown, red & yellow, all act alike, as one, as bros.," Malcolm wrote. "People with blue eyes to blonde hair, bowing in complete submission to Allah, beside those with black skin & kinky hair. As they give the same honor to the same God, they in turn give <u>same</u> (equal) honor to each other."

Malcolm arrived in Jeddah on Friday, April 17, 1964. But airport officials refused to allow Malcolm to go into the country. To go to Mecca.

Only true Muslims were allowed to enter the Holy City of Mecca. Members of Elijah's Nation were not considered true Muslims.

Malcolm had to go before the hajj court in Jeddah to prove he was truly a Muslim. But the hajj court was closed on Fridays.

Malcolm found a bed in the fourth-floor dormitory at the airport. It housed hundreds of Muslims going to their hajj. The area with all those beds overlooked a large courtyard. Malcolm liked the atmosphere. "Muslims from everywhere, hugging, embracing, warm friendly spirit," he wrote in his diary. "The whites don't seem white—Islam actually removed differences." One White man "followed me around, offering the hospitality of eating with his family." The "pilgrims from Nigeria & Ghana, very vocal & confident."

Malcolm soon felt lonely. He did not know anyone. Few Muslims spoke English. Other languages were spoken, especially Arabic. "Not being able to speak the language is like being in a fish bowl," Malcolm thought, "everyone looking at me, talking about me & to me, and me not able to understand (hear) or to answer back."

Most of all, Malcolm sat there worried. Because he did not have much time. The hajj had to be started by April 20 in 1964 to be official.

The sun set in Jeddah. Malcolm got on his knees with other Muslims to pray. Muslims pray to Allah five times a day. At dawn. Noon. Midafternoon. Sunset. And evening.

After his prayer, maybe Malcolm took out his book. *The Eternal Message of Muhammad* by Abd al-Rahman Azzam. Maybe that's when Malcolm remembered. His spiritual teacher in New York, Dr. Shawarbi, had written the name and phone number of the author's son. Dr. Omar Azzam, who lived in Jeddah.

Malcolm got Omar on the phone.

Chapter 69
HAJJ

Omar rushed up to the airport. Malcolm saw a tall and "power-fully built man." Probably six foot three. Polished. Came from money. In the United States, some people would have seen this Arab man as White. By his appearance. Malcolm certainly did. But his antiracist behavior was so different from almost every American White man Malcolm had met.

"Why didn't you call before?" Omar asked Malcolm. "Come!"

Omar talked to airport officials. Got Malcolm out of the airport. His father, Abd al-Rahman Azzam, had a spacious three-room suite at the beautiful Jeddah Palace Hotel. It had a porch with a picturesque view of the Red Sea. Abd al-Rahman allowed Malcolm to stay in his suite while the author stayed with his son. And they all dined together at Omar's home that night. Malcolm told them about his need to go before the hajj court. These powerful men agreed to help. Washing away all Malcolm's worry.

Malcolm reflected on the night in his diary. He thought of the author, Abd al-Rahman Azzam. "Never have I met a more educated, intellectual" than him. Elijah, distant from his mind now. Malcolm thought of all the Azzams had given him. "Such hospitality," he wrote in his diary. "Never so honored."

In that beautiful suite, Malcolm could not help but think. He began to seriously question his racist views about White people. Views taught to him by Elijah. Views taught to Elijah by Wallace Fard, the White founder of the Nation of Islam. The day before, Omar had treated Malcolm like a brother. Abd al-Rahman Azzam had treated Malcolm like a son.

In the United States today, Omar and Abd would be considered MENA, people of Middle Eastern and North African descent. But back then, they looked White to Malcolm. And Malcolm's views of White people as devils did not match the loving way these two people had treated him. His views did not match the antiracist way Muslims from Europe had treated him since he arrived in Cairo and Jeddah.

Later that day, Abd al-Rahman Azzam went with Malcolm to the hajj court. Spoke for Malcolm. Told the judge Malcolm had left the Nation of Islam. Told the judge Malcolm had adopted the true Muslim faith. The judge also received word that Prince Faisal supported Malcolm's hajj. And named Malcolm an official guest of the nation of Saudi Arabia. Of course, the judge approved him. The judge recorded Malcolm's name in the holy register as a true Muslim.

Off Malcolm went to Mecca later that day after the sun set. After his prayer. Saudi Arabia provided a special car and driver and guide for Malcolm, as a guest of the nation.

Malcolm's first impression came from looking out his car window. "Mecca is as ancient as time itself, and looks it, except for the cars," he wrote in his diary. Indeed, Muslims had been making this spiritual journey to Mecca for thirteen hundred years.

They parked at the Great Mosque. To do the most important ritual in the hajj. The night air touched Malcolm's nerves. He followed his guide inside and around.

Malcolm saw it. The Kaaba, a huge stone in the middle of the Great Mosque that represents the holy center of Islam. Malcolm saw the ṭawāf: thousands of praying and chanting Muslims—"all sexes, sizes, colors"—walking around the Kaaba seven times. His guide led Malcolm around the Kaaba seven times. After the seventh time, Malcolm fell to the floor in prayer. His guide and another companion had to hold back the crowd from stepping on Malcolm.

Malcolm rose up. His guide led him over to do the sa'y, where Muslims run back and forth seven times between two small hills. Malcolm ran back and forth seven times. The ritual repeats Hagar's desperate search of water for her thirsty son in the desert. Hagar, a revered mother of Islam, maintained her faith in God. And water appeared out of nowhere in the form of the well of Zamzam.

Malcolm drank from the water of Zamzam. As the water went down, Malcolm probably felt a cleansing. A cleansing of his sins. All the lawbreaking before the Nation of Islam. And then as one of Elijah's ministers, preaching what he now considered a false faith.

Over the next four days, Malcolm completed the other rites of the hajj, including visiting Mount Arafat—where the Prophet Muhammad delivered his final sermon—casting stones at the devil, and repeating the ṭawāf and sa'y. Tired but inspired, Malcolm sat down to write letters back home. He wrote a letter to his wife, Betty. A similar letter to his older sister Ella. A similar letter to Dr. Shawarbi. A similar letter to Elijah's son Wallace. A similar letter to his assistants at the Muslim Mosque, Inc. Asked his assistants to copy the letter and send it to the media for all Americans to read.

Malcolm writing Arabic words in his notebook, 1964

Chapter 70
ALL THE SAME

From the heart, Malcolm wrote:

"Never have I witnessed such sincere hospitality and the overwhelming spirit of true brotherhood as is practiced by people of all colors and races here in this Ancient Holy Land . . . For the past week, I have been utterly speechless and spellbound by the graciousness I see displayed all around me by people *of all colors.*"

Malcolm described his upcoming plans and his first night in Mecca. What he did. What he saw. "There were tens of thousands of pilgrims from all over the world. They were of all colors, from blue-eyed blonds to black-skinned Africans . . . displaying a spirit of unity and brotherhood that my experiences in America had led me to believe could never exist between the white and the non-white."

No one in the United States was more known over the previous ten years for preaching that Islam was the Black man's religion. No one was more known for teaching that White people were devils. But here Malcolm was. Taking back those viewpoints. Which meant the problem was not White people, but White racism. Which meant Black people did not need to separate themselves from White people. Which meant it was possible for White people to be antiracist (and Muslim). Possible for Malcolm to work with antiracist White Americans. Possible for people of all races to come together and fight racism. To build an antiracist society where there would be equity and justice for all.

"You may be shocked by these words coming from me. But on this pilgrimage, what I have seen, and experienced, has forced me to *re-arrange* much of my thought-patterns previously held, and to *toss aside* some of my previous conclusions," Malcolm wrote. "This was not too difficult for me. Despite my firm convictions, I have always been a man who tries to face facts, and to accept the reality of life as new experience and knowledge unfolds it. I have always kept an open mind, which is necessary to the flexibility that must go hand in hand with every form of intelligent search for truth."

Malcolm recognized the truth that he had "eaten from the same plate, drunk from the same glass, and slept in the same bed (or on the same rug)—while praying to the *same* God—with fellow Muslims, whose eyes were the bluest of blue, whose hair was the blondest of blond, and whose skin was the whitest of white. And in the *words* and in the *actions* and in the *deeds* of the 'white' Muslims, I felt the same sincerity that I felt among the black African Muslims of Nigeria, Sudan, and Ghana. We were *truly* all the same . . .

"I could see from this, that perhaps if white Americans could accept the Oneness of God, then perhaps, too, they could accept *in reality* the Oneness of Man—and cease to measure, and hinder, and harm others in terms of their 'differences' in color . . .

"All praise is due to Allah, the Lord of all the Worlds.

"Sincerely, El-Hajj Malik El-Shabazz."

• • •

Completing the hajj, Malcolm X took on a new Arabic name, El-Hajj Malik El-Shabazz.

Malcolm reread the letter before mailing. Even *he* was shocked by what he wrote, by how much this trip had changed him already. Then again, he had changed before. His whole life, he reflected, "had been a chronology of—*changes*."

Now, Malcolm headed to West Africa, for more changes.

23-11 97th Street
East Elmhurst 69, N. Y.
U. S. A.
January 15, 1965

Miss Maya Maka
c/o J. Mayfield
P.O. Box 2052
Accra, Ghana

Dear Maya,

I was shocked and surprised when your letter
arrived but I was also pleased because I only had
to wait two months for this one whereas previously
I had to wait almost a year. You see I haven't
lost my wit. (smile)

I am very happy to learn that Sylvia returned
rejuvenated and has since been rejuvenating all
the rest of us there. It is true that I certainly
have wished many times that you and Alice and
Helen were here in the states again because all
of you gave so much on the ball it seems to be
almost a waste of time. For some strange reason
I never get any mail from Alice. Since I've
written her several times, I have began to wonder
if she gets my mail. When you write to her call
this to her attention.

Your analysis of our peoples tendency to
talk over the head of the masses in a language
that is too far above and beyond them is certainly
true. You can communicate because you have
plenty of (soul) and you always keep your feet
firmly rooted on the ground. This is what makes
you, you. Where is Helen and what is she doing
and what is her address?

What is Nana and Nketsia's position in the
field of culture there? A girl who has been
highly instrumental in helping us get the OAAU
started here is planning on coming there. Her
boyfriend is an artist who's last name is
Feelings. He is there already and you have
probably met him, at least, I know he has met
Efua Southerland and was highly impressed by
her as I myself was also highly impressed by

Malcolm writing to legendary writer and poet
Maya Maka (Angelou), January 15, 1965

Chapter 71
OMOWALE

They called it "refugee night." A refugee is someone who is forced to leave their home country due to a natural disaster, like an earthquake or hurricane that destroys whole communities. Or a human disaster like war. Or poverty. Or racism. Just as Malcolm's father fled White supremacists in Georgia to go up North.

Right now, more than one hundred million refugees are fleeing violence and poverty in the Middle East, Latin America, Eastern Europe, and Africa. In places like Palestine, Honduras, Ukraine, Sudan, and the Democratic Republic of the Congo. All the African Americans walking into that house on May 11, 1964, felt like refugees. Refugees from the United States. Racism forced them to flee the country of their birth.

They walked into the home of the unofficial leader of the refugees. A writer named Julian Mayfield. His Puerto Rican wife, Dr. Ana Livia Cordero, was a physician. She had prepared the delicious food.

A few years back, Malcolm met Julian at the New York home of his good friends actors Ruby Dee and Ossie Davis. Malcolm and Julian remained in touch. Even when Julian fled the United States like a refugee and ended up in Accra, the capital city of Ghana. Malcolm notified Julian that after his hajj, he planned to tour West Africa. Julian told fellow African Americans living in Accra.

They all got so excited! But they did not know exactly when

Malcolm was coming. They did not know exactly which plane he was arriving on. A group actually met three different planes at the airport! Thinking Malcolm was on each one. Only to be disappointed when they did not see him.

Malcolm did not immediately fly from Saudi Arabia to Ghana after his hajj. He traveled to Beirut, the seaport capital of Lebanon, in the Middle East.

From Lebanon, Malcolm flew back to Cairo, and then he flew over to West Africa.

On this first trip, Malcolm did not go to Ghana first. He went to Nigeria. Of the fifty-four countries in Africa today, Nigeria has the most people.

Malcolm landed in Lagos, the extremely busy capital city of Nigeria at the time. He hung out with E. U. Essien-Udom, who had written one of the first major books on the Nation of Islam as a graduate student in Chicago. That's how they first met. Now Essien-Udom was teaching at the University of Ibadan in Nigeria. Malcolm spoke there. He urged African Americans to develop alliances with Africans. He proclaimed the need for African nations to go before the United Nations and charge the United States with violating the human rights of African Americans. Students honored Malcolm with a new name: Omowale. Meaning "the son who has come home," in Yoruba, a Nigerian language. Malcolm was deeply honored.

From Lagos, Nigeria, Malcolm flew east. Over the West African nations of Benin and Togo. When Malcolm landed in Accra, Ghana, on May 10, 1964, none of the African American refugees were at the airport waiting for him. But when he called Julian the next day, it set off a hectic week of meetings and speeches.

The first: refugee night at Julian's house.

Chapter 72
GHANA

A s much as racism pushed these African Americans away from the United States, they were pulled by the promise of Ghana. They felt both like refugees and at home.

Let's back up. When Malcolm left prison in 1952, people across the continent of Africa felt imprisoned by European nations. Almost all of Africa had been violently colonized by European nations like Great Britain, France, Belgium, Portugal, and Spain. Meaning Europeans had ruled these majority-Black areas in Africa for decades—just as White Americans ruled majority-Black areas in the United States. Just as Britain colonized America. The American Revolution against Britain led to the creation of the United States.

Europeans colonized Africa—as they did Asia and the Americas—to get rich off the natural and human resources. Africans across the continent had been fighting for their independence for a long time. A young Malcolm sat spellbound watching his father shout "Africa for the Africans." Malcolm's father spreading the word of Marcus Garvey and African revolutions in living rooms across middle America.

The first group of African people south of the Sahara Desert to win their independence were led by an admirer of Marcus Garvey. A man who went to college in the United States. His name: Kwame Nkrumah. In 1957, Malcolm rejoiced when he learned that Kwame had helped establish the nation of Ghana after securing for his people freedom from British colonial rule. President Nkrumah went about supporting other liberation struggles around Africa. Calling for workers to rule rather than their rich bosses. Calling for African people across the continent to unite and become more powerful together. To gain control of their lands. To ensure Africa for the Africans!

President Nkrumah helped found the Organization of African Unity in 1963. Thirty-two African nations—most of which had just won their independence from European colonizers in the 1950s and early 1960s—came together to form the organization. Despite all their differences. Exactly what Malcolm had been calling for in the United States! Black Americans coming together despite their differences. Malcolm was so inspired by the group that he approved the naming of his own political organization after it: the Organization of Afro-American Unity. Malcolm founded the OAAU in 1964. "Its purpose is to unite Afro-Americans and their organizations around a non-religious . . . constructive program for Human Rights," Malcolm announced to potential supporters. The OAAU focused on defending Black people against racist violence, providing antiracist education, building Black economic and political power, assisting Black Americans "who have lost their place in society" to get back on their feet, and promoting Black history and culture to unlearn racist ideas.

But Malcolm's OAAU, like his Muslim Mosque, Inc., struggled to get off the ground. And make much of an impact. Attacks in the United States were coming from all sides. From the Nation of Islam. From the police. From racist Americans. From some civil rights leaders. He felt he had more support in Africa. He saw that spirit of unity. Especially in Ghana. While there, he wrote in his diary: "Moving my family out of America may be good for me personally but bad for me politically."

President Nkrumah welcomed African Americans fleeing American racism to help him build the new nation of Ghana. In 1961,

President Nkrumah recruited to Ghana the most eminent African American scholar, W. E. B. Du Bois. His talented wife, Shirley, came too. By the time Malcolm arrived in 1964, Du Bois had died. But Shirley was directing Ghana's national television station and publishing house. Today, the Du Bois home is a memorial, hosting tourists from around the world.

But on this night, Malcolm's second night in Ghana, Julian and his wife, Ana, were the hosts. Their home, the memorial. All the people that night never forgot that dinner. The Mayfield home, all but twenty feet from the Du Bois home.

Standing against walls and sitting on chairs and couches were a number of Black people born in the United States who were filling key roles in the new nation, with access to President Nkrumah.

Julian Mayfield, editing a local magazine and writing speeches for President Nkrumah.

Vicki Garvin, teaching English to people working in the embassies of China, Cuba, and Algeria.

Alice Windom, working as secretary to the Ethiopian ambassador to Ghana.

Julia Wright, daughter of novelist Richard Wright, serving as a translator and journalist.

Preston King, teaching philosophy at the University of Ghana.

Leslie Alexander Lacy, also teaching at the University of Ghana.

Robert and Sara Lee, practicing dentistry.

Maya Angelou, working in the theater department at the University of Ghana. (When Maya returned to the United States in 1964, she became a legendary writer and poet, inspiring the mother of President Barack Obama to name his sister Maya.)

Of course, the refugees had heard about Malcolm's split from the Nation of Islam. Asked him why. Malcolm said he wanted to engage in political activism, but Elijah was holding him back. Malcolm said Elijah was breaking his own rules against sex outside marriage. Malcolm said Elijah had at least six children with some of his young secretaries. And wasn't supporting them.

Julian's houseguests gasped. Malcolm assured them it was all true. The rumors they probably heard about Elijah all the way over in Ghana were true.

The bulk of the conversation on refugee night had nothing to do with Elijah Muhammad. Malcolm almost certainly presented his plan to encourage African nations to charge the United States with violating the human rights of African Americans. Malcolm talked about bringing the challenges African Americans were facing before the whole world. Those African Americans gathered in Ghana likely debated the plan. Most of them likely supported the plan.

Julian and his fellow African American refugees had heard about the letter Malcolm sent back to the United States from Mecca. About his changing views about White people. They asked Malcolm about it. Malcolm made clear he was *not* going from attacking all White people to attacking no White people. "We had some" good White people, he said. We had some White abolitionists. Like John Brown. Like the Quakers who helped Black people find freedom from slavery through the Underground Railroad. "I found on my trip to Mecca that there were more people outside of the United States who could identify with us without the badge of skin color or racism," Malcolm said. "And so I think I'm going to give them a chance, but they have to prove something to me."

Prove that they could see Black people and treat them equally. As human beings. With rights. Because we all have human rights.

In Nigeria and again in Ghana, Malcolm pushed back against American officials and businesspeople who had been coming to Africa. These American officials and businesspeople were claiming that there was racial progress in the United States. Encouraging African people to trust Americans, to do business with Americans, to ally with the United States. So the US State Department and the Central Intelligence Agency, which are responsible for US interests abroad, followed Malcolm's public speeches closely. And state department and CIA officials were not happy that Malcolm was making the United States look bad. Even if what Malcolm was saying was true. Image mattered. Not truth.

American officials were most concerned about Malcolm's plans to encourage African nations to go before the United Nations and charge the United States with violating the human rights of Black Americans. He talked about it a lot in speeches in Nigeria and Ghana.

But Malcolm knew presidents in Africa needed to sign off on such an action. Which is why he was so excited when he secured a meeting in Ghana with none other than President Kwame Nkrumah.

23-11 97th Street
East Elmhurst 69, N. Y.
U. S. A.
June 1, 1964

Mr. Joseph Iffreoh
Federal Ministry of Works and Surveys
Lagos, Nigeria

My dear brother,

May these few lines find you in good health, enjoying
wealth and happiness. I want you to know that I had
a fine time with you while I was in Lagos and will
never forget you for showing me the many different
aspects of that wonderful and beautiful country.
Nigeria impressed me as being one of the most
beautiful and wealthiest countries I've ever visited.

I want to thank you also for seeing that my bag of
film was sent from Lagos to Accra. My stay in Ghana
was quite fruitful. I saw Nkrumah for over an hour,
spoke to the Ghanian Members of Parliament, lectured
at the University of Accra, and the Kwame Nkrumah
Ideological Institute. So my stay in Ghana was quite
fruitful. Please write to me and send me the name of
the writer who wrote that headline story in the
West African Pilot so I can correspond with him. He
gave me his name. It's written in my book but I
can't quite understand it.

Best wishes to all and I hope to hear from you soon.

                              Sincerely,

            ✢

MX:max   Malcolm X.

**Malcolm recounting his visit to Ghana and meeting with President
Nkrumah to a Nigerian government official, June 1, 1964**

Chapter 73

PRESIDENT NKRUMAH

Malcolm appeared at Christiansborg Castle. It was like Ghana's White House, where the president lived and worked. Europeans had built the castle three hundred years prior. For a long time, Europeans held human beings in chains in this castle before they were shipped to the Americas to labor in slavery. When Great Britain colonized the area, British officials ruled from the castle. When President Nkrumah liberated Ghana, he took it over.

The castle is no longer the president's house in Ghana. But tourists and presidents from other countries—like US presidents Bill Clinton and Barack Obama—still visit the castle on their trips to Ghana. To learn about Ghana's history. To learn about slavery and the human trade of African people.

President Nkrumah's security detail searched Malcolm hard and long. To make sure he did not have any weapons. People had already tried to kill President Nkrumah. European leaders and businesspeople and their major ally—the United States—were hardly happy that African leaders like President Nkrumah were claiming their independence and using their resources to benefit Africans, as opposed to foreigners under colonialism.

Malcolm entered the long office. He probably smiled watching President Nkrumah come from behind his desk—at the far side of the room. The two men walked toward each other. Malcolm saw the president's smile. They shook hands. Sat down at a nearby couch. And talked.

They agreed on the need for unity. The need for Africans across the continent to come together. The need for Black people across the world to come together. To fight against racism. Fight against non-Black people who were trying to control their lands and peoples.

All that talk of unity, of the challenges Black Americans were facing—Malcolm had high hopes when he probably raised the question. Can you, President Nkrumah, can Ghana go before the United Nations and charge the United States with violating the human rights of African Americans?

President Nkrumah hated how horribly Black Americans were being treated. But Ghana could not help. He could not go before the UN. If Ghana interfered in affairs of the United States, then the United States could interfere in the affairs of Ghana, the president perhaps said.

President Nkrumah knew US officials were upset that he wasn't allowing US businesses to control Ghanaian resources. And that President Nkrumah had been working with the enemies of the United States, those communists in the Soviet Union and China. Since the end of World War II, the capitalist United States and the communist Soviet Union had been fighting a Cold War for global supremacy. They each tried to gain influence in decolonized nations like Ghana.

President Nkrumah's worries about Europeans and Americans were spot-on. Local army and police officials wanted to join with Europeans and Americans in growing rich off Ghanaian resources as Ghanaians grew poor. These army and police officials didn't care about their fellow Ghanaians. They only cared about themselves.

Two years after his meeting with Malcolm, the CIA helped the Ghanaian army and police officials push President Nkrumah out of office—and out of Ghana.

When Malcolm's friends picked him up from the castle, they could tell he was sad. They could tell something went wrong during his meeting with President Nkrumah. But he did not say anything about the likely rejection. His friends did not ask.

Maybe Malcolm questioned himself on that car ride back to his hotel. Questioned whether he should stop pushing the UN plan. Questioned whether African leaders would support it. Then again, when Malcolm put his mind to something, there was no stopping him. And there was no stopping his travels in Africa.

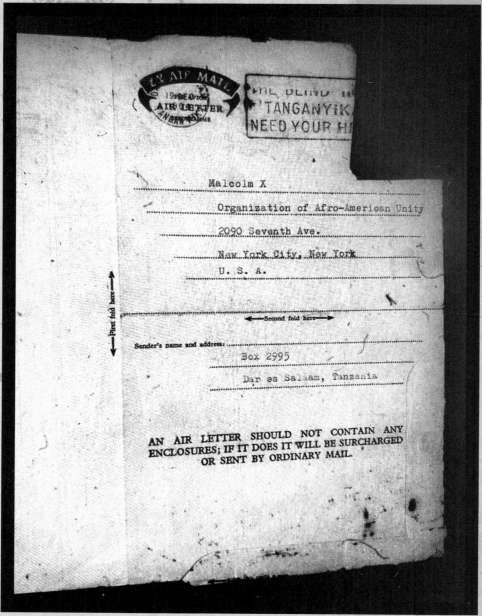

Malcolm X

Organization of Afro-American Unity

2090 Seventh Ave.

New York City, New York

U.S.A.

First fold here

Second fold here

Sender's name and address:

Box 2995

Dar es Salaam, Tanzania

AN AIR LETTER SHOULD NOT CONTAIN ANY
ENCLOSURES; IF IT DOES IT WILL BE SURCHARGED
OR SENT BY ORDINARY MAIL.

Air letter sent from Tanzania to Malcolm at the
Organization of Afro-American Unity, 1964

Chapter 74

CHANGES

Malcolm left Ghana a few days after first meeting with President Nkrumah. He flew to Senegal, where he signed many autographs at the airport in Dakar. Then on to Morocco, a Muslim nation, where he toured Casablanca. He arrived in Algiers, the capital of Algeria, on his thirty-ninth birthday on May 19, 1964. His taxi driver shared with him the many atrocities of French colonizers. Algerians had just won their independence from the French in 1962 after a long and violent war.

These travels changed Malcolm's ideas. He stopped identifying as a Black nationalist. The more he traveled across the world, the more he realized White supremacy was global. He met Black people in other countries fighting for their independence, fighting against White supremacy. The more antiracist Black people he met in other countries, the more Malcolm connected with potential allies African Americans had abroad. Identifying himself as a Black *nation*alist focused him on his nation, the United States. Cutting off his allies abroad. It was similar to his urging Black Americans to fight for human rights instead of just civil rights. Demanding civil rights, he realized antiracist activists had to pressure the United States. Demanding human rights, antiracist activists could take the United States before the entire world.

Malcolm's travels also caused him to question the sexist ideas of the Nation of Islam. Sexist ideas that positioned women as submissive wives and mothers and daughters. Sexist ideas that positioned men as leaders and women as followers. But Malcolm was exposed to the critical role of antiracist women leaders, like those powerful women in Ghana. Like Maya Angelou, who helped organize refugee night and steer him around the country. Wherever he went in Africa, he met women who were central to liberation struggles. Perhaps as he marveled about the power of these women, he thought about his powerful wife, Betty. Perhaps he thought about his growing daughters, Attallah, Qubilah, and Ilyasah—not wanting anyone to hold them back from leadership when they came of age.

African leaders, especially socialists like President Nkrumah, urged Malcolm to rethink capitalism. They urged him to join with a growing number of people around the world challenging capitalism as forcefully as they challenged racism. But coming out of the capitalist Nation of Islam, Malcolm still had much to learn about capitalism and socialism.

Malcolm flew on a Pan American jet back home. He landed at JFK airport at 4:25 P.M. on May 21, 1964. Apparently, journalists had learned Malcolm was coming. Because about fifty or sixty reporters and photographers were there when Malcolm appeared in the airport terminal. All their cameras and recorders and pens ready.

When Malcolm saw them, he wondered what celebrity was on his plane. Then they came at him with questions.

They asked him about his "Letter from Mecca" and his changed views of White people. Malcolm was ready to speak on them.

The hajj broadened his mind, he said. "I saw all *races*, all *colors*—blue-eyed blonds to black-skinned Africans—in *true* brotherhood! In unity! Living as one! . . .

"In the past, yes, I have made sweeping indictments of *all* white people. I never will be guilty of that again—as I know now that some white people *are* truly sincere, that some truly are capable of being brotherly toward a black man. The true Islam has shown me that a blanket indictment of all white people is as wrong as when whites make blanket indictments against blacks."

It was as if the reporters did not believe Malcolm had changed. Then again, even before he changed, Malcolm had not been involved in any violence against White individuals. But some Black teens in Harlem had just killed some White people. They called themselves the Blood Brothers. Malcolm had never met these Blood Brothers. But that did not stop racist White reporters from claiming Malcolm had trained them to kill White people. That did not stop racist White reporters from asking him about it at the airport as if it were true.

Malcolm probably smiled. The questions reminded him he was back in the United States. The reporters did not anticipate Malcolm's response. He pointed out the hypocrisy. When White youth kill innocent White people, you wonder why. But when Black youth kill innocent White people, you are outraged. You look for someone to blame! Look for someone to hang! Where is your outrage when White supremacists kill Black people! This is why we must go to the United Nations and charge the United States with denying us our human rights, Malcolm declared.

Reporters weren't ready to discuss Malcolm's plan. But a group of African American leaders were.

22-11 97th Street
East Elmhurst 69, N. Y.
July 8, 1964

22-11 97th Street
East Elmhurst 69, N. Y.
July 8, 1964

Mrs. Ruby Williams
1810 E. Wood St.
Phoenix, Arizona   85040

As-Salaam-Alaikum

In the name of Allah the Beneficent the Merciful.

Dear Sister Ruby,

I was very happy to receive your letter this
evening and to know that you both are still well and
thinking with a clear mind. It is difficult to be as
sincere as we were and admit to ourselves that the
man when we were following could be so wrong and so
hypocritically

If you wish to send me the manuscript that you
wrote I can probably see that it gets published. Send
me a copy of it if you want to. I am leaving today
for another trip to Africa. I plan to attend the
meeting of African heads of states, (Organization of
African Unity) that is being held in Cairo on July 17th,
at which time I hope to present the truth to these
African heads of states concerning the plight of 22-
million Afro-Americans in this country, and ask their
help in getting our problem brought before the world
court or the United Nations. I hope your letters will
be waiting for me when I return.

As-Salaam-Alaikum

Your brother,

MX:mex   Malcolm X.

Malcolm acknowledging receipt of Ruby Williams's inside
knowledge of Elijah's immorality and sharing his own plans to
meet with the Organization of African Unity in Cairo, July 8, 1964

Chapter 75

SECRET MEETING

Not long after he arrived back in the United States, Malcolm traveled about thirty-three miles upstate to Pleasantville, New York. He arrived at the home of a famous Hollywood actor that all the African Americans in Ghana knew. Sidney Poitier.

Sidney gathered a small but powerful group of Black leaders and actors.

Whitney Young, the head of the National Urban League.

Benjamin Davis of the Communist Party.

A representative of A. Philip Randolph, the man behind the March on Washington in 1963.

A leader from the Congress of Racial Equality.

Actors Ruby Dee and Ossie Davis.

And Clarence Jones, the lawyer of Martin Luther King Jr., jailed at the time for protesting segregation in St. Augustine, Florida. Martin authorized Clarence Jones to speak for him.

The leaders presented different ideas for challenging American racism. Most of the leaders thought Malcolm's idea was the best presented that night. Clarence Jones, speaking for Martin, suggested they present their case before the United Nations when it met in September, in a few months. Malcolm agreed! The group tasked Malcolm with reaching out to governments in Africa and the Middle East that would support them. Malcolm was all for it!

The media could not report on this meeting. It was supposed to be secret. But the FBI—engaged in surveillance of Black leaders—

found out. The FBI reported that there was a "discussion of general future of civil rights movement in US" and that "the best idea presented" was Malcolm's "idea to internationalize the civil rights movement by taking it to the United Nations." The FBI shared this "urgent" report with the State Department, military intelligence agencies, and the CIA. Malcolm was gaining an enemy in not just the powerful Nation of Islam. But the all-powerful US government.

Before he left again for Africa, he had two personal matters to take care of. One brought him joy: Betty and Malcolm welcomed their fourth daughter, Gamilah Lumumba, on July 1, 1964. They named her after Patrice Lumumba, a leader of Congo's independence movement. He became the nation's first prime minister in 1960. Belgian and American agents were involved in his assassination the next year.

The other personal matter brought Malcolm and Betty nothing but stress. The Nation of Islam was still trying to kick Malcolm's family out of their house.

Chapter 76

COURT CASE

When Malcolm first left the Nation in March 1964, he only said good things about Elijah. In open letters. In public speeches. But things had changed by the time he arrived in Africa, by the time he returned to the United States in May. It isn't hard to figure out why.

Almost as soon as Malcolm left Elijah's Nation back in March, Elijah ordered him to leave his house. A house the Nation of Islam purchased for Malcolm and his family in 1960. Not far from where he lived before in East Elmhurst, Queens.

The thought of being evicted from their home of the last four years caused all sorts of pain for Betty, Malcolm, and their daughters. All sorts of fears of being houseless. They did not have any money to buy a new house. All the money Malcolm could have saved over the years to move his family had gone to the Nation of Islam. And now, the Nation was taking him to court to get him out! Oh, Malcolm and Betty were angry!

The summer after Malcolm returned from Africa, the eviction trial against Malcolm started. Brought by the Nation of Islam, to get a judge to force Malcolm and his family to leave the house.

Malcolm told the judge that the Queens house was a gift to him for his loyal service to Elijah. And it should remain with his family. Malcolm also argued he remained a loyal follower of Elijah. But his starting the Muslim Mosque, Inc., showed that wasn't true.

What upset Malcolm most of all during the trial was Elijah's lawyer claiming Malcolm had been stealing money from the Nation of Islam for years. That the Nation of Islam had been allowing Malcolm to live like a rich man. Dishonoring Malcolm to protect the honor of Elijah! Malcolm was furious.

So, in his private meetings in Ghana and when he returned home to the United States, Malcolm had no problem telling the ugly truth about Elijah. At a rally for the Muslim Mosque, Inc., in Harlem on June 7, 1964, someone asked a question about Elijah. This was before the trial. For the first time, Malcolm went into detail about Elijah's sexual life. Before a crowd of about 450 people. No doubt including Elijah's supporters and FBI agents. There spying. Malcolm said the Nation of Islam would rather kill someone than let word of Elijah's misbehavior get out.

Malcolm was right. The next morning, someone called Malcolm's house. Betty picked up the phone. The person threatened to kill Malcolm. The first of hundreds of death threats. On some days, the phone constantly rang. Fearful, Betty did not want to pick up.

On July 2, 1964, Lucille Rosary and Evelyn Williams filed paternity suits against Elijah. Elijah had been saying that they were lying—and Malcolm was lying—about Elijah being the father of Lucille's and Evelyn's children. A paternity suit could prove Elijah was the father. And then those mothers could get money from him to help support their children. Elijah was probably upset when he got news of the lawsuits. Upset at the women. Upset at Malcolm.

Two evenings later, as fireworks and sparklers went off in celebration of the Fourth of July, Malcolm walked out of his front door to move his car. A group of men rushed at him. Malcolm saw murder in their eyes. He ran into his car. Drove away. Believing they wanted to kill him. Not his daughters and their babysitter inside the house. Betty was in the hospital. Recovering from having their fourth baby.

Sometime later, Malcolm returned home. He drove into his

driveway. He ran into his home through the back door. He probably grabbed his rifle. He patrolled the house. He looked out windows, keeping an eye out for Elijah's assassins.

In leaving for Africa again, not long after, Malcolm probably saved his own life.

TO: DIALLO TELLI
       SECRETARY GENERAL
       ORGANIZATION OF AFRICAN UNITY
       SECRETARIATE

TO: DIALLO TELLI
       SECRETARY GENERAL
       ORGANIZATION OF AFRICAN UNITY
       SECRETARIATE
       ADDIS ABABA, ETHIOPIA

(MESSAGE)

THE VIOLENT AND BRUTAL ATTACKS BY SAVAGE RACISTS POLICEMEN IN AMERICA AGAINST
INNOCENT AND DEFENSELESS AFROAMERICANS MEN WOMEN AND CHILDREN HAS INCREASED
SINCE THE AFRICAN SUMMIT CONFERENCE ENDED LAST WEEK HERE IN CAIRO STOP
THESE INHUMAN ACTS BY AMERICAN RACISTS POSING AS POLICEMEN NOT ONLY VIOLATE
THE HUMAN RIGHTS OF YOUR TWENTYTWO MILLION AFROAMERICAN BROTHERS AND SISTERS
BUT IS ALSO AYE DIRECT SLAP IN THE FACE TO THE HEADS OF THE INDEPENDENT AFRICAN
STATES WHO PARTICIPATED IN THIS RECENT AFRICAN SUMMIT CONFERENCE STOP
BEFORE WESTERN IMPERIALISTS AND NEOCOLONIALISTS SUCCEED BY USING RACISM TO
TURN AMERICA COMPLETELY INTO AYE FACIST STATE THAT CAN SERIOUSLY THREATEN THE
PEACE AND SECURITY OF THE ENTIRE WORLD COMMA THE ORGANIZATION OF AFROAMERICAN
UNITY CALLS UPON OUR ELDER BROTHERS OF THE ORGANIZATION OF AFRICAN UNITY TO
DEMAND THAT THE UNITED NATIONS COMMISSION ON HUMAN RIGHTS LAUNCH AN IMMEDIATE
INVESTIGATION INTO THE INHUMAN DESTRUCTION OF AFROAMERICAN LIFE AND PROPERTY
WHICH THE PRESENT UNITED STATES GOVERNMENT SEEMS EITHER UNABLE OR UNWILLING TO
PROTECT STOP
BECAUSE OF THE URGENCY OF THIS EXPLOSIVE RACIAL SITUATION IN AMERICA EYE REQUEST
YOU TO INITIATE IMMEDIATE CONTACTS WITH MEMBER STATES OF THE OOAAUU FOR THE
PURPOSE OF CONVENING AN EXTRAORDINARY SESSION OF THE COUNCIL OF MINISTERS OF
THE OOAAUU AT THE EARLIEST POSSIBLE TO ACT UPON THE ABOVE PROPOSAL BEFORE ITS
TOO LATE END

                              (SIGNED) MALCOLM X, CHAIRMAN
                              ORGANIZATION OF AFROAMERICAN UNITY
                              HOTEL 1919, SUITE 213
                              CAIRO, UAR

JULY 28, 1964

Letter from Malcolm to the secretary general of the
Organization of African Unity, requesting support for an
investigation of the United States by the UN, July 28, 1964

Chapter 77

AFRICAN UNITY

In July 1964, Malcolm traveled to Cairo, Egypt. That year, Malcolm spent almost as much time in Africa (five months) as he did in the United States (seven months). On his first trip, Malcolm spent about two weeks in Africa. He had returned to the United States for seven weeks. About a week in May. All of June. Several days in July. On this second trip, he stayed in Africa and the Middle East until November.

Malcolm went to Cairo first to attend the second meeting of the Organization of African Unity. Leaders gathered from thirty-four African independent nations with 240 million people who spoke eight hundred languages—on a continent four times as large as the United States. A decade earlier, only four of these nations were independent, while the rest were still colonies.

Malcolm spoke nonstop to leaders from African countries about his plan. On July 17, 1964, he sent all the leaders an eight-page memorandum.

> Your Excellencies:
>
> The Organization of Afro-American Unity has sent me to attend this historic African summit conference as an observer to represent the interests of 22 million African-Americans whose *human rights* are being violated daily by the racism of American imperialists.
>
> Since the 22 million of us were originally Africans,

who are now in America not by choice but only by a cruel accident in our history, we strongly believe that African problems are our problems and our problems are African problems . . .

We, in America, are your long-lost brothers and sisters . . .

During the past ten years the entire world has witnessed our men, women and children being attacked and bitten by vicious police dogs, brutally beaten by police clubs, and washed down the sewers by high-pressure water hoses that would rip the clothes from our bodies and the flesh from our limbs . . .

The American government is either unable or unwilling to protect the lives and property of your 22 million brothers and sisters. We stand defenseless, at the mercy of American racists who murder us at will for no reason other than we are black and of African descent.

And not just African Americans. Africans too. Malcolm described how three students from Kenya were "brutally beaten" by police officers. Two diplomats from Uganda "were also beaten by the New York City police, who mistook them" for African Americans.

"Our problem is your problem. No matter how much independence Africans get here on the mother continent," he wrote. "When you visit America, you may be mistaken for us" and beaten. "You will never be fully respected until and unless we are also respected. You will never be recognized as free human beings until and unless we are also recognized and treated as human beings.

"Our problem is your problem . . . This is a world problem; a problem for humanity. It is not a problem of civil rights but a problem of human rights . . .

"Many of you have been led to believe that the much publicized, recently passed civil-rights bill is a sign that America is making a sincere effort to correct the injustices we have suffered there." But don't fall for that trick, Malcolm implored.

Ten years earlier, the US Supreme Court had ruled that segregation in public schools was unconstitutional. But the federal government had not forced states to follow this ruling. If the United States won't enforce this rule, Malcolm asked African leaders, what makes you think it will enforce the Civil Rights Act?

"These are nothing but tricks," Malcolm wrote. "Surely, our intellectually mature African brothers will not fall for this trickery . . .

> We beseech the independent African states to help us bring our problem before the United Nations, on the grounds that the United States government is morally incapable of protecting the lives and the property of 22 million African-Americans . . .
>
> May Allah's blessings of good health and wisdom be upon you all. Salaam Alaikum.
>
> Malcolm X, Chairman, Organization of Afro-American Unity.

● ● ●

It was a powerful letter. But the Organization of African Unity decided not to go before the United Nations. It did pass a resolution that said it was "deeply disturbed" by ongoing racism. It did call on the US government to eliminate racism.

Malcolm pressed on. He stayed in Africa to meet with presidents in different countries about his plan. Like President Nkrumah, these presidents led their people out of colonialism in the 1950s and early 1960s. And now led their countries. He connected with Jomo Kenyatta of Kenya. Sékou Touré of Guinea. Julius Nyerere of

Tanzania. Gamal Abdel Nasser of Egypt. Nnamdi Azikiwe of Nigeria. And Milton Obote of Uganda.

Malcolm heard from most of them what he first heard from President Nkrumah. They were upset at American racism. But did not want to get into US affairs, which might embolden the United States to get into theirs.

The United States, through the CIA, got into the affairs of these nations anyway. US businesspeople wanted access to Africa's natural resources for cheap. So they could make products cheaper and make more money. US political leaders wanted Africa's political leaders to align with the United States and not the Soviet Union. The CIA supported African leaders who supported US interests. The CIA assassinated or pushed from power African leaders who supported their own people's interests. Let alone the interests of Black Americans.

These African leaders were in a tough spot. Colonialism had kept their people very poor. They needed money to improve their lives. Money to create jobs. Money to build roads and schools and hospitals. But their former colonizers had the money. The United States had the money. The Soviet Union had the money. But to take the Soviet Union's money, African leaders would anger the United States and the CIA.

Colonialism ended. But did it really? Or did it just change? Did colonizers get better at hiding their colonialism? People can't challenge what they can't see.

Malcolm wanted to see, so he could help others to see. He took a two-day trip outside Africa. It best allowed him to see the new colonialism. And a new unity.

Chapter 78

GAZA

On September 5, 1964, Malcolm traveled just over the border of Egypt into Gaza.

Gaza is at the eastern end of the Mediterranean Sea that separates Europe from Africa. On a map, Gaza looks like a rectangle.

For weeks before visiting Gaza, Malcolm spent a lot of time with Muslim scholars. Learning about the religion of Islam. Learning about the history of Muslims.

Maybe he already knew about the history of Palestine. Maybe he read about Palestine's history in prison. Maybe he learned that this land between Egypt and Lebanon had been home for centuries to mostly Palestinians, who commonly practice Islam. Jews and Christians had lived there for centuries too. But some Jews wanted their own Jewish homeland in Palestine. They are known as Zionists.

The British occupied Palestine during World War I in 1918. Before this occupation, in 1917, the British Foreign Secretary had promised to help Zionists secure a "a national home for the Jewish people." They had an ulterior motive: Some British leaders wanted to rid so-called Christian Europe of Jews. For centuries, antisemitic Europeans believed Jews were evil and dangerous. They harmed their Jewish neighbors. Kept Jews feeling unsafe.

Home is supposed to feel safe. Amid all this antisemitism, many Jews didn't feel that the countries where they lived were their homes. A feeling the *old* Malcolm could relate to.

As Elijah's spokesman, Malcolm spent years preaching to Black people that they were not Americans. Because "if you were an American, you wouldn't catch hell," Malcolm liked to say. Elijah and Malcolm spent years urging the United States to turn over land to Black people so they could separate from White Americans. Build their own nation. Where Black people would feel safe. "Land is the basis of all independence," Malcolm once said. "Land is the basis of freedom, justice, and equality."

While Elijah's spokesman, Malcolm did not believe Black people and White people could live together in peace. Malcolm had viewed White people as evil and dangerous. As people who could only terrorize Black people. Especially in nations where White people were in the majority.

Remember Malcolm's trip to Mecca earlier that year? That's when Malcolm had stopped viewing White people as evil and dangerous. That's when Malcolm stopped pushing the United States for land to create a separate Black homeland. But Zionists did not stop pushing the British for land.

While Malcolm was growing up, antisemitism kept Jews fleeing to Palestine from around the world. These Jews were encouraged by Zionists eager to bolster their numbers. Palestinians tried to stop new Zionist settlements. Sometimes violently, sometimes peacefully. But the British backed the Zionists, divided Palestinian leaders, and stopped the peaceful protests of Palestinians. Took away their weapons. Allowed Zionists to build up armies.

Now Palestinians were defending against Zionist colonizers *and* British occupiers. The more Palestinians fought to keep their lands, the more Zionists came to view them as evil and dangerous. As people who could only terrorize Jews. These Zionists did not believe Jews could be safe. Especially if Palestinians were in the majority.

Many Jews still remained in Europe. Germany's Adolf Hitler saw them as evil and dangerous. Hitler used the cover of World War II to murder six million Jews. Tried to rid Europe of this so-called internal threat. This is known as a genocide. This genocide is called the Holocaust.

The Holocaust and World War II ended in 1945, when Malcolm was twenty years old. This is the war Malcolm's act got him out of fighting.

After the war and genocide, Zionist demands for a Jewish homeland in Palestine grew louder. Palestinians made up about two-thirds of the population. They still demanded an independent Palestine. Free of British occupiers. Free of Zionists pushing for a Jewish nation. But in November 1947, the newly created United Nations allocated 55 percent of Palestine to Zionists to create a new Jewish nation. The rest of the lands were provided to Palestinians to build their own nation. One of the places allocated to Palestinians: Gaza, which Malcolm visited in 1964.

Palestinians rejected the UN's two-state solution. They refused to give up their lands. So in 1948, Zionist armies started driving Palestinians out. Thousands were murdered. Palestinians called this catastrophe the Nakba.

Troops from other Arab nations failed to stop the Nakba. On May 14, 1948, Zionists declared the creation of Israel, and British troops left. By the end of 1948, Israel had expanded its territory to 77 percent of Palestine. Around 750,000 Palestinians were forced from their homes.

• • •

Zionists and Palestinians have been warring over the land ever since. Many Israelis have died. Many more Palestinians have died.

On October 7, 2023, the Palestinian group that governs Gaza, named Hamas, attacked Israel. Hamas killed around 1,200 Israelis and non-Israelis. Took 251 hostages.

Israel invaded Gaza in response. Rescued very few hostages over the next year.

Israel's invasion killed more than forty thousand Palestinians in the year after the initial Hamas attack. A genocide.

Israeli bombs destroyed most of Gaza, with many of them made by the United States. Angering many Americans. Including many Jewish Americans.

Not all Jews identify as Zionists. There have also been anti-Zionist Jews and organizations like Jewish Voice for Peace that do not consider Palestinians to be evil terrorists. They protest Israeli Zionists instead.

• • •

On September 5, 1964, Malcolm visited a hospital in Gaza. (Israel likely bombed or raided this hospital if it was still in operation when the war began in 2023.)

Malcolm also visited the Khan Younis refugee camp in Gaza. It housed Palestinians whom Zionist soldiers had driven from their homes in 1948. (In the 2023 war, Israeli troops drove nearly all of Gaza's 2.3 million people from their homes too. Many fleeing Palestinians ended up again in the Khan Younis refugee camp.)

After leaving the camp, Malcolm lunched with Palestinian religious leaders. He heard a poem from Harun Hashim Rashid.

We must return
No boundaries should exist
No obstacles can stop us
Cry out refugees: "We shall return"

Malcolm had an evening prayer with religious leaders. Possibly at the Great Omari Mosque, which Israeli troops destroyed in the 2023 war. "The spirit of Allah was strong," Malcolm wrote in his diary.

The next day, Sunday, September 6, 1964, Malcolm left Gaza around noon.

Back in Cairo, Malcolm met with Aḥmad Shuqayrī, the first leader of the Palestine Liberation Organization, on September 15, 1964. The PLO had just been founded a few months earlier. Its plans: Unify Palestinians. Represent Palestinians internationally. Confront Zionism. End Israel. Build the nation of Palestine, where Christians, Muslims, and Jews would have equal rights. Some PLO members later organized horrific attacks on civilians inside and outside of Israel to achieve their goals.

But the PLO's goals when Malcolm met with Aḥmad Shuqayrī in 1964 resembled Malcolm's plans for his new Organization of Afro-American Unity. Unify Black Americans. Represent Black Americans internationally. Confront racism. Malcolm saw Zionists as desiring a Jewish nation built on Jewish *supremacy*. For Malcolm, this resembled the racism of White American nationalists—like the Ku Klux Klansmen he thought killed his father. They desired the United States to be a White nation built on White supremacy. And those Klansmen hated Jewish Americans as they hated Black and Muslim Americans.

Maybe PLO leaders shared with Malcolm how some African leaders were allying with Zionists. Maybe they asked for his help. Because after the meeting, Malcolm wrote an essay for the *Egyptian Gazette*. It appeared on September 17, 1964, titled "Zionist Logic."

In it, Malcolm argued that Zionists had led the way in creating a "new kind of colonialism." They "camouflage" it so well that "African masses" submit to their "authority and guidance, without . . . being aware that they are still colonized."

In this new colonialism, Israelis, Americans, and Europeans get "their potential victims to accept their friendly offers of economic 'aid,' and other tempting gifts." Malcolm called this "dollarism." Once these African nations accept these dollars, they rely on these dollars. Once they rely on these dollars, the new colonizers can control them. Can divide Arab nations from one another. Can divide Arab nations from African nations. Malcolm pushed back against this African-Arab disunity.

"Did the Zionists have the legal or moral right to invade Arab Palestine, uproot its Arab citizens from their homes and seize all Arab property for themselves just based on the 'religious' claim that their forefathers lived there thousands of years ago?" Malcolm answered no.

Malcolm probably felt inspired visiting Gaza, meeting with PLO leaders, writing this piece. In two weeks, he finally had something to celebrate.

Chapter 79
FULL CIRCLE

The highlight of Malcolm's efforts in Africa came on October 15, 1964. He spoke before the legislators of Kenya. They passed a resolution of support for the human rights struggles of Black Americans. Malcolm was overjoyed. It prompted an angry reaction from US officials. Malcolm had more luck getting support from African legislators and diplomats than presidents.

• • •

When Malcolm returned to the United States in November 1964, he returned to the Nation of Islam still trying to kick him out of his house. Death threats had turned into actual attempts to kill Malcolm. In Boston, Philadelphia, New York City, Chicago, and Los Angeles. The attempts on his life in Los Angeles—where Elijah's men followed him constantly—really affected him. All these assassination attempts affected him deeply.

Maybe what affected him most was what would happen to the people he loved if he died. His wife and four daughters would be penniless and without a house. He could not get the courts to allow him to stay in their house. He could not get any company to give him life insurance. "They refused to insure my life," Malcolm complained to a friend.

African presidents had offered him jobs to save his life and livelihood. But Malcolm kept saying no. He could not bring himself to leave Black Americans to the wolves of American racism. He could not bring himself to leave the fight. He could not bring himself to leave the Organization of Afro-American Unity. He could not bring himself to become a refugee and flee, like those African Americans he met in Ghana.

Malcolm grew depressed. His friends knew something was up when they saw him in the final weeks of 1964. For years, Malcolm arrived at meetings dressed well and full of energy. Now his shoes weren't shined. His clothes were wrinkled. He arrived tired. He lived "like a man who's already dead," as Malcolm told a reporter. Perhaps thinking more and more about his father. Who suffered an early death. Perhaps thinking more and more about his mother. Who faced down the Klan without his father. Perhaps thinking more and more about when his childhood home was set on fire by racist White people who wanted him out. Life can be a circle.

Chapter 80

TIRING

Imagine if Malcolm lived. Was alive today and walking by his old house. He would barely recognize the outside. The dark-brown bricks have been painted over. A light, almost lime green—of all colors. Very bright like Malcolm's old zoot suits. Very bright like the red on the outside walls of LaGuardia Café. This café now sits to the left of Malcolm's old house. On a street renamed in his honor in 2005: Malcolm X Place.

Malcolm's old house is small. Imagine if you were standing out front in 1965. Walk up steps to go in through the front door. A dining room to the left. A living room to the right. Walk down the hallway. There is a baby's nursery to the right. Malcolm and Betty's bedroom to the left. At the back of the house is another children's bedroom to the left and the kitchen to the right. Upstairs there is a small attic. A room Malcolm turned into his office.

• • •

Malcolm sat in his upstairs office. The date, February 13, 1965. It was late at night. Malcolm probably sat worried. Worried that this may be the last night in this house. He had lost the court case against the Nation of Islam. A judge ruled that the Nation owned the house and Malcolm's family had to leave. He had one last hearing the day after next, February 15, before a judge. But he knew the judge was unlikely to allow him to keep the house. (And the judge did not.)

Malcolm probably tried to get his mind off the eviction. He probably outlined his speech for the next day in Detroit. On index cards, as he normally did for speeches. When he finished preparing the speech, he looked over a list of questions given to him by the editors of *Al-Muslimoon*, an Arabic-language monthly magazine. He met the editors when he visited the Islamic Centre of Geneva in Switzerland during his travels in 1964.

Back in Malcolm's day, there were no laptops. Just typewriters. Which are like keyboards and printers in one. Put a blank white page into the typewriter. Push a letter on the typewriter's keyboard, and a metal lever punches a ribbon wet with ink, instantly transferring the letter onto the page.

Malcolm worked there in his attic, typing out answers to the questions.

"What were the reasons behind Elijah Muhammad being against you immediately after the assassination of Kennedy, and then behind your breakaway from the Movement as a whole?"

"Elijah Muhammad allowed himself to become insanely jealous of my own popularity which went even beyond his own followers and into the non-Muslim community," Malcolm typed. "Elijah feared that my position of influence in the movement was a threat to him and his other children who were now controlling the Movement and benefitting from its wealth . . .

"At the time they announced I was to be suspended and silenced for 90 days, they had already set in motion the machinery to have me completely ousted from the movement, and Elijah Muhammad himself had already given the order to have me killed because he feared I would expose to his followers the secret of his extreme immorality."

It creeped past midnight. Quite early for Malcolm. He often spent several more hours working in his attic office as his family slept. But on this night, he found himself tiring. And tiring fast.

Long flights across time zones tire out people. Malcolm had just got back home earlier in the day after speaking in England, after trying to speak in France. But French authorities refused to let Malcolm into their country. Some people think the French government learned of a CIA plot to assassinate Malcolm. French authorities didn't want him killed on French soil. Whatever the reason, being denied entry into France opened Malcolm's eyes. When he returned, he told his friends he had been making a "serious mistake" focusing all his attention on the Nation of Islam. He started to believe that the US government wanted him dead too.

I would do nothing to harm your image or your work or Islam, but I don't hesitate one minute to attack and expose these vicious hypocrites who are trying to make it appear that I am the hypocrite.

Brothers who were sent out to kill me ended up confessing their intentions to me, and who sent them to do it. This is a very bad thing, and there are too many Muslims in the Mosque who know that this wicked plot is true. So when the officials stand on the Rostrum and try to deny it, it not only makes them look very bad but it casts reflections on the integrity of the Nation of Islam itself. If they would be quiet and stop maligning me from the Rostrum I would be quiet. But as long as they tell lies they force me to tell the truth. I know what they are doing. They are trying to maneuver me into making an open verbal attack and indictment upon you. I am just as much a defender of yours today as I have been all of my life. On the other hand, I refuse to defend those around you because in my humble opinion they are worse enemies to you than the devil himself.

They sent me an ultimatum to move out of this house. I told them in no uncertain words that it was my house, but that it was purchased in the name of the Mosque and that you yourself was well aware of this and that they should consult with you before coming to me with their ignorant plans. I told them that on the other hand if they brought me before the general body at Mosque #7 and permitted me to defend myself against the charges they had been levelling at me, and the Muslims then asked me to give up the house, I would give it up without a word. But I will never let a hand full of hypocrites posing as officials think they can frighten or harass me. You made me a Muslim and your message has removed all fear from me. I have started a new Mosque only because the hypocrites in the Nation of Islam refused to let me and many other well-meaning Muslims like me attend the Mosque. All of us are out in the street. There are more out than there are in. Yet, all believe in you, and all of us have been driven out by those around you. Since the Nation doesn't want them, I will take them, organize them, unite them and show them how to take your message and raise the dead. We are as faithful to you as those who are in the Nation of Islam.

Malcolm noting the attempts on his life in a letter to Elijah Muhammad, March 21, 1964

Chapter 81

REHEARSAL

Why would American officials want Malcolm dead?

No, Malcolm did not get the Organization of African Unity to stand against the United States in the way it stood against apartheid in South Africa, where a White minority ruled by violence and segregation. No, Malcolm did not get African presidents to go before the United Nations and charge the United States with violating the human rights of Black Americans. No, Malcolm did not unite antiracist Black American organizations. There were so many things Malcolm tried to achieve that would have left the US government feeling threatened—and couldn't.

But after he came home from his travels, Malcolm *did* start to see American racism brought up more and more by African and Asian delegates at the United Nations. He did start to see more and more civil rights leaders—namely Martin Luther King Jr.—talk about internationalizing the struggle. Malcolm did start seeing more and more young Black activists turning from civil rights to human rights since racism is "a problem for all humanity."

Malcolm did start seeing more and more young Black people turning from being ashamed of being Black to having pride in being Black.

Malcolm did start seeing more and more young Black people turning from attacking poor people to attacking their exploiters.

Malcolm did start seeing more and more young Black people turning from nonviolence to self-defense.

Malcolm did start seeing more and more young Black activists turning from pushing to integrate White neighborhoods and institutions to gaining power over Black neighborhoods and institutions.

Malcolm did start seeing more and more young Black activists transforming the civil rights movement into the Black Power movement that exploded onto the American scene in the late 1960s. And many of these young Black people were writing to Malcolm, were sending in money to the offices of his Organization of Afro-American Unity. Like Bobby Seale, who would go on to cofound the Black Panther Party, the most prominent Black Power organization, in 1966.

Malcolm did start to connect more and more with revolutionaries in Africa, Latin America, and Asia. Malcolm did start to connect more and more with Southern civil rights leaders, like Mississippi's Fannie Lou Hamer, who spoke at a rally in Harlem alongside Malcolm to support the Mississippi Freedom Democratic Party on December 20, 1964. Malcolm did venture down South to Alabama in early February 1965. He spoke before three thousand students at Tuskegee University and the next day in nearby Selma. Martin Luther King Jr. and activists with the Student Nonviolent Coordinating Committee sat in jail during a major campaign to press for Black voting rights—a campaign that helped compel Congress to pass the Voting Rights Act later that year. In Selma, Malcolm did meet with Coretta Scott King, Martin's wife, about working together.

Malcolm did meet with Elijah's son Wallace, who first told Malcolm about Elijah's misbehavior. The two men talked about building a major Black Muslim organization with Wallace as the spiritual leader. These members could become soldiers in the battle against racism.

"This is the era of revolution," Malcolm said days after returning from his travels in Africa. He spoke on and on about the African revolutionaries he met who used every means available to them to free their country from racist Europeans. He contrasted them with some American civil rights leaders who didn't believe in seizing power by any means necessary. "Whenever you hear a man saying he wants freedom, but in the next breath he is going to tell you what he won't do to get it," Malcolm said, "he doesn't believe in freedom."

Malcolm again made a distinction between antiracist White Americans and racist White Americans who "don't act all right."

"When I say white man, I'm not saying all of you," Malcolm said, "because some of you might be all right."

Malcolm had come to realize that the grand battle was not between White people and people of color. "We are today seeing a global rebellion of the oppressed against the oppressor, the exploited against the exploiter," Malcolm said in his last public address, at the Barnard College gymnasium in Harlem.

This is what racist government officials wanted to halt: Malcolm's nonstop efforts to generate a revolution against American racism from within and abroad. These efforts were slowly snowballing in late 1964 and early 1965. His efforts were nonstop because Malcolm knew he could die at any moment.

Malcolm had every reason to fear that officials in the American policing and intelligence agencies wanted him dead. Malcolm did not know this, but FBI agents and local police agents had planted bugs to surveil Malcolm's conversations and activities. A White NYPD officer named Gerry Fulcher secretly listened to conversations at Malcolm's office at the Hotel Theresa in Harlem. The more he listened to Malcolm, the more he agreed with Malcolm, making Gerry unpopular with his fellow officers, who hated Malcolm as much as they hated Black people. Gene Roberts, a Black police officer, worked undercover on Malcolm's security detail. Roberts reported Malcolm's movements to police officials, who shared them with the FBI.

At an OAAU rally in Harlem on February 15, 1965, Gene Roberts saw a commotion at the back of the crowd.

"Get your hand outta my pocket!" one person shouted to another.

"Cool it, brothers," Malcolm said. And they did. Just like that.

For Gene, it looked suspicious. It looked like they were practicing a diversion. "I just think I saw a dress rehearsal for this man's assassination," Gene reported to police headquarters.

A.

Report.

Gene.

Did.

Not.

Share.

With.

Malcolm.

A police officer refusing to serve and protect a citizen. Only serving and protecting the racist government that Malcolm wanted to overthrow.

Afterward, the NYPD sharply *reduced* the number of police at certain speaking events of Malcolm's. Why would the NYPD reduce police protection when they suspected Elijah's followers were about to kill Malcolm? Why would the NYPD not be protecting Malcolm at his home—as he sat there drifting off to sleep? Only one explanation makes sense. Did they want to make it easier for the Nation of Islam to kill Malcolm?

Chapter 82

2:30 A.M. AGAIN

"**H**ave any of Elijah Muhammad's followers left the Movement with you, and do you think that your breakaway from the Movement has affected its main body in any considerable way?"

"Yes, many of Elijah's followers could not go along with his present 'immorality,' and this opened their eyes to the other falsities of his doctrine," Malcolm typed in his attic office while fighting off exhaustion.

"*Do you have any course of action in mind towards establishing some new organisation in the field?*"

"With what little finance we could raise, we have founded the Muslim Mosque, Inc., with headquarters here in Harlem. Our sole interest is to help undo the distorted image we have helped spread about Islam . . .

"We have established another organisation which is non-religious, known as the Organization of Afro-American Unity (OAAU), and which is designed to unite all Black Americans regardless of the religious affiliation into a group that can fight against American racism and the economic, political and social evils that stem from white racism here in this American society."

It was about 12:30 A.M. on Valentine's Day, February 14, 1965. Malcolm could barely keep his eyes open as he typed answers to the questions from the editors of *Al-Muslimoon*. At some point, he fell asleep in his study.

His wife, Betty, pregnant with twins, slept in her and Malcolm's bedroom downstairs, across the hall from their seven-month-old baby daughter, Gamilah. Sleeping in their room nearby were their six-year-old daughter, Attallah; their four-year-old daughter, Qubilah; and their two-year-old daughter, Ilyasah.

As Malcolm and his family slept, some members of Malcolm's old mosque parked near his house. They acted on orders from Elijah. To get Malcolm's family out of this house—if not kill them. Elijah had ordered Malcolm to be killed by Saviour's Day, the annual gathering of Elijah's followers, which was upcoming on February 26, 1965.

Under the cover of night, Elijah's followers walked toward Malcolm's home. They held low-budget bombs. What are known as Molotov cocktails. Each a large glass bottle full of gasoline and a rag. Part of the rag stuffed in the bottle, part hanging out of it, working like a wick. They quietly took their positions around the front and back windows of Malcolm's house.

The man at the front window lit a rag with fire. Smashed open the window. Tossed the Molotov cocktail inside the living room. It exploded. Fire engulfed the space. Black smoke too.

One of Malcolm's daughters screamed. Waking up Malcolm. He saw the smoke. He smelled the fire in the living room. He immediately knew what was happening. It was shortly after 2:30 A.M. The same time White supremacists firebombed Malcolm's home back in Lansing, Michigan, when he was four years old.

Malcolm jumped up. Focused, like he'd been here before. Malcolm heard a second bomb explode in the living room. A third bomb hit off a rear window and did not explode. The arsonists ran. Hopped into their car and sped away.

Malcolm gathered up their seven-month-old daughter. Then raced to the children's room. He brought their three scared and coughing daughters to Betty, who was waiting near the open back door. They hurried the children outside. They all breathed the fresh cold winter air. They all saw the fire and smoke engulfing the house and the few items they owned.

Maybe in that moment, Malcolm remembered what his parents did. How his parents ran back into their burning house to save some stuff from the fire. As Malcolm, at four years old, looked on. Scared. Hoping the fire did not get them. Because almost as soon as he and Betty got the children outside, Malcolm was running back into his burning house. To grab important things. As his four-year-old daughter, Qubilah, looked on. Scared. Hoping the fire did not get him.

Mural of Malcolm's solidarity with Palestinians by
Muslim artist Mohammed Ali, Birmingham, Alabama

Chapter 83
FATHER TO SON

The fire did not get Malcolm. He managed to save several personal items that his family needed.

At least the firefighters came this time. Remember, the firefighters refused to come for Malcolm's parents' house back in Lansing. Giving Malcolm one of his first lessons in American racism.

Malcolm. Betty. Attallah. Qubilah. Ilyasah. Baby Gamilah. The family shivered in the February cold. Watching flames rush out of windows. Watching firefighters hosing the flames.

Friendly neighbors came outside to support Malcolm's family. Family friends heard about the fire. And came. So did journalists. Who crowded around Malcolm. Who asked him who he thought set the fire.

"It could have been done by any one of the many," Malcolm said. "I'm not surprised that it was done. It doesn't frighten me. It doesn't quiet me down in any way or shut me up."

Malcolm's family was now houseless. His wife, his girls needed him—as much as he needed them. After one of the worst nights of their lives. But Malcolm was not thinking about the needs of his family. Or his needs.

Malcolm decided right then and there he would still fly to Detroit in a few hours and speak. He notified Betty. She became very upset. Rightfully so. But she knew there was no changing his mind. She knew only death could stop Malcolm at this point. Then again, not even death. Because death stops a person in the world. But death cannot stop a person's message to the world.

• • •

It did not take long for firefighters to put out the fire. Everything was burnt in the front part of the house. The dining room and the living room. But neighbors went through the back to get some items that did not burn. They probably retrieved things for the baby. They certainly got clothes in the dressers. They did not see any large bottles with gasoline.

Police detectives arrived. They ordered everyone out of the house to start their investigation. That was when Malcolm believed something unjust happened. Malcolm thought someone dressed as a police officer or an actual police officer secretly carried an unlit Molotov cocktail into the home. Placed the bottle of gasoline with a rag sticking out on the dresser in the children's room.

Time passed. Police allowed Betty to go back into the house. She noticed the bottle of gasoline. It looked like a bottle of alcohol. Which was weird. She did not drink alcohol. Malcolm didn't either. She pointed out the bottle to the firemen.

After gathering all their stuff, Betty and the four girls were taken to a friend's house in Queens. Malcolm was off to Detroit.

• • •

Captain Joseph, a leader from Malcolm's old Harlem Mosque, supervised the firebombing of Malcolm's home. But he told the media Malcolm set fire to his own home "to get publicity" and sympathy from the public. And then on February 17, 1965, a story came out in the *New York Times*: "Bottle of Gasoline Found on a Dresser in Malcolm X Home." Detectives were investigating.

The same thing happened to Malcolm's father after White supremacists firebombed his house. Police accused Malcolm's father.

Now, the police were suspecting Malcolm. And Malcolm was suspecting the police were working with his enemies to kill him. Just as Malcolm's father had suspected the same thing.

● ● ●

Malcolm pressed on, as his father did amid the death threats. He promoted the next event of his Organization of Afro-American Unity. By word of mouth. At his college lectures. In radio interviews.

He announced his plans to reveal the names of Elijah's followers who firebombed his home. He announced plans to unveil the program of the OAAU.

The event was being held on Sunday, February 21, 1965. At 2:00 P.M.

In the meantime, Malcolm did not want his family to be in danger. So he checked into a hotel. He did not really tell anyone which hotel. Somehow his enemies found out.

It was the morning of the event. The phone rang in Malcolm's hotel room.

"Wake up, brother," one of his enemies said.

7. Devise Original Educational Methods.

8. Stimulate International Economic and Political
Awareness.

9. Act as an Overseas "Voice" for Afro-Americans.

10. To Provide A Means to Defend Ourselves by Any
Means Necessary from Racist Oppression where
the Government Proves It Is Unwilling and/or
Unable To Do So.

O.A.A.U. HEADQUARTERS:
write – HOTEL THERESA
2090 7th AVE.
(Corner of 125th St. & 7th Ave.)
NEW YORK CITY, NEW YORK

or call – UN. 6-3300 Extension-128

JOIN THE O.A.A.U.

"BE A BUILDER — NOT A BEGGAR"
WRITE OR CALL TODAY!

"FROM DARKNESS
TO LIGHT"

OAAU, Inc. Seal

ORGANIZATION
OF
AFRO-AMERICAN UNITY
INC.

•

AIMS & OBJECTIVES

Organization of Afro-American Unity leaflet, 1964

Chapter 84
AUDUBON

Malcolm arrived at the entrance of the event. Standing outside were four security men, including undercover cop Gene Roberts. The spy and three security guards were standing in front of the double doors under an awning with the sign: AUDUBON BALLROOM. They escorted Malcolm into the building and over to the small office near the stage.

Malcolm held the event in the same place he had been holding OAAU events over the past year. The Audubon Ballroom had hosted famous musicians, like Duke Ellington and Count Basie, for years. The type of place a wide-eyed teenager named Malcolm Little loved to go—with his zoot suit and dance moves—before robbing houses. Before being incarcerated. Before meeting Elijah Muhammad. Before emerging as one of the most influential speakers of his time. Before fleeing the Nation of Islam. Before fearing for his life. Before freeing his spirit and mind during life-changing trips to Mecca, Gaza, and African nations. Before giving birth to the Muslim Mosque, Inc., and the Organization of Afro-American Unity. Before giving birth to what became the Black Power movement. Before urging his fellow Black Americans to unite and transform their civil rights struggle into a human rights struggle. Before trying to get a foreign nation to charge the United States with violating the human rights of Black Americans.

Before people talked about Malcolm as someone who hated White people, when he really hated racism. Before people talked about him as violent, when he really hated violence against Black people. Before people talked about him as so different from Martin Luther King Jr., when both men really wanted freedom.

Before Malcolm was this world figure, he was just like any other young person. Finding his way in an unknown world.

The Audubon was not in Harlem, but up the road in Washington Heights. An area, like Harlem, with many Black Americans in 1965. Since then, many African Americans have moved out. Many Latino Americans have moved in. Especially Dominican Americans. The Community Association of Progressive Dominicans has its offices today at the Audubon.

Correction: in the building that once was the Audubon. The Audubon is no more. The building has been almost totally renovated. Most of the building is part of the medical center of Columbia University, the very university that hosted Malcolm's last speech. Most of the building is Columbia's Mary Woodard Lasker Biomedical Research Building. Biomedical researchers look for ways to prevent or remedy diseases that harm humans and animals. Not all diseases. Not diseases of the mind. Like racist ideas. Or like jealousy. Which caused Malcolm to fear for his life.

Malcolm arrived at the Audubon upset. The leaders of his new Organization of Afro-American Unity had not finished the organization's charter. A charter is like a constitution. Not having it ready made Malcolm and the OAAU look bad.

Malcolm had been saying all week he planned to present the OAAU's charter at the event. Encouraging people to come to hear it. He billed the event as momentous. Is this why he asked Betty and his four daughters to come? He rarely asked them to attend his public events.

Malcolm sat there troubled in the office. Likely trying to figure out what to say about the OAAU. His assistant, James 67X, had to tell Malcolm more bad news. Reverend Milton Galamison, a school desegregation activist in Brooklyn, and Ralph Cooper, a prominent Harlem DJ, weren't able to appear at the event as planned. James 67X didn't know what hotel Malcolm was staying in the night before. So he called Malcolm's home and told Betty. But Betty hadn't told Malcolm.

"Why didn't you tell me?" Malcolm asked James 67X.

"I called your wife and I told her," James 67X replied.

"You should have told me," Malcolm said, enraged.

Whenever Malcolm got really angry, you could see a large vein in the middle of his forehead. Everyone in the office noticed that vein.

Malcolm was the type of person who was always on time and highly organized. From not having the OAAU charter ready to the last-minute program changes, Malcolm could not have been more annoyed.

"Get out, get out," Malcolm shouted.

Everybody left the office. Some of his colleagues went out into the ballroom. Noticed the room starting to fill up. Malcolm had insisted that visitors *not* be checked for weapons. He did not want to alienate people who were interested in the OAAU. The order angered his security personnel. Except for Gene Roberts. Who notified the NYPD, who likely notified the FBI. Did an FBI agent notify John Ali, Elijah's secretary and the FBI informant?

Because five armed men walked into the ballroom, knowing no one would be checking for their weapons. These men were from the Newark mosque of the Nation of Islam with orders to kill Malcolm X. The Newark mosque had a squad of men well known in the Nation of Islam for inflicting severe punishment on anyone who crossed Elijah Muhammad, for anyone who crossed their own minister.

James Shabazz, the minister of the Newark mosque, hated Malcolm. He hated Malcolm because he envied Malcolm. He envied

Malcolm because Malcolm—not he—had become the national spokesman, drawing crowds and attention. Instead of appreciating Malcolm's talents, he looked down on Malcolm. "Look at him," James said one day, watching Malcolm speak, "he's nothing but a Hollywood actor." Most of all, James probably hated Malcolm's politics. James reflected the politics of some ministers in the Nation of Islam, including Elijah Muhammad, who were using the organization to enrich themselves rather than advance Black people. Malcolm—obsessed with liberating Black people. Elijah and James—obsessed with killing Malcolm X.

Chapter 85

HOLD IT, HOLD IT

Benjamin 2X, Malcolm's assistant minister, went back into the office. He had primed crowds for Malcolm at events for years.

"How are you going to open up?" Malcolm asked Benjamin.

Benjamin told Malcolm that he planned to prepare the crowd for the fact the OAAU charter wasn't ready. Malcolm approved.

Sometime later, Benjamin walked out to the stage. He stood behind the wooden podium as the crowd of four hundred people hushed. He started talking about a captain steering a ship to a destination. He plans to get there on time. Based on the speed the ship's going. Then a storm hits the ship. Out of nowhere. The storm slows the ship down. Now the ship can't get to its destination on time.

Benjamin spoke about the unexpected storm making the ship late to explain that things came up, making the OAAU charter late.

Malcolm walked onto the stage. He took a seat behind the speaker. Benjamin did not see Malcolm come onstage. Perhaps because he was focused on his speech and two men near the front. They looked like Muslims, but he did not recognize them. They had their coats slung over their arms. Like they were hiding something. And they were expressionless. Silent. Unmoved by anything Benjamin was saying.

Malcolm reached for an index card on a chair behind him. Probably to jot down something he wanted to say. That's when Benjamin first noticed Malcolm back there.

"Make it plain," Malcolm said, his way of telling Benjamin to finish up.

Benjamin brought his remarks to an end. "I now introduce to you a man that would give his life for his people."

Malcolm stood up. Asked Benjamin to leave the stage—something Malcolm never asked him to do. Benjamin left confused.

Malcolm was now alone onstage. Security guards stood on the floor in front of him.

Malcolm walked to the podium. Organized his index cards. Gathered himself and his unusually hoarse voice.

"As-Salaam-Alaikum," Malcolm said. There were many non-Muslims in the audience. So not many people responded with "Wa-Alaikum-Salaam."

Two assassins stood up four rows back. Acted like they were fighting. Looking like they were drunk. One shouted, "Get your hands out of my pocket."

Near the back, another assassin tossed a low-budget smoke bomb. The smoke and the sounds of the two men fighting snatched everyone's attention.

Including Malcolm's security guards, who went toward the fight. Leaving Malcolm exposed.

Malcolm stepped from behind the podium, body exposed, and said, "Now, now, brothers break it up . . . hold it, hold it, hold it . . ."

William 25X, one of the men Benjamin had been eyeing, had a shotgun under his coat. With Malcolm's body exposed, he charged the stage and shot Malcolm. The gunshot set off a stampede as people took cover or fled the hall. Two other assassins, Talmadge X and Leon X, ran up to the stage and shot Malcolm too.

"They're killing my husband," Betty screamed. "They're killing my husband."

William and Leon dropped their weapons. Talmadge was

supposed to drop his weapon too. But he did not. The three assassins ran into the crowd, rushing out of the hall. They planned to blend into the crowd to get away.

But the crowd—including Malcolm's security guards—noticed Talmadge's weapon. They tackled him to the ground outside. Malcolm's supporters were beating Talmadge up when the police arrived. The police hauled Talmadge into a police car and on to the hospital. The other four assassins got away.

A FBI spy in the ballroom called the FBI field office in New York. "Malcolm X has been shot and I think he's dead." The FBI had informants in the Newark mosque, where the assassins came from. The FBI knew the attempt on Malcolm's life was coming on February 21, 1965. The FBI did nothing to stop the assassination.

FBI director J. Edgar Hoover was one of the first to know about the shooting and quickly relayed the news to President Lyndon B. Johnson. The CIA probably heard the news too—after trying for months to stop Malcolm from getting an African head of state to charge the United States with violating the human rights of African Americans. "The American government is either unable or unwilling to protect the lives and property of your 22 million African-American brothers and sisters," Malcolm wrote the previous year in his appeal to the African heads of state.

His shooting—the latest example.

• • •

Malcolm X died on that stage. He was thirty-nine years old.

11 Court Drive
Huntington Station, N
11746
2/28/65

Concerned Mothers -
  Dear friends -
      The enclosed check is for the
family of Malcolm X. Although I never
met him, I felt that he was a man of
integrity, who was continually growing
and reaching out in a search for true
brotherhood. His example in this respect
and his courage should make his
children proud of him.
                    Sincerely yours,
                  Frederick S. Lightfoot

Donation and condolence letter addressed to the
Committee of Concerned Mothers for Mrs. Malcolm X
and Family, organized after Malcolm's death to provide
financial support to his family, February 28, 1965

Chapter 86

ANCESTOR

Thomas Jefferson, who enslaved more than six hundred Black people during his lifetime, wrote the Declaration of Independence that established the United States in 1776. "We hold these truths to be self-evident, that all men are created equal, that they are endowed by their Creator with certain unalienable Rights, that among these are Life, Liberty and the pursuit of Happiness," Jefferson wrote. "To secure these rights, Governments are instituted."

Human rights: Life, Liberty, and the Pursuit of Happiness. Human rights that the US government had never secured for Black Americans, had never secured for Malcolm Little as a child or Malcolm X as an adult. Racist violence had stolen his happiness at every stage of his life—even before he was born, when Klansmen threatened his mother while pregnant with him. Racist policies had stolen his liberty at every stage of his life too.

Thomas Jefferson added that "whenever any Form of Government becomes destructive" of securing the rights of life, liberty, and the pursuit of happiness, "it is the Right of the People to alter or to abolish it." It is a line that justified the American Revolution against Great Britain. But when Malcolm attempted to build a revolution against American racism, the US government did not acknowledge that right. Racist government authorities, especially the police, did all they could to stop him. And Malcolm lost his life as a revolutionary, fighting to liberate Black people from racism.

When he died on that stage in the Audubon, the police did all they could to cover up the assassination. Talmadge X was charged. But likely only because he was caught at the scene. New York prosecutors charged Norman 3X and Thomas 15X, both members of Mosque Number Seven in Harlem. These three men were convicted of murdering Malcolm. Norman and Thomas spent two decades in prison for a murder they did not commit. The four other assassins, the lookouts and getaway drivers, the planners like James Shabazz and John Ali, Elijah who ordered the hit, the police who knew about the hit—none of them were ever held accountable for murdering Malcolm X.

It was all too much for Betty to bear—the brutal assassination of her beloved husband before her eyes, before the eyes of their children. She looked at the struggles ahead of raising her children as a single parent—just as Malcolm's mother had to raise seven and then eight children after the tragic death of Malcolm's father. But Betty persevered. She gave birth to twins, Malaak and Malikah, seven months after Malcolm's death.

She raised Attallah, Qubilah, Ilyasah, Gamilah, Malaak, and Malikah together. Raised them resolute like her, like their father. Betty fiercely protected her daughters' lives and her husband's legacy.

Betty gave speeches in the budding Black Power movement— that revolution against White supremacy in the late 1960s and 1970s her husband inspired. She went back to college. Earned three degrees. Became Dr. Shabazz. Worked as a professor. Later an administrator at Medgar Evers College in Brooklyn.

All to come.

But in the hours and days after Malcolm's death, a pregnant Betty had to figure out how to support her family. She had to figure out how she was going to give people from around the world sending condolences to her the opportunity to pay their respects to her husband.

Two days after Malcolm's murder, Betty placed her husband's body for public viewing at the Unity Funeral Chapel in Harlem. *Unity*, a word Malcolm died loving. Malcolm was like a deceased president lying in state. Because about thirty thousand people came by to see him give his first speech in the afterlife. A silent one. A personal speech for every person inspired by Malcolm in some way. As each person viewed the body, in their grief, they probably thought about something Malcolm said or did that moved them, even as he could not move now. But they could. They could forge a movement against racism. Many of them did. Many people are still being anti-racist today, moved by Malcolm's life.

Betty called around Harlem to secure a church for Malcolm's funeral. Church officials kept declining. Fearing those who came for Malcolm would come for them. Finally, a courageous bishop named Alvin A. Childs opened the doors to the Faith Temple Church of God in Christ. A church building that has since been demolished, like many places from Malcolm's life.

But Malcolm's ideas and thoughts still stand after all these years. Betty and Malcolm's daughters did not allow his legacy to be demolished. They built it up. And today, people can listen to Malcolm's speeches, see his pictures, read his words, learn about his life.

The day of the funeral came on February 27, 1965. People filled every seat in the six hundred–seat auditorium and lined the walls to pay their respects to Malcolm X. Betty asked Malcolm's close friend, actor Ossie Davis, to give the eulogy.

"Many will say turn away—away from this man, for he is not a man but a demon, a monster, a subverter and an enemy of the black man—and we will smile," Davis said to a nodding audience. "And we will . . . say unto them: Did you ever talk to Brother Malcolm? Did you ever touch him, or have him smile at you? Did you ever really listen to him? . . .

"For if you did you would know him. And if you knew him you

would know why we must honor him," Davis said. "And, in honoring him, we honor the best in ourselves."

They killed Malcolm X. Then again, they failed to kill Malcolm X. Because Malcolm did great things in his thirty-nine years on this Earth. He told Black people to love themselves. He fought for human rights. He fought against racism. He fought against global White supremacy. He tried to generate an antiracist revolution so Black people—so all people—could finally be respected and secure in their human rights.

In the African sense, when you die, you have the opportunity to live as an ancestor. You can live as an ancestor if you have done great things. When you have done great things, people remember you. When people remember you, they speak your name. When people speak your name, you live.

Like history, Malcolm lives.

ACKNOWLEDGMENTS

It was in 2005, twenty years before this book's publication, that I began my intensive study of Malcolm X. It began with Malcolm's spoken words. I listened to his speeches on my drives between Temple University in Philadelphia, where I attended graduate school, and my parents' home in Manassas, Virginia. It was during those drives, thinking about Malcolm's words, that I first thought about learning about his life beyond what I heard in his speeches and read in old books. For me to want to learn about a subject is for me to want to research a subject and to ultimately write out that research, in this case the life story of Malcolm X.

The year after I finished graduate school, historian Manning Marable published a biography of Malcolm. In 2020, historian Peniel E. Joseph released a joint biography of Martin Luther King Jr. and Malcolm X, and Les and Tamara Payne finished their long-awaited life story of Malcolm. After reading and coming to cherish these three thorough biographies, I no longer thought about adding another to the bookshelf.

Aside from writing an essay or giving a speech here or there, studying Malcolm's life became a private affair for me. I continued to research for a book I never thought I'd write. Then again, studying Malcolm's life inspired the books I *did* write. His recognition that Black people could hold assimilationist ideas gave me the courage to chronicle those ideas in my history of racist ideas, *Stamped from the Beginning*. His self-reflection and radical growth inspired me to share in *How to Be an Antiracist* my own "chronology of changes," which is how Malcolm described his antiracist life.

As I reflected on Malcolm's youth, I couldn't help but reflect on my own. I realized we were both around twenty-three years old when we really started reading. And when we both started reading, we really started reading about racism. And as we understood more about racism, we understood more about what we had gone through as young people. It all frustrated me. Because five decades after Malcolm became an ancestor, there were still very few antiracist books for young people. So I teamed up with talented editors and writers like Nic Stone, Jason Reynolds, Sonja Cherry-Paul, and the late Zora Neale Hurston to create some. All the while learning how young people like their books written. All the while witnessing the magic when young people discover their world (and themselves) through a book.

I am sorry for the long windup to my acknowledgments. But I had to tell you the backstory to the day when Farrar Straus Giroux Books for Young Readers and Malcolm X's estate presented me with the opportunity of a lifetime. An opportunity that I didn't know I had been working toward for years, through studying Malcolm, through applying Malcolm's message to our time, through producing books for young people. I am talking about the opportunity to write this official biography of Malcolm X for young readers.

And so I must first sincerely thank Attallah Shabazz, Qubilah Shabazz, Ilyasah Shabazz, Gamilah Lumumba Shabazz, Malaak Shabazz, and the late Malikah Shabazz for this opportunity. I want to express my immense gratitude for all your work caretaking your father and mother's legacies with a diligence and fierceness so they can continue to inspire revolutionaries and human rights activists in the twenty-first century.

I want to acknowledge the most recent biographers of Malcolm, specifically Marable, Joseph, and the Paynes. Writing such excellent biographies for adults ended up sending me down a path to write this first major biography for young people since the late great

Walter Dean Myers published one in 1993. I must acknowledge all the writers who wrote books for young people with me, and the young people who read these books and offered their thoughts to me. I learned so much from you, learning I poured into this book.

I must sincerely acknowledge my editor, Grace Elizabeth Kendall, for all your passion and commitment and dogged determination for us to create a powerful and inspirational testament to Malcolm. Thank you immensely to the rest of the team at Macmillan who helped us usher this book into the world, namely Asia Harden, Mallory Grigg, Allyson Floridia, Elizabeth Peskin, Sara Elroubi, Chantal Gersch, Melissa Zar, Samantha Fabbricatore, and Allison Verost.

Thank you, as always, to my wonderful literary agent, Ayesha Pande, for navigating the winding path in order for us to arrive at this special opportunity. I must sincerely thank Dr. Heather Sanford and Hunter Moyler for helping me research and fact-check this book. With all the fiction surrounding Malcolm's life, I am thankful for being able to work diligently with you to ensure *Malcolm Lives!* is fact-based.

I must sincerely thank my oldest daughter, Imani. Your voice was always in my ear alongside Malcolm's voice as I composed the book's prose. In the background, of course, has been your little Sissy, screaming "DADA" with all that force we love.

Finally, I must acknowledge my parents, my brother, my friends, and my other relatives—you know who you are—and my loving partner, Sadiqa. Your steady presence amid the emotional roller coaster in writing about the life, death, and afterlife of Malcolm could not have been more crucial. I am grateful for you steadying me, so I can show how history lives.

The Ballot or th Bullet

① Moderator
Rev. Cleage   Milton + Michael Henry
Ballot Bin...

The Ballot or th Bullet

1. This is the year of: The Ballot or th Bullet

1. First: my personal position
2. Still a Muslim, Islam.
3. Still credit MM for what I know & what I am.
4. Minister of newly founded M.M.I (Theresa Hotel)

1. Powell — CM — Abys — political struggle
2. King — CM — Atl — civil rights
3. Galamison — CM — Brklyn — School Boycotts
4. Cleague — CM — Det — Freedom Now Party
5. I — MMI — ready to fight on all fronts
6. I am a Black Nationalist Freedom Fighter

Malcolm's notes for "The Ballot or the Bullet" speech, 1964

SOURCE NOTES

Introducing Malcolm

3 THE NEBRASKA HISTORICAL MARKER: The marker's words can be seen in the photo at National Park Service, "Nebraska: Malcolm X House Site Omaha," May 9, 2020, www.nps.gov/places/nebraska-malcolm-x-house-site-omaha.htm.

3 "I'M FOR TRUTH, NO MATTER WHO TELLS IT": *The Autobiography of Malcolm X*, with Alex Haley (New York: Grove, 1965; New York: Ballantine Books, 1992), 421. Citations refer to the Ballantine edition. Hereafter cited as *Autobiography*.

Chapter 1: Louise

5 THE SIX OR SO WHITE MEN ON HORSES: Details about this visit to intimidate the Little family, including the quotes, are drawn from *Autobiography*, 3; and Les Payne and Tamara Payne, *The Dead Are Arising: The Life of Malcolm X* (New York: Liveright, 2020), 3–6. Hereafter cited as Payne and Payne.

6 POWERFUL PORTUGUESE WRITERS CONSTRUCTED *RACE* IN THE 1400s: Gomes Eanes de Zurara's *Chronicle of the Discovery and Conquest of Guinea*, published in 1453, was the first book in this construction project. To learn more about the construction of race to justify the enslavement of Africans, see Jason Reynolds, *Stamped: Racism, Antiracism, and You* (New York: Little, Brown, 2020), a young readers' adaptation of Ibram X. Kendi, *Stamped from the Beginning: The Definitive History of Racist Ideas in America* (New York: Nation Books, 2016).

6 EXPERTS CAN'T FIND ANY BIOLOGICAL OR GENETIC DIFFERENCES: Michael Yudell et al., "Taking Race Out of Human Genetics," *Science* 351, no. 6273 (February 5, 2016): 564–65, doi.org/10.1126/science.aac4951; Simon Worrall, "Why Race Is Not a Thing, According to Genetics," *National Geographic*, October 24, 2017, www.nationalgeographic.com/science/article/genetics-history-race-neanderthal-rutherford; Alan Goodman, "Race Is Real, But It's Not Genetic," *Sapiens*, March 13, 2020, www.sapiens.org/biology/is-race-real; and "Race in Clinical Practice: A Reckoning," Kaiser Permanente Bernard J. Tyson School of Medicine, March 6, 2024, medschool.kp.org/news/race-in-clinical-practice-a-reckoning.

7 ANNOUNCED THEMSELVES AS THE "KNIGHTS" OF THE KU KLUX KLAN: Payne and Payne, 3.

7 THE KLAN AND OTHER RACIST MOBS HAD KIDNAPPED THOUSANDS: W. E. Burghardt Du Bois, *Black Reconstruction: An Essay Toward a History of the Part Which Black Folk Played in the Attempt to Reconstruct Democracy in America, 1860–1880* (New York: Russell & Russell, 1935), 674–87; and "Lynchings: By State and Race, 1882–1968," Tuskegee University Archives Repository, accessed March 20, 2024, archive.tuskegee.edu/repository/wp-content/uploads/2020/11/Lynchings-Stats-Year-Dates-Causes.pdf.

7 **RUMOR WAS HER WHITE FATHER HAD RAPED HER BLACK MOTHER:** Manning Marable, *Malcolm X: A Life of Reinvention* (New York: Penguin Books, 2012), 16.

7 **RACISM AND SEXISM SHUT BLACK WOMEN OUT OF OTHER JOBS:** *The Canadian Encyclopedia*, s.v., "Racial Segregation of Black People in Canada," by Natasha Henry-Dixon, May 28, 2019, www.thecanadianencyclopedia.ca/en/article/racial-segregation-of -black-people-in-canada.

8 **"UP, YOU MIGHTY RACE":** Roi Ottley, *"New World A-Coming": Inside Black America* (Boston: Houghton Mifflin, 1943), 72.

8 **"I AM THE EQUAL OF ANY WHITE MAN":** Rollin Lynde Hartt, "The Negro Moses and His Campaign to Lead the Black Millions into Their Promised Land," *Independent*, February 26, 1921, 206.

8 **"GET THAT [N-WORD] OUT HERE, NOW!":** Wilfred Little (Malcolm's older brother), interview by Les Payne, April 26, 1991, quoted in Payne and Payne, 3.

Chapter 2: Earl

9 **DID NOT THINK BLACK KIDS NEEDED TO GO TO SCHOOL:** Payne and Payne, 8.

9 **ONLY WANTED BLACK PEOPLE TO LEARN HOW TO PICK COTTON AND MAINTAIN WHITE HOMES:** Payne and Payne, 8.

9 **DID NOT LIKE THAT EARL ACTED AS IF HE WAS EQUAL:** Payne and Payne, 9–10; and Marable, *Malcolm X*, 15.

9 **JOINED THE GREAT MIGRATION OF NEARLY SIX MILLION BLACK PEOPLE:** Marable, *Malcolm X*, 16; and "The Great Migration (1910–1970)," National Archives, accessed March 20, 2024, www.archives.gov/research/african-americans/migrations/great -migration.

10 **TERRORIZED ASIAN AMERICANS, NATIVE AMERICANS, AND LATINO AMERICANS:** Marable, *Malcolm X*, 21; and *The Encyclopedia of Oklahoma History and Culture*, s.v. "Ku Klux Klan," by Larry O'Dell, January 15, 2010, www.okhistory.org/publications/enc /entry?entry = KU001. See also Juan O. Sánchez, *The Ku Klux Klan's Campaign Against Hispanics, 1921–1925: Rhetoric, Violence and Response in the American Southwest* (Jefferson, NC: McFarland, 2018).

10 **EVEN WHITE AMERICANS, ESPECIALLY CATHOLICS AND JEWS AND UNION ORGANIZERS AND ANTI-RACISTS:** Marable, *Malcolm X*, 21; Payne and Payne, 27; and Thomas R. Pegram, *One Hundred Percent American: The Rebirth and Decline of the Ku Klux Klan in the 1920s* (Chicago: Ivan R. Dee, 2011), 34, 176–80.

10 **AROUND FORTY THOUSAND KLANSMEN:** Payne and Payne, 28.

10 **"THE GOOD CHRISTIAN WHITE PEOPLE":** *Autobiography*, 3.

Chapter 3: Lansing

13 **FOR YEARS, FBI AGENTS TRIED TO FIND A LAW GARVEY BROKE:** Payne and Payne, 35, 45, 53. The FBI itself states, "In the aftermath of World War I, the FBI began investi-

gating Garvey's activities, looking to deport him as an undesirable alien." See the Marcus Garvey file, FBI Records: The Vault, vault.fbi.gov/marcus-garvey.

14 **"SPIRITUAL ADVISER"**: S. E. Rougere, "Milwaukee, Wis.," News and Views of UNIA Divisions, *Negro World*, January 29, 1927, 6.

14 **"RELEASE MARCUS GARVEY"**: Earl Little, W. M. Townsend, and Robert Finney to President Calvin Coolidge, June 8, 1927, in *The Marcus Garvey and Universal Negro Improvement Association Papers*, ed. Robert A. Hill, vol. 6, *September 1924–December 1927* (Berkeley: University of California Press, 1989), 561.

14 **CONVICTION OF A CRIME LIKE MAIL FRAUD MADE AN IMMIGRANT LIKE GARVEY SUBJECT TO DEPORTATION**: US National Commission on Law Observance and Enforcement, *Report on The Enforcement of the Deportation Laws of the United States* (Washington, D. C.: Government Printing Office, 1931), 34.

14 **DEPORTED "PROMPTLY" AND "BY OPERATION OF THE LAW"**: James Finch to John Sargent, November 22, 1927, in *The Marcus Garvey and Universal Negro Improvement Association Papers*, vol. 6, *September 1924–December 1927*, ed. Robert A. Hill (Berkeley, CA: University of California Press, 1989), 613.

14 **"MENTAL ENERGY"**: Wilfred Little interview, quoted in Payne and Payne, 62.

15 **WHITE PEOPLE CALLED THE "[N-WORD] SECTION"**: Wilfred Little interview, quoted in Payne and Payne, 62.

Chapter 4: 2:30 A.M.

17 **"SAID LOT SHALL NOT BE OCCUPIED BY A COLORED PERSON"**: *Parmalee v. Morris*, 218 Mich 625 (1922) (Record at 2), books.google.com/books?id = sChAt_UbD5AC.

18 **IN 2019, A MICHIGAN LEGISLATOR FROM LANSING INTRODUCED A BILL**: Prohibited Restrictive Convenants Act, House Bill 4676, Michigan Legislature, May 24, 2019, www .legislature.mi.gov/documents/2019–2020/billintroduced/House/htm/2019-HIB -4676.htm.

18 **REP. SARAH ANTHONY HAD YET TO GET HER INITIAL BILL PASSED**: Ryan Stanton, "Ann Arbor Subdivision Reckoning with Its Racist Past, Repealing 1947 Whites-Only Policy," MLive, February 13, 2022, www.mlive.com/news/ann-arbor/2022/02/ann-arbor -subdivision-reckoning-with-its-racist-past-repealing-1947-whites-only-policy.html.

18 **IN DECEMBER 2022, MICHIGAN GOVERNOR GRETCHEN WHITMER SIGNED INTO LAW**: Discharge of Prohibited Restrictive Covenants Act, Michigan Public Act 234 of 2022, legislature.mi.gov/documents/2021–2022/publicact/htm/2022-PA-0234.htm.

18 **PROBABLY AT A LOWER PRICE**: Payne and Payne, 64.

19 **RACIST WHITE CARPENTERS WOULD START TROUBLE**: Payne and Payne, 62–63.

Chapter 5: Blame

21–22 **LANSING FIRE DEPARTMENT REFUSED TO COME**: G. W. Waterman, report of investigation of suspected arson, case 2155, started November 8, 1929, in *The Portable*

Malcolm X Reader, ed. Manning Marable and Garrett Felber (New York: Penguin Books, 2013), 11.

22 **BLACK RESIDENTS OF NEW ORLEANS:** "Race an Issue in Katrina Response," CBS News, September 3, 2005, www.cbsnews.com/news/race-an-issue-in-katrina-response/; and Christopher Flavelle, "Why Does Disaster Aid Often Favor White People?" *New York Times*, June 7, 2021, www.nytimes.com/2021/06/07/climate/FEMA-race -climate.html.

22 **HOUSELESS BLACK PEOPLE:** "Homelessness and Racial Disparities," National Alliance to End Homelessness, December 2023, endhomelessness.org/homelessness -in-america/what-causes-homelessness/inequality/.

22 **BLACK PEOPLE WHO CALLED THE POLICE:** Abigail Abrams, "Black, Disabled and at Risk: The Overlooked Problem of Police Violence Against Americans with Disabilities," *Time*, June 25, 2020, time.com/5857438/police-violence-black-disabled/.

22 **LOCAL POLICE WASTED PRECIOUS TIME INVESTIGATING EARL:** Waterman, report of case 2155; Payne and Payne, 65–66; and Marable, *Malcolm X*, 25–26.

22 **A HOUSE IN A WHITE NEIGHBORHOOD NEAR EAST LANSING:** "United States Census, 1930," database with images, *FamilySearch* (familysearch.org/ark:/61903 /3:1:33S7–9RHH7TB?cc = 1810731&wc = QZF32QB%3A648805801%2C650103101% 2C648942101%2C1589282600 : 8 December 2015), Michigan > Ingham > Lansing > ED 50 > image 62 of 174; citing NARA microfilm publication T626 (Washington, D.C.: National Archives and Records Administration, 2002).

22 **FACED WITH CONSTANT HARASSMENT FROM RACIST NEIGHBORS:** *Autobiography*, 6.

23 **"THE NIGHTMARE NIGHT IN 1929, MY EARLIEST VIVID MEMORY":** *Autobiography*, 5.

Chapter 6: Bullies

25 **MANY PEOPLE TREAT LIGHT-SKINNED BLACK KIDS BETTER:** Lance Hannon, Robert DeFina, and Sarah Bruch, "The Relationship Between Skin Tone and School Suspension for African Americans," *Race and Social Problems* 5 (2013), 282, 292–93; and Jandel Crutchfield, Latocia Keyes, Maya Williams, and Danielle R. Eugene, "A Scoping Review of Colorism in Schools: Academic, Social, and Emotional Experiences of Students of Color," *Social Sciences* 11, no. 1 (2022): 15.

25 **"IF ANYBODY WAS PASSING BY OUT ON THE ROAD":** *Autobiography*, 10–11.

26 **A PICKANINNY IS A RACIST PICTURE:** Philbert Little (Malcolm's brother), interview by Les Payne, November 15, 1990, quoted in Payne and Payne, 74; Stephanie Polsky, *The Dark Posthuman: Dehumanization, Technology, and the Atlantic World* (Punctum Books, 2022), 144; and Debbie Olson, *Black Children in Hollywood Cinema: Cast in Shadow* (Cham, Switzerland: Palgrave Macmillan, 2017), 83–84.

27 **"IF YOU FEEL THE WHITE KIDS ARE BETTER THAN YOU":** Louise Little's words are re-created, based on what Malcolm's brother Wilfred Little remembered learning as

a child: "If you acted like you were inferior, that's the way they related to you. If you didn't act like you were inferior, then they would be forced to treat you as an equal." Payne and Payne, 75.

27 "CHICKEN MONEY": Manning Marable, *Malcolm X: A Life of Reinvention* (New York: Penguin Books, 2012), 30.

Chapter 7: A Vision

29 "SUNDOWN TOWNS": Sundown towns were entire communities that had purposely kept Black people out for decades. From 1890 to around 1968, White people established thousands of sundown towns all across the United States. They were very common in the Midwest. James W. Loewen, *Sundown Towns: A Hidden Dimension of American Racism* (New York: New Press, 2005), 4–5, 55.

29 EAST LANSING WAS THIS WAY: *Autobiography*, 10.

29 BLACK PEOPLE CALLED THE TOWN "WHITE CITY": *Autobiography*, 10.

29 THESE SECRET MEETINGS WERE USUALLY HELD: Details of the UNIA meetings, including Earl Little's quotes, come from *Autobiography*, 9–10.

30 "ALWAYS WORKING—COOKING, WASHING, IRONING, CLEANING": *Autobiography*, 10.

31 "HAD ALWAYS HAD A STRONG INTUITION" AND "WHEN SOMETHING IS ABOUT TO HAPPEN": *Autobiography*, 12.

31 "EARLY! EARLY!" SHE SCREAMED: *Autobiography*, 12.

Chapter 8: Accident?

34 TOO MANY POLICE OFFICERS ARE SECRETLY WHITE SUPREMACISTS: Michael German, "Hidden in Plain Sight: Racism, White Supremacy, and Far-Right Militancy in Law Enforcement," Brennan Center for Justice, August 27, 2020, www.brennancenter .org/our-work/research-reports/hidden-plain-sight-racism-white-supremacy-and -far-right-militancy-law.

34 MICHIGAN HAD AROUND 75,000 KLANSMEN: David M. Chalmers, *Hooded Americanism: The History of the Ku Klux Klan*, 2nd ed. (New York: New Viewpoints, 1981), 195; and Kenneth T. Jackson, *The Ku Klux Klan in the City, 1915–1930* (New York: Oxford University Press, 1967), 129n4.

34 MURDER CONVICTION OF INDIANA KLAN LEADER: Gwyneth Harris, "D.C. Stephenson," Digital Civil Rights Museum, Ball State University, accessed March 22, 2024, www .digitalresearch.bsu.edu/digitalcivilrightsmuseum/items/show/111.

34 NEW TERRORIST GROUP, THE BLACK LEGION: Peter H. Amann, "Vigilante Fascism: The Black Legion as an American Hybrid," *Comparative Studies in Society and History* 25, no. 3 (July 1983): 490–524; Marable, *Malcolm X*, 30; and Payne and Payne, 80.

34 A FORMER DETROIT POLICE OFFICER: Amann, "Vigilante Fascism," 505–6.

34 **MANY POLICE OFFICERS AND PUBLIC OFFICIALS:** Marable, *Malcolm X*, 30; Amann, "Vigilante Fascism," 506, 508–9; and Kenneth R. Dvorak, "Terror in Detroit: The Rise and Fall of Michigan's Black Legion" (PhD diss., Bowling Green State University, 2000), 131–33, rave.ohiolink.edu/etdc/view?acc_num = bgsu1668786652702366.

34 **"NEGROES IN LANSING":** *Autobiography*, 13.

Chapter 9: Great Depression

37 **BY 1933, ALMOST HALF OF US BANKS CLOSED THEIR DOORS:** Bank closures and job losses during the Depression come from *Encyclopedia Britannica*, s.v., "Great Depression: Facts & Related Content," accessed March 22, 2024, www.britannica.com/facts/Great-Depression.

37 **BLACK BUSINESSES GENERALLY HAD FEWER RESOURCES:** Information about the Depression's unequal effect on Black businesses comes from Cheryl Lynn Greenberg, *To Ask for an Equal Chance: African Americans in the Great Depression* (Lanham, MD: Rowman & Littlefield Publishers, Inc., 2011), 31–32; and Mary-Elizabeth B. Murphy, "African Americans in the Great Depression and New Deal," *Oxford Research Encyclopedia of American History*, November 19, 2020, doi.org/10.1093/acrefore /9780199329175.013.632; and Robert E. Weems Jr., "Making a Way Out of No Way: The History of Black Business in America" (proposal, Racism and the Economy: Focus on Entrepreneurship webinar, Federal Reserve Bank of Minneapolis, June 2, 2021), www.minneapolisfed.org/-/media/assets/events/2021/racism-and -the-economy-focus-on-entrepreneurship/weems-proposal.pdf.

37 **BLACK WORKERS HAD OFTEN BEEN THE LAST HIRED:** Information about the Depression's unequal effect on Black workers comes from Murphy, "African Americans in the Great Depression"; and "Race Relations in the 1930s and 1940s," Great Depression and World War II, 1929–1945, U.S. History Primary Source Timeline, Library of Congress, accessed March 22, 2024, www.loc.gov/classroom-materials /united-states-history-primary-source-timeline/great-depression-and-world-war-ii -1929–1945/race-relations-in-1930s-and-1940s/.

38 **"COME HOME CRYING, BUT TRYING TO HIDE IT":** *Autobiography*, 15.

38 **"DIDN'T CONTRIBUTE ANYTHING":** *Autobiography*, 15.

39 **WHEN A PARENT IS INCARCERATED:** "Children with an incarcerated parent were more than three times more likely to have behavioral problems or depression than similar children without an imprisoned parent." Paola Scommegna, "Parents' Imprisonment Linked to Children's Health, Behavioral Problems," Population Reference Bureau, December 3, 2014, www.prb.org/resources/parents-imprisonment-linked -to-childrens-health-behavioral-problems/.

39 **WHEN A PARENT IS SEPARATED FROM A CHILD BEING SENT TO FOSTER CARE:** John DeGarmo, "Children in Foster Care & Mental Health Disorders," *Fostering Families Today*, February 6, 2023, fosteringfamiliestoday.com/fostering-families-today-feature /children-in-foster-care-mental-health-disorders/.

39 **ONE IN EIGHT HOUSEHOLDS IN THE UNITED STATES:** Matthew P. Rabbitt, Laura J. Hales, Michael P. Burke, and Alisha Coleman-Jensen, *Household Food Security in the United States in 2022*, no. ERR-325 (US Department of Agriculture, Economic Research Service, October 2023), iv, www.ers.usda.gov/webdocs/publications /107703/err-325.pdf; and Annie Nova, "Another public health crisis: 1 in 8 U.S. households struggle with food insecurity, government report finds," CNBC, October 27, 2023, cnbc.com/2023/10/27/1-in-8-us-households-struggle-with-hunger-food -insecurity-usda.html. The official statistic is 12.8 percent of US households are food insecure, meaning they don't have access to enough food due to a lack of resources. (A household is one or more people living in a single housing unit.)

39–40 **BLACK CHILDREN ARE MORE LIKELY TO GO HUNGRY:** The race-based statistics, which have been rounded to the nearest whole number, represent rates of food insuffi-ciency in the United States, showing the percentage of households where an adult "said children in the household were not eating enough 'sometimes' or 'often' in the last 7 days because the household could not afford enough food." Laura J. Hales and Matthew P. Rabbitt, "Child Food Insufficiency Continues to Vary Widely Across Racial and Ethnic Groups," Economic Research Service, US Department of Agriculture, last updated April 6, 2023, www.ers.usda.gov/data-products/chart -gallery/gallery/chart-detail/?chartId = 106257.

40 **TEASED MALCOLM FOR EATING "FRIED GRASS":** *Autobiography*, 17.

40 **"I NEVER WANTED TO WAIT FOR ANYTHING":** *Autobiography*, 19.

Chapter 10: Cold

43 **"LOOKED JUST LIKE MY FATHER":** Wilfred Little interview, quoted in Payne and Payne, 98–99.

44 **MARCUS GARVEY URGED BLACK PEOPLE TO BE SELF-RELIANT:** Marable, *Malcolm X*, 30; and Payne and Payne, 29.

45 **"THEY WERE TRYING TO GET HER TO KNEEL":** Wilfred Little, interview, January 27, 1992, for documentary film by Blackside Inc., excerpted in companion book, Che-ryll Y. Greene, ed., *Malcolm X: Make It Plain*, text by William Strickland (New York: Viking, 1994), 28.

45 **STATE ONLY GAVE AROUND $1.75:** Reba F. Harris, *Mothers' Pensions in Michigan: Report of a Study Made by the State Welfare Department* (Lansing, MI: State Wel-fare Department, 1934), 8–9, quoted in Susan Stein-Roggenbuck, *Negotiating Relief: The Development of Social Welfare Programs in Depression-Era Michigan, 1930–1940* (Columbus: Ohio State University Press, 2008), 36.

45 **AND SOMETIMES, MOTHERS WITH EIGHT CHILDREN:** Harris, *Mothers' Pensions in Mich-igan*, quoted in Stein-Roggenbuck, *Negotiating Relief*, 36.

45 **WELFARE OFFICIALS WERE CONSTANTLY COMING TO THE HOME:** Walter Dean Myers, *Mal-colm X: By Any Means Necessary* (New York: Scholastic Focus, 2020), 24–25; and Marable, *Malcolm X*, 34–35.

45 **"as vicious as vultures":** *Autobiography*, 22.

46 **"paranoid condition, probably dementia praecox":** E. F. Hoffman, physician's certificate for Louise Little, January 3, 1939, in *The Portable Malcolm X Reader*, ed. Manning Marable and Garrett Felber (New York: Penguin Books, 2013), 31.

47 **could have been experiencing what's called postpartum depression:** Jolie Solomon, "Overlooked No More: Louise Little, Activist and Mother of Malcolm X," *New York Times*, March 19, 2022, www.nytimes.com/2022/03/19/obituaries /louise-little-overlooked.html.

47 **may have been suffering from postpartum psychosis:** Louise's symptoms were consistent with those that people with postpartum psychosis may experience. See "Postpartum Depression," Mayo Clinic, accessed March 22, 2024, www.mayoclinic .org/diseases-conditions/postpartum-depression/symptoms-causes/syc-20376617.

Chapter 11: Homeless

49 **because white teachers and school officials believed he was disobedient and disrespectful:** Payne and Payne, 100, 116.

49 **he earned four cs:** Malcolm's 1938–1939 grades appear in a letter from Robert E. Lott of the Lansing School District to William T. Noble of the *Detroit News*, January 17, 1966, quoted in Payne and Payne, 116.

49 **Educators used to use e:** "Apparently, some professors worried that students would think the grade stood for 'excellent,' since *F* stood for 'failure.'" Brian Palmer, "E Is for Fail," *Slate*, August 9, 2010, slate.com/news-and-politics/2010/08 /how-come-schools-assign-grades-of-a-b-c-d-and-f-but-not-e.html.

50 **that was a no-no then and, with some people, now:** In a Gallup poll taken July 6–July 21, 2021, 4 percent of American adults said they disapproved of marriage between Black people and White people. "Question 26: Bi-Racial Marriage Approval," Gallup Poll Social Survey, July 2021, in Justin McCarthy, "U.S. Approval of Interracial Marriage at New High of 94%," Gallup, September 10, 2021, news .gallup.com/poll/354638/approval-interracial-marriage-new-high.aspx.

50 **"go ahead, pull the trigger, whitey":** John Davis Jr. (Malcolm's friend) recalled this scene in interview by Les Payne, September 1, 1993, quoted in Payne and Payne, 122.

50 **"that way," he said, "everyone can see you":** *Autobiography*, 30.

50 **these homes had been organized in almost every state:** Charles H. Warner, "County Children's Courts," *Juvenile Court Record*, February 1919, 12.

51 **black boys were more likely to be forced into detention homes:** Mary Huff Diggs, "The Problems and Needs of Negro Youth as Revealed by Delinquency and Crime Statistics," *Journal of Negro Education* 9, no. 3 (July 1940), 316, table iv.

51 **that is still the case today:** "Black youth were 4.7 times as likely to be placed (i.e., detained or committed) in juvenile facilities as their white peers," according to

nationwide data from Easy Access to the Census of Juveniles in Residential Placement (C. Puzzanchera, T. J. Sladky, and W. Kang, 2023). Joshua Rovner, "Black Disparities in Youth Incarceration," The Sentencing Project, December 12, 2023, www.sentencingproject.org/fact-sheet/black-disparities-in-youth-incarceration/.

Chapter 12: Mr. Kaminska

53 MR. KAMINSKA WAS MALCOLM'S EIGHTH-GRADE ENGLISH TEACHER: Although Malcolm's *Autobiography* uses the fake name "Mr. Ostrowski" for this teacher, Malcolm's former classmates eventually revealed that this teacher's real name was Richard Kaminska. James Cotton (Malcolm's classmate), interview by Les Payne, June 20, 1992, quoted in Payne and Payne, 140.

54 "MALCOLM, YOU OUGHT TO BE THINKING ABOUT A CAREER": Quotes from this exchange between Malcolm and Mr. Kaminska appear in *Autobiography*, 43.

55 SIXTY-ONE BLACK MALE LAWYERS: US Census Bureau, "Michigan: Table 13. Race and Age of Employed Persons [. . .] by Occupation and Sex for the State, and Cities of 100,000 or More," in *1940 Census of Population*, vol. 3, *The Labor Force: Occupation, Industry, Employment, and Income*, pt. 3, *Iowa–Montana* (Washington, DC: US Government Printing Office, 1943), 606, www2.census.gov/library /publications/decennial/1940/population-volume-3/33973538v3p3ch6.pdf.

55 RACIST BARRIERS PREVENTING BLACK PEOPLE FROM BECOMING LAWYERS: For information on some of these barriers today, see Marisa Manzi and Nina Totenberg, "'Already Behind': Diversifying The Legal Profession Starts Before The LSAT," NPR, December 22, 2020, www.npr.org/2020/12/22/944434661/already-behind-diversifying -the-legal-profession-starts-before-the-lsat.

56 A FEW DOZEN BLACK PEOPLE AMID NEARLY THREE THOUSAND WHITE PEOPLE: US Census Bureau, "Michigan: Table 28. Race and Age, by Sex, with Rural-Farm Population, for Minor Civil Divisions, by Counties," in *1940 Census of Population*, vol. 2, *Characteristics of the Population*, pt. 3: *Kansas–Michigan*, 844, www2.census.gov /library/publications/decennial/1940/population-volume-2/33973538v2p3ch7 .pdf.

56 "IT JUST NEVER DAWNED UPON THEM": *Autobiography*, 32.

57 "IT WAS THEN THAT I BEGAN TO CHANGE—INSIDE": *Autobiography*, 44.

57 "WHAT'S WRONG?" AND "NOTHING": *Autobiography*, 44–45.

Chapter 13: Ella

60 THE LYNCHINGS: Between 1882 and 1930, White mobs lynched 423 Black people in Georgia. The racist violence in the state was second only to Mississippi, where 462 Black people were lynched by White mobs. Stewart E. Tolnay and E. M. Beck, *A Festival of Violence: An Analysis of Southern Lynchings, 1882–1930* (Urbana: University of Illinois Press, 1995), 273, table C-4.

60 "WE LITTLES HAVE TO STICK TOGETHER": *Autobiography*, 40.

60 **23,679 BLACK PEOPLE IN BOSTON, ABOUT 676 TIMES AS MANY:** US Census Bureau, "Massachusetts: Table 34. Race and Age, by Sex, for Cities of 50,000 or More by Wards," in *1940 Census of Population*, vol. 2, *Characteristics of the Population*, pt. 3, 666, www2.census.gov/library/publications/decennial/1940/population-volume-2 /33973538v2p3ch6.pdf; and US Census Bureau, "Michigan: Table 28," 844.

Chapter 14: Boston

63 **"YOU DON'T HAVE TO START HUNTING FOR A JOB RIGHT AWAY":** Ella's words are re-created, based on *Autobiography*, 47–48: "About my second day there in Roxbury, Ella told me that she didn't want me to start hunting for a job right away, like most newcomer Negroes did. She said that she had told all those she'd brought North to take their time, to walk around, to travel the buses and the subway, and get the feel of Boston, before they tied themselves down working somewhere, because they would never again have the time to really see and get to know anything about the city they were living in. Ella said she'd help me find a job when it was time for me to go to work."

63 **FEWER THAN 20 PERCENT AND 4 PERCENT:** Education statistics are from US Census Bureau, "United States Summary: Table 13. Persons 25 Years Old and Over, by Years of School Completed, Race and Sex for the United States, Urban and Rural," in *1940 Census of Population*, vol. 2, *Characteristics of the Population*, pt. 1, *United States Summary and Alabama–District of Columbia*, 41, www2.census.gov/library /publications/decennial/1940/population-volume-2/33973538v2p1ch2.pdf.

64 **BOSTON WAS 96.7 PERCENT WHITE AND 3.1 PERCENT BLACK IN 1940:** US Census Bureau, "Massachusetts: Table 34," 666.

64 **THEY WERE KNOWN AS "HILL NEGROES":** *Autobiography*, 48–49, 53.

65 **HAD A SINGLE PARAGRAPH ON BLACK AMERICAN HISTORY:** *Autobiography*, 35.

65 **A HISTORY TEXTBOOK RECOMMENDED:** The textbook was *History of the United States of America* by Henry William Elson, which appeared on a 1937 list of books that the Michigan superintendent of public instruction and the state librarian recommended for school libraries. See Grace S. McClure and Eugene B. Elliott, *Preferred List of Books for School Libraries, State of Michigan*, rev. ed. (Lansing, MI: Franklin DeKleine, 1937), 55.

65 **"MILLIONS OF ILLITERATE FREEDMEN":** The textbook's quotes can be found in Henry William Elson, *History of the United States of America* (New York: Macmillan, 1904), 795, 803.

66 **HIS MOTHER WAS A MEMBER OF THE WAMPANOAG NATION:** Eric Hinderaker, *Boston's Massacre* (Cambridge, MA: Belknap Press of Harvard University Press, 2017), 160.

68 **"NICE YOUNG PEOPLE":** *Autobiography*, 51.

69 **"EVEN THOUGH I DID LIVE ON THE HILL":** *Autobiography*, 51.

Chapter 15: New Look

71 **"WELL, I GUESS IT HAD TO HAPPEN"**: *Autobiography*, 62.

72 **"I ENDURED ALL OF THAT PAIN"**: *Autobiography*, 64.

Chapter 16: Other Malcolm

73 **"HI, RED"**: Quotes from Malcolm X's recollection of his first meeting with Malcolm Jarvis appear in *Autobiography*, 52–53. Jarvis was the main source for the book's composite character Shorty. Payne and Payne, 158.

74 **"GIVE IT BACK"**: Jarvis's recollection of their first meeting comes from Malcolm Jarvis, interview by Les Payne, December 9, 1992, quoted in Payne and Payne, 159.

75 **"MALCOLM, YOU HAVEN'T HAD ANY EXPERIENCE"**: *Autobiography*, 55.

Chapter 17: Ballroom

77 **"GET HERE EARLY . . ."**: Kenneth's instructions are from *Autobiography*, 55–56.

78 **MOST OF THE DANCES AT THE ROSELAND HAD WHITE BANDS**: *Autobiography*, 58; and Payne and Payne, 156.

78 **"WHITES ONLY" WAS IN THE NORTH TOO IN THE 1940s**: Gunnar Myrdal, *An American Dilemma: The Negro Problem and Modern Democracy* (New York: Harper & Brothers, 1944), 630–31; and *To Secure These Rights: The Report of the President's Committee on Civil Rights* (New York: Simon and Schuster, 1947), 78.

78 **THESE DANCES WERE NOT BLACK ONLY**: *Autobiography*, 60; and Payne and Payne, 156.

78 **"SOME COUPLES WERE SO ABANDONED"**: *Autobiography*, 60.

Chapter 18: Girlfriend

82 **LEGISLATION HAD BEEN INTRODUCED**: Zebulon Miletsky, "The Dilemma of Interracial Marriage: The Boston NAACP and the National Equal Rights League, 1912–1927," *Historical Journal of Massachusetts* 44, no. 1 (Winter 2016), 138–40, 149.

82 **"A WRECK OF A WOMAN"**: *Autobiography*, 80.

82 **"HE WAS A REAL HONEST-TO-GOODNESS MESS"**: Ella Collins, interview transcript for "Malcolm X: The Real Story," CBS News, aired December 3, 1992, quoted in Payne and Payne, 162.

83 **MALCOLM KNEW THAT RACIST WHITE PEOPLE LOVED**: *Autobiography*, 88.

Chapter 19: Harlem

86 **"WITHIN THE FIRST FIVE MINUTES IN [SMALLS']"**: *Autobiography*, 85.

87 **"HAD NEVER SEEN SUCH FEVER-HEAT DANCING"**: *Autobiography*, 86.

87 **"INCUBATOR FOR THE HARLEM RENAISSANCE":** Sandra E. Garcia, "The Visionary Community of the Harlem Y.M.C.A." *New York Times Style Magazine*, October 15, 2021, www.nytimes.com/2021/10/15/t-magazine/harlem-ymca-black-culture.html.

88 **"RENT-RAISING PARTIES":** *Autobiography*, 89.

Chapter 20: Home, Home

91 **"SKIN ME, DADDY-O!":** *Autobiography*, 92.

91 **SIGNED AUTOGRAPHS "HARLEM RED":** *Autobiography*, 93.

Chapter 21: Seventh Heaven

93 **THE TOP BLACK-OWNED NIGHTCLUB IN HARLEM:** Kathleen Drowne, "Small's Paradise," in *Encyclopedia of the Harlem Renaissance*, vol. 2, ed. Cary D. Wintz and Paul Finkelman (New York: Routledge, 2004), 1120–21.

93 **SOME WHITE OWNERS OF HARLEM CLUBS BARRED GUESTS OF COLOR:** *Autobiography*, 96; and Shane Vogel, "Nightclubs," in *Encyclopedia of the Harlem Renaissance*, vol. 2, 909–10.

94 **SMALLS' PARADISE WAS "SEVENTH HEAVEN":** *Autobiography*, 94.

94 **CONNECTING SOLDIERS TO WOMEN FOR MONEY WAS AGAINST MILITARY RULES:** Payne and Payne, 180.

95 **"PLEASE! PLEASE DON'T BEAT MY FACE!":** *Autobiography*, 113.

Chapter 22: Crazy Red

97 **DOUBLE V CAMPAIGN:** For more information on the campaign, see Lee Finkle, "Origins and Aims of the 'Double V,'" in *Forum for Protest: The Black Press During World War II* (Cranbury, NJ: Associated University Presses, 1975) 108–28.

97 **RACISM CLOSES LEGAL PATHWAYS OUT OF POVERTY:** David J. Maurrasse, *Listening to Harlem: Gentrification, Community, and Business* (New York: Routledge, 2006), 23–25.

97 **"ALMOST EVERYONE IN HARLEM NEEDED SOME KIND OF HUSTLE":** *Autobiography*, 106.

97 **"ALL OF US—WHO MIGHT HAVE PROBED SPACE":** *Autobiography*, 104.

99 **LITTLE OPPORTUNITY TO GO TO ONE OF THE BIG UNIVERSITIES:** Wilfred had left Michigan to study a trade at Wilberforce University, a historically Black university in Ohio. *Autobiography*, 92. Around this time only 1.2 percent of Black people completed four years of college. US Census Bureau, "United States Summary: Table 13. Years of School Completed," 41. The *Detroit News* reported that even at the end of the 1940s, Black students at the University of Michigan only "made up about 0.5% of the enrollment and were mostly barred from Ann Arbor's shops and restaurants. Most rental rooms were closed to them, too, and Black students couldn't get a

haircut in the Michigan Union." Myesha Johnson, "Project Spotlights the Faces of Black History at the University of Michigan," *Detroit News*, August 9, 2022, www.detroitnews.com/story/news/education/2022/08/10/7788349001.

Chapter 23: Actor

101 COUNTLESS PROTESTS: Christopher Gray, "Look Familiar, Men? Maybe You Were There," *New York Times*, May 7, 2009, www.nytimes.com/2009/05/10/realestate/10scapes.html; and "Picket in Front of U.S. Army Building, First-Ever U.S. Gay Rights Protest," NYC LGBT Historic Sites Project, accessed March 26, 2024, www.nyclgbtsites.org/site/picket-in-front-of-u-s-army-building-first-ever-u-s-gay-rights-protest/.

101 THEY DID NOT WANT GAY MEN IN THE ARMY: During World War II "homosexuality was classified as a mental illness by the medical community; mental illness was one condition that disqualified young people from service." Adam Foreman, "'Coming Out Under Fire': The Story of Gay and Lesbian Servicemembers," review of 1994 film *Coming Out Under Fire*, National WWII Museum, June 25, 2020, www.nationalww2museum.org/war/articles/gay-and-lesbian-service-members.

101 "CRAZY-O, DADDY-O, GET ME MOVING": *Autobiography*, 122.

103 "DADDY-O, NOW YOU AND ME, WE'RE FROM UP NORTH HERE": *Autobiography*, 124.

103 "THE SUBJECT WAS FOUND MENTALLY DISQUALIFIED": Payne and Payne, 187. See also FBI file no. 105–899, notes on Malcolm K. Little's Selective Service records, December 3, 1954, in "Malcolm Little (Malcolm X) New York File," pt. 39 of 41, 11, FBI Records: The Vault, vault.fbi.gov/malcolm-little-malcolm-x/malcolm-little-malcolm-x-new-york-file-39-of-41.

Chapter 24: Hunted

105 THAT YEAR VIOLENT REBELLIONS BROKE OUT IN FORTY-SEVEN CITIES: Charles S. Johnson, "Review of the Month," *Monthly Summary of Events and Trends in Race Relations* 1, no. 6 (January 1944), 2.

105 HAD GROWN FRUSTRATED: Lizabeth Cohen, *A Consumers' Republic: The Politics of Mass Consumption in Postwar America* (New York: Vintage Books, 2004), 96–98; and Luis Alvarez, *The Power of the Zoot: Youth Culture and Resistance During World War II* (Berkeley: University of California Press, 2008), 224.

105 BLACK-OWNED BUSINESSES, LIKE SMALLS' PARADISE, WERE SPARED: Alvarez, *Power of the Zoot*, 221.

105 SIX BLACK PEOPLE HAD BEEN KILLED: The six men who died are named in "Dead in Harlem," *New York Times*, August 3, 1943, 10, and "6th Man Dies in Harlem Riot," *New York Post*, August 7, 1943, 6. Injuries and arrests come from Dominic J. Capeci Jr., *The Harlem Riot of 1943* (Philadelphia: Temple University Press, 1977), 102; and Alvarez, *Power of the Zoot*, 221.

106 **OFFICIALS BLAMED THE IMMORALITY OF THE PEOPLE:** "Harlem Disorders Bring Quick Action by City and Army," *New York Times*, August 2, 1943, 1, 16; and Alvarez, *Power of the Zoot*, 227.

107 **"I DON'T KNOW WHERE RED IS":** Malcolm Jarvis recounted this episode, including Sammy's and Malcolm's words, in his interview with Les Payne, quoted in Payne and Payne, 190.

Chapter 25: Daring

109 **ONE OF THE FIRST MAJOR NIGHTCLUBS IN THE AREA:** The following information on Little Harlem and Little Dixie comes from Richard Vacca, *The Boston Jazz Chronicles: Faces, Places, and Nightlife, 1937–1962* (Belmont, MA: Troy Street, 2012), 25–29, and Richard Vacca, "Feb 27, 1937: City Bureaucrats Hit 'Lawless Nightclubs,'" blog, February 27, 2013, richardvacca.com/on-february-27–1937/.

110 **FIRST BLACK-OWNED NIGHTCLUB IN NEW ENGLAND:** "History," Wally's Cafe Jazz Club, accessed March 26, 2024, wallyscafe.com/history/.

110 **"LOOK, IF THAT WAS YOUR MOTHER":** Jarvis interview, quoted in Payne and Payne, 201.

111 **"SHOULD DO ANYTHING THAT HE WAS SLICK ENOUGH":** *Autobiography*, 155.

112 **"OH, WE'VE GOT MORE THAN THAT":** Jarvis interview, quoted in Payne and Payne, 201.

112 **REALLY DANGEROUS AT THE TIME WERE POLICE BRUTALITY AND RACISM:** Police violence against Black people at this time was "routine, unaddressed and overlooked," says Kenneth W. Mack, a law and history professor at Harvard. Returning Black veterans were often the victims. Olivia B. Waxman, "How a 1946 Case of Police Brutality Against a Black WWII Veteran Shaped the Fight for Civil Rights," *Time*, March 30, 2021, time.com/5950641/blinding-isaac-woodard/.

112 **SOUTHERNERS IN CONGRESS INSISTED THAT THESE BENEFITS SHOULD BE ADMINISTERED LOCALLY:** Ira Katznelson, *When Affirmative Action Was White: An Untold History of Racial Inequality in Twentieth Century America* (New York: W.W. Norton & Company, 2005), 122–124, 126–127.

112 **BLOCKED MANY BLACK VETERANS FROM RECEIVING BENEFITS:** Alexis Clark, "Returning from War, Returning to Racism," *New York Times Magazine*, July 30, 2020, www.nytimes.com/2020/07/30/magazine/black-soldiers-wwii-racism.html.

112 **BLACK WORKERS WERE THE FIRST FIRED:** The experience of Black workers in the postwar years and the related statistics all come from *To Secure These Rights: The Report of the President's Committee on Civil Rights* (New York: Simon and Schuster, 1947), 55–58, 61.

113 **"THE WARTIME GAINS":** Fair Employment Practice Committee, *Final Report, June 28, 1946* (Washington, DC: US Government Printing Office, 1947), viii.

113 **THRILL OF HANGING OUT WITH THREE "BAD" BLACK MEN:** Rodnell P. Collins, *Seventh Child: A Family Memoir of Malcolm X*, with A. Peter Bailey (Secaucus, NJ: Carol, 1998), 45; and Payne and Payne, 208.

113 **"I'M BORED." "LET'S BREAK INTO"**: Quotes are based on Malcolm Jarvis's recollection: "One of the girls, I think it was Joyce, said she was bored . . . And somebody said, 'Let's break into a house.' You see, this is the way they [wealthy white women who seemed to enjoy the thrill of hanging out with 'bad' black men] think. We said, 'Yeah, that's a good idea.'" Jarvis interview, quoted in Payne and Payne, 208.

Chapter 26: Arrest

116 **A LONG LINE OF WHITE WOMEN HAD LIED**: Daniele Selby, "From Emmett Till to Pervis Payne—Black Men in America Are Still Killed for Crimes They Didn't Commit," Innocence Project, July 25, 2020, innocenceproject.org/emmett-till-birthday-pervis -payne-innocent-black-men-slavery-racism; and Jamelle Bouie, "The Deadly History of 'They're Raping Our Women,'" *Slate*, June 18, 2015, slate.com/news-and -politics/2015/06/the-deadly-history-of-theyre-raping-our-women-racists-have-long -defended-their-worst-crimes-in-the-name-of-defending-white-womens-honor.html.

116 **"TEACH HIM A LESSON"**: Ella Collins, interview transcript for "Malcolm X: The Real Story," quoted in Payne and Payne, 214.

116 **"YOU HAD NO BUSINESS WITH WHITE GIRLS!"**: *Autobiography*, 173.

116–117 **MALCOLM LATER CLAIMED THAT TWO YEARS WAS THE AVERAGE BURGLARY SENTENCE**: *Autobiography*, 173.

117 **GAVE MALCOLM AND JARVIS LONGER SENTENCES**: Manning Marable, *Malcolm X: A Life of Reinvention* (New York: Penguin Books, 2012), 68; and *Autobiography*, 173.

117 **"YOU'RE SENDING MY BOY TO PRISON"**: Bill Cunningham and Daniel Golden, "Malcolm: The Boston Years," *Boston Globe Magazine*, February 16, 1992, 30.

Chapter 27: Caged

119 **"ANY PERSON WHO CLAIMS TO HAVE A DEEP FEELING"**: *Autobiography*, 176.

120 **OLDEST PRISON IN THE COUNTRY STILL IN USE**: John G. Harris, "Officials Clear Way to Replace Ancient Charlestown Prison," *Boston Globe*, June 21, 1949, 8; and "Dever Breaks Ground for Modern Prison at Norfolk," *Boston Globe*, May 13, 1952, 14.

120 **PRESIDENT JEFFERSON ENSLAVED HUNDREDS OF BLACK PEOPLE**: Thomas Jefferson Foundation, "Slavery FAQs–Property," Thomas Jefferson's Monticello, accessed March 27, 2024, www.monticello.org/slavery/slavery-faqs/property/.

120 **"NEITHER SLAVERY NOR INVOLUNTARY SERVITUDE, *EXCEPT AS A PUNISHMENT FOR CRIME*"**: US Constitution, Amendment XIII, Section 1.

120 **SLAVERY STILL EXISTS IN THE UNITED STATES**: To learn more, see Dyjuan Tatro, "US Prison Labor Is Cruel and Pointless Legalized Slavery. I Know First-Hand," *Guardian*, September 22, 2023, www.theguardian.com/commentisfree/2023/sep/22/us -prison-labor-is-cruel-and-pointless-legalized-slavery-i-know-first-hand; and "End the Exception," Abolish Slavery National Network, endtheexception.com/.

120 **"YOU NEVER HEARD YOUR NAME, ONLY YOUR NUMBER"**: *Autobiography*, 176.

120 **THE PRISON POPULATION IN MASSACHUSETTS WAS ABOUT 91 PERCENT WHITE:** US Census Bureau, "Table 36. Age of Persons in Correctional Institutions, by Type of Control of Institution, Color, and Sex, for States: 1950–Con.," in *US Census of Population: 1950*, vol. 4, *Special Reports*, pt. 2, ch. C, Institutional Population, 74, www2.census.gov/library/publications/decennial/1950/population-volume-4/41601752v4p2ch4.pdf.

121 **PROVIDING MORE MONEY TO "FIGHT CRIME":** See Elizabeth Hinton, "We Were Warned About a Divided America 50 Years Ago. We Ignored the Signs," *Washington Post*, March 16, 2021, www.washingtonpost.com/opinions/2021/03/16/kerner-comission-police-reform/; and James Cullen, "The History of Mass Incarceration," Brennan Center for Justice, July 20, 2018, www.brennancenter.org/our-work/analysis-opinion/history-mass-incarceration.

121 **140,079 PEOPLE IN STATE AND FEDERAL PRISONS:** Bureau of Justice Statistics, "Prisoners 1925–81," *Bureau of Justice Statistics Bulletin*, December 1982, p. 2, table 1, bjs.ojp.gov/content/pub/pdf/p2581.pdf.

121 **1,230,100 PEOPLE IN STATE AND FEDERAL PRISONS:** E. Ann Carson and Rich Kluckow, *Prisoners in 2022—Statistical Tables* (Bureau of Justice Statistics, November 2023), 1, 13, bjs.ojp.gov/document/p22st.pdf.

Chapter 28: Satan

124 **"CAN HAVE HER GOSPEL":** Malcolm X to Ella Collins, April 12, 1946, quoted in Collins, *Seventh Child*, 72.

124 **FELLOW INCARCERATED MEN CAME UP WITH A NICKNAME:** *Autobiography*, 177.

Chapter 29: John

125 **INCARCERATED PEOPLE WORKED FOR LITTLE PAY:** "Incarcerated workers typically earn little to no pay at all, with many making just pennies an hour. They earn, on average, between 13 cents and 52 cents per hour nationwide . . . In seven states, incarcerated workers are not paid at all for the vast majority of work assignments." American Civil Liberties Union, "Captive Labor: Exploitation of Incarcerated Workers," ACLU, June 15, 2022, www.aclu.org/news/human-rights/captive-labor-exploitation-of-incarcerated-workers.

125 **"WHAT'CHA KNOW, DADDY?":** *Autobiography*, 178.

126 **"WHAT FASCINATED ME WITH HIM MOST OF ALL":** *Autobiography*, 178.

Chapter 30: Back to School

128 **"I DIDN'T KNOW A VERB FROM A HOUSE":** *Autobiography*, 179.

128 **"MY DEAR SISTER":** Malcolm X to Ella Collins, December 14, 1946, quoted in Payne and Payne, 227.

129 **"GLUED TO THE RADIO":** *Autobiography*, 179.

Chapter 31: Nation of Islam

131 "NATURAL RELIGION FOR THE BLACK MAN": *Autobiography*, 179.

132 "MALCOLM, DON'T EAT ANY MORE PORK": *Autobiography*, 180.

133 PREACHING THAT THE BIBLE SAID BLACK PEOPLE: Noel Rae, "How Christian Slaveholders Used the Bible to Justify Slavery," *Time*, February 23, 2018, time.com/5171819/.

133 GREW EUROPE'S WEALTH AND AFRICA'S POVERTY: Daron Acemoglu, "The Economic Impact of Colonialism," VoxEU, Center for Economic and Policy Research, January 30, 2017, cepr.org/voxeu/columns/economic-impact-colonialism.

133 SAID IT WAS ABOUT CIVILIZING AFRICAN PEOPLE: "The Berlin Conference of 1884–1885," *Africa's Great Civilizations*, PBS for Teachers, pbslearningmedia.org/resource/6031c3a2-ada9-42b4-8045-52006e2a2b07/.

Chapter 32: Moorish Science Temple

135 FOUNDED THE MOORISH SCIENCE TEMPLE IN NEWARK IN 1913: C. Eric Lincoln, *The Black Muslims in America* (Boston: Beacon Press, 1961), 51. For more information about the creation of the Moorish Science Temple, see Payne and Payne, 235–44.

135 URGED HIS FOLLOWERS TO THINK OF THEMSELVES AS ASIANS: On Timothy's teaching, see Payne and Payne, 240.

136 CLAIMED THIRTY THOUSAND MEMBERS IN 1928: Payne and Payne, 244.

136 MIDDLE EASTERN POPULATION IN THE DETROIT AREA: In 2020, there were 16,238 people of Middle Eastern or North African descent living in Detroit, and 59,938 in neighboring Dearborn. US Census Bureau, "Detailed Demographic and Housing Characteristics File A," in *Decennial Census*, 2020, table T01001, accessed on May 2, 2024, data.census.gov/table/DECENNIALDDHCA2020.T01001.

136 ARAB AMERICANS WERE NOT LEGALLY CONSIDERED WHITE: Khaled A. Beydoun, "Between Muslim and White: The Legal Construction of Arab American Identity," *New York University Annual Survey of American Law* 29, no. 1 (2013), ssrn.com/abstract=2529506.

136 "ARABS AS A CLASS ARE NOT WHITE": *In Re Ahmed Hassan*, 48 F.Supp. 843 (E.D. Mich. 1942).

137 FIRST MOSQUE IN DETROIT: *Autobiography*, 303; and "Elijah Muhammad–I," Columbia Center for Teaching and Learning, accessed April 10, 2024, ccnmtl.columbia.edu/projects/mmt/mxp/people/753_I.html. The Nation of Islam called its places of worship "temples" until around 1960, when Elijah Muhammad began referring to them as "mosques" after a trip to Muslim countries. For clarity, "mosque" is used throughout this book except in quoted material, which appears as originally said or written.

137 "THE SPIRITUAL REINCARNATION OF DREW ALI": Christopher C. Alston, interview with Les Payne, September 19, 1993, quoted in Payne and Payne, 250.

137 **"BLUE-EYED DEVIL":** Payne and Payne, 250.

137 **MADE UP A STORY THAT A BLACK SCIENTIST NAMED YAKUB:** Elijah Muhammad, "The White Man's Claim to Divine Superiority," Mr. Muhammad Speaks, *Pittsburgh Courier*, July 4, 1959, 14.

Chapter 33: Elijah

139 **WALLACE WAS A WHITE MAN FROM NEW ZEALAND:** FBI special agent in charge, Los Angeles, to FBI director, AIRTEL memo re "Changed: W. D. Fard, was," October 18, 1957, in "Wallace Fard Muhammad," pt. 2 of 7, p. 10, FBI Records: The Vault, vault.fbi.gov/Wallace Fard Muhammed/Wallace Fard Muhammed Part 2 of 7.

140 **"IN CONNECTION WITH THE CULT ACTIVITIES":** FBI, correlation summary of files on Wallace Don Ford, January 15, 1958, in "Wallace Fard Muhammed," pt. 5 of 7, p. 115, FBI Records: The Vault, vault.fbi.gov/Wallace Fard Muhammed/Wallace Fard Muhammed Part 5 of 7.

140 **RUMORS OF "HUMAN SACRIFICE":** Erdmann Doane Beynon, "The Voodoo Cult Among Negro Migrants in Detroit," *American Journal of Sociology* 43, no. 6 (May 1938), 903–4.

140 **"FARD MUHAMMAD DIRECTED HIMSELF BACK TO THE HEAVENS":** John Muhammad (Elijah Muhammad's brother), interview with Les Payne, September 18, 1993, quoted in Payne and Payne, 257.

140 **"MESSENGER OF ALLAH":** Payne and Payne, 258.

141 **"WHY DON'T YOU LEAVE THIS MAN ALONE?":** Wilfred Little interview, quoted in Payne and Payne, 230–31.

Chapter 34: Devils

143 **"MALCOLM, IF A MAN KNEW EVERY IMAGINABLE THING":** This conversation between Malcolm and Reginald comes from *Autobiography*, 183–84. "All white people are devils" is based on the line "He told me that all whites knew they were devils."

144 **A PARADE OF WHITE PEOPLE:** For Malcolm's own account of this "parade," see *Autobiography*, 184–85.

Chapter 35: Forgiveness

147 **"THE DEVIL WHITE MAN":** All Reginald's words are from *Autobiography*, 186.

147 **"THE HONORABLE ELIJAH MUHAMMAD":** All the quotes from the letters come from *Autobiography*, 186–88.

148 **SAW HIMSELF AS EVIL, AS SATAN:** *Autobiography*, 196, 344.

149 **"LIKE SNOW OFF A ROOF":** *Autobiography*, 196.

Chapter 36: A to Z

151 "IN FACT, UP TO THEN, I NEVER HAD BEEN SO TRULY FREE": *Autobiography*, 199.

152 INCARCERATED MEN AT CHARLESTOWN STATE PRISON LARGELY CONSTRUCTED: "Secrets of the Norfolk Prison," Boston.com, January 13, 2013, www.boston.com /uncategorized/noprimarytagmatch/2013/01/13/secrets-of-the-norfolk-prison.

152 CRITICS CALLED THE PRISON A "COUNTRY CLUB": "Secrets of the Norfolk Prison."

152 REDEMPTION THROUGH EDUCATION AND COMMUNITY IS NO LONGER THE FOCUS: Jennifer Roesch et al., "Howard B. Gill: Architect of the Fallen Community Prison Model," States of Incarceration, accessed March 28, 2024, statesofincarceration.org/story /howard-b-gill-architect-fallen-community-prison-model.

152 A DISPROPORTIONATE AMOUNT OF PEOPLE BEING PUNISHED IN THIS WAY TODAY ARE BLACK: Less than 7 percent of the people in Massachusetts are Black, but 31 percent of the state's prison population is Black. Rachel Jollie and Kristen M. Budd, *Massachusetts Should Restore Voting Rights to Over 7,700 Citizens*, Sentencing Project, February 2024, www.sentencingproject.org/app/uploads/2024/01/Massachusetts -Voting-Rights-Brief.pdf; and Massachusetts Department of Correction, "Frequently Asked Questions," January 1, 2024, Commonwealth of Massachusetts, www.mass.gov/doc/frequently-asked-questions-july-2023–0/download.

153 "NEGROES' FEET ARE SO BIG THAT WHEN THEY WALK": *Autobiography*, 201.

153 "THE WORLD'S MOST MONSTROUS CRIME": *Autobiography*, 202.

153 EUROPEANS ENSLAVED AND SOLD MORE THAN TWELVE MILLION AFRICAN PEOPLE: "The Transatlantic Slave Trade," Equal Justice Initiative, accessed March 28, 2024, eji .org/report/transatlantic-slave-trade; and SlaveVoyages, accessed May 2, 2024, www.slavevoyages.org/.

153 "I COULD SPEND THE REST OF MY LIFE READING": *Autobiography*, 207.

153 "LIGHTS OUT" EVERY NIGHT: *Autobiography*, 200.

153 "BAPTISM INTO PUBLIC SPEAKING": *Autobiography*, 210.

153–154 AGAINST SOME OF THE NATION'S BEST DEBATE TEAMS: Payne and Payne, 269.

Chapter 37: Faith

155 "ISLAM AND MR. ELIJAH MUHAMMAD HAD CHANGED MY WHOLE WORLD": *Autobiography*, 214.

156 "IF YOU ONCE BELIEVED IN THE TRUTH": *Autobiography*, 215.

157 BLACK AMERICA'S CHIEF PROSECUTOR OF THE UNITED STATES: See Peniel E. Joseph, *The Sword and the Shield: The Revolutionary Lives of Malcolm X and Martin Luther King Jr.* (New York: Basic Books, 2020).

157 RELIGIOUS FREEDOM IN PRISON: Courts did not recognize many of the religious rights of incarcerated people, including dietary practices, until decades later. ACLU

National Prison Project, *Know Your Rights: Freedom of Religion*, July 2005, www
.aclu.org/sites/default/files/images/asset_upload_file78_25744.pdf. Even today,
"jails and prisons throughout the country frequently violate the religious rights
of prisoners." American Civil Liberties Union, "Religious Freedom in Prison,"
accessed March 28, 2024, www.aclu.org/issues/prisoners-rights/civil-liberties
-prison/religious-freedom-prison.

158 "WHAT COLOR WAS PAUL?": Malcolm's exchange with the White teacher is from
Autobiography, 219.

158 JESUS WAS NOT WHITE: "Judaeans of this time were closest biologically to Iraqi
Jews of the contemporary world. In terms of a colour palette then, think dark-
brown to black hair, deep brown eyes, olive-brown skin. Jesus would have been
a man of Middle Eastern appearance." Joan E. Taylor, "What Did Jesus Really
Look Like, as a Jew in 1st-Century Judaea?," *Irish Times*, February 9, 2018, www
.irishtimes.com/culture/books/1.3385334. Taylor is a professor of Christian origins
and the author of the book *What Did Jesus Look Like?* (London: Bloomsbury, 2018).

158 "MY MAN! YOU EVER HEARD ABOUT SOMEBODY NAMED": *Autobiography*, 219.

Chapter 38: Meeting

159 "HIGHWAY ROBBERY": *Autobiography*, 222.

Chapter 39: Belief

163 THE "WHITE MAN" HAD BRAINWASHED THE "SO-CALLED NEGRO": Quotes from this
speech come from *Autobiography*, 226–27.

164 MOST NEWLY BUILT HOUSES IN THE UNITED STATES TODAY: US Census Bureau, "High-
lights of 2022 Characteristics of New Housing," accessed March 28, 2024, www
.census.gov/construction/chars/highlights.html.

165 HIS ECONOMIC PROGRAM OF BLACK-OWNED BUSINESSES: Nafeesa Muhammad, "The
Nation of Islam's Economic Program, 1934–1975," BlackPast, April 1, 2020, www
.blackpast.org/african-american-history/the-nation-of-islams-economic-program
-1934–1975/.

165 THE FIRST FLOOR IS BEING RESTORED: For details on the restoration and the house
museum, see Wendy L. Muhammad, interview by Hermene Hartman on the Elijah Muhammad House, N'DIGO, April 19, 2021, ndigo.com/2021/04/19/interview
-with-wendy-muhammad-on-the-elijah-muhammad-house/.

Chapter 40: Thousands

167 "THERE ARE SUPPOSED TO BE THOUSANDS": This conversation between Malcolm and
Elijah appears in *Autobiography*, 228.

168 "MY MAN, LET ME PULL YOUR COAT TO SOMETHING": *Autobiography*, 229.

168 "AW, MAN, GET OUT OF MY FACE!": *Autobiography*, 231.

168 **"MY BROTHERS AND SISTERS, OUR WHITE SLAVEMASTER'S CHRISTIAN RELIGION":** *Autobiography*, 231.

169 **"AND THUS QUIT BEING EXPLOITED BY THE WHITE MAN":** *Autobiography*, 235.

169 **"YOU WANT TO KNOW HOW TO SPREAD MY TEACHINGS?":** *Autobiography*, 236.

Chapter 41: Emmett Till

174 **THE US ARMY WAS SEGREGATED ABROAD:** Tyler Bamford, "African Americans Fought for Freedom at Home and Abroad During World War II," National WWII Museum, February 1, 2020, www.nationalww2museum.org/war/articles/african-americans-fought-freedom-home-and-abroad-during-world-war-ii.

174 **FOR ACTS HE LIKELY DID NOT COMMIT:** See John Edgar Wideman, *Writing to Save a Life: The Louis Till File* (New York: Scribner, 2016).

Chapter 42: Growing

177 **"I WOULDN'T HAVE EXPECTED ANYONE SHORT OF ALLAH":** *Autobiography*, 246.

178 **"RELIGIOUS KICK":** *Autobiography*, 246.

178 **"WHAT YOU KNOW, DADDY?":** *Autobiography*, 247.

178 **"I KNEW, FROM WHAT I HAD BEEN WHEN I WAS WITH THEM":** *Autobiography*, 247.

178 **"I KNOW YOU DON'T REALIZE THE ENORMITY":** This and the following quotes from Malcolm's living room speeches can be found in *Autobiography*, 244–45.

179 **PHILADELPHIA HAS ONE OF THE LARGEST BLACK MUSLIM POPULATIONS:** Tom MacDonald, "Group Representing Black Muslims Wants to Be Heard Nationally," WHYY, March 8, 2024, whyy.org/articles/black-muslim-leadership-council-philadelphia-biden/.

Chapter 43: Massive Resistance

181 **THE SYSTEM OF SHARECROPPING:** "Sharecropping in Mississippi," *American Experience*, "The Murder of Emmet Till," aired April 15, 2023, PBS, www.pbs.org/wgbh/americanexperience/features/emmett-sharecropping-mississippi/; and "Sharecropping," *Slavery by Another Name*, aired February 13, 2012, PBS, www.pbs.org/tpt/slavery-by-another-name/themes/sharecropping/.

182 **RACIST LAWS ALLOWED AUTHORITIES TO ARREST AND FINE UNEMPLOYED BLACK PEOPLE:** For more information on these laws and the practice known as "convict leasing" described in this paragraph, see David M. Oshinsky, "Convict Labor in the Post-Civil War South: Involuntary Servitude after the Thirteenth Amendment," in *The Promises of Liberty: The History and Contemporary Relevance of the Thirteenth Amendment*, ed. Alexander Tsesis (New York: Columbia University Press, 2010), 100–118.

182 **RACIST WHITE BUSINESSES' REFUSAL TO PAY BLACK WORKERS EQUAL WAGES:** During a debate in Congress in 1937 about providing equal pay for equal work, representative J. Mark Wilcox of Florida proclaimed there had "always been a difference in the wage

scale of white and colored labor" in the South. He said "grave social and racial conflicts" would result if the federal government were to "prescribe the same wage for the Negro that it prescribes for the white man." 82 Cong. Rec. H1404 (December 13, 1937).

182 GENERATIONS OF BLACK PEOPLE WERE UNABLE TO RISE OUT OF POVERTY: For more on the links between these racist policies and economic inequities today, see Danyelle Solomon, Connor Maxwell, and Abril Castro, "Systematic Inequality and Economic Opportunity," Center for American Progress, August 7, 2019, www .americanprogress.org/article/systematic-inequality-economic-opportunity/.

182 EMMETT BEGGED HIS COUSINS: Simeon later wrote a firsthand account of the events leading up to Emmett's murder. See Simeon Wright, *Simeon's Story: An Eyewitness Account of the Kidnapping of Emmett Till*, with Herb Boyd (Chicago: Lawrence Hill Books, 2010).

184 "LET THE PEOPLE SEE WHAT THEY DID TO MY BOY": "Battered Body of Till Boy Arrives Here," *Chicago Sun-Times*, September 2, 1955.

185 RACIST AND SEXIST PRACTICES DID NOT ALLOW BLACK PEOPLE OR WOMEN TO SERVE: Although the US Supreme Court found in *Norris v. Alabama* in 1935 that the exclusion of Black people from juries violated the Constitution, courts and prosecutors still found ways to exclude Black people; they continue to do so today. State laws barred women from jury service into the 1960s, theorizing they were too fragile. Only in 1975 did the Supreme Court rule in *Taylor v. Louisiana* that excluding women from a jury violated a defendant's right to a fair trial. Equal Justice Initiative, *Race and the Jury: Illegal Racial Discrimination in Jury Selection* (Montgomery, AL: 2021), 16–17, 22, 43–45, eji.org/wp-content/uploads/2005/11 /race-and-the-jury-digital.pdf.

185 JURIES STILL SAY NOT GUILTY: Rebekah Riess and Theresa Waldrop, "Former Texas Police Officer Acquitted of Jonathan Price Murder by Jury," CNN, September 23, 2022, www.cnn.com/2022/09/23/us/jonathan-price-murder-officer-acquitted /index.html; and Peter Holley, "Jonathan Price Was Wolfe City's Hometown Hero. On Saturday, He Was Killed by Police," *Texas Monthly*, October 6, 2020, www .texasmonthly.com/news-politics/jonathan-price-wolfe-city-hometown-hero/.

Chapter 44: Mosque Number Seven

187 THOUSANDS OF BLACK PEOPLE WHO HAD BEEN LYNCHED: Jessie P. Guzman and W. Hardin Hughes, "Table 2. Lynchings by States and Race 1882–1946," in *Negro Year Book: A Review of Events Affecting Negro Life*, ed. Guzman (Tuskegee, AL: Tuskegee Institute, 1947), 306–307.

187 MORE THAN TEN THOUSAND PEOPLE CAME TOGETHER: "10,000 in Harlem Protest Verdict," *New York Times*, September 26, 1955, 10.

187 CONGRESS DID NOT PASS AN ANTI-LYNCHING BILL UNTIL 2022: Emmett Till Anti-Lynching Act, Pub. L. No. 117–107, 136 Stat. 1125 (03/29/2022).

188 **ABOUT ONE THOUSAND AMERICANS A YEAR:** "On average, police in the United States shoot and kill more than 1,000 people every year, according to an ongoing analysis by the *Washington Post*." Jennifer Jenkins et al., "Fatal Force: 1,141 People Have Been Shot and Killed by Police in the Past 12 Months," *Washington Post*, updated May 27, 2024, www.washingtonpost.com/graphics/investigations/police -shootings-database.

188 **DISPROPORTIONATELY PACIFIC ISLANDER OR BLACK OR BROWN OR NATIVE AMERICAN:** Mapping Police Violence, updated November 25, 2024, mappingpoliceviolence.org.

188 **TYPICALLY SPOKE OUTSIDE THE HOUSE OF COMMON SENSE:** C. Gerald Fraser, "Lewis Michaux, 92, Dies; Ran Bookstore in Harlem," *New York Times*, August 27, 1976, www.nytimes.com/1976/08/27/archives/lewis-michaux-92-dies-ran-bookstore-in -harlem.html; and Howard Rambsy II, "Black Bookstores in NYC: Toward a History," *Cultural Front* (blog), March 31, 2018, www.culturalfront.org/2018/03/black -bookstores-in-nyc-toward-history.html.

188 **WORLD HISTORY BOOK OUTLET:** Jim Peppler, *Signs and Merchandise in Front of the House of Common Sense and Home of Proper Propaganda in Harlem*, photograph, 1966, Jim Peppler Southern Courier Photograph Collection, Alabama Department of Archives and History, digital.archives.alabama.gov/digital/collection/peppler/id/1469.

188 **HAD TWO HUNDRED THOUSAND BOOKS:** Fraser, "Lewis Michaux, 92, Dies."

Chapter 45: Louis

191 **"COME TO HEAR US, TOO, BROTHER":** For the following quotes from Malcolm's recruitment attempts, see *Autobiography*, 251–53.

192 **ADULTS NEED AT LEAST SEVEN HOURS OF SLEEP A NIGHT:** Office of Disease Prevention and Health Promotion, "Healthy Living: Get Enough Sleep," US Department of Health and Human Services, last updated August 4, 2023, health.gov /myhealthfinder/healthy-living/mental-health-and-relationships/get-enough-sleep.

Chapter 46: Betty

196 **"WELL, YOU SURE WAITED LONG ENOUGH":** *Autobiography*, 262–63.

197 **PRESIDENT ROOSEVELT BELIEVED THESE RACIST IDEAS:** "Knowing the Presidents: Theodore Roosevelt," National Portrait Gallery, Smithsonian Institution, accessed March 29, 2024, www.si.edu/spotlight/knowing-the-presidents-theodore -roosevelt; Nora McGreevy, "The Racist Statue of Theodore Roosevelt Will No Longer Loom over the American Museum of Natural History," *Smithsonian*, June 23, 2020, www.smithsonianmag.com/smart-news/statue-theodore-roosevelt -removed-reexamination-racist-acts-180975154; and Jeremy Hobson, "Teddy Roosevelt's Complicated Legacy 100 Years After His Death," WBUR, March 21, 2019, www.wbur.org/hereandnow/2019/03/21/teddy-roosevelt-legacy-100-years.

197 **DID NOT REMOVE THIS STATUE:** Robin Pogrebin, "Roosevelt Statue to Be Removed from Museum of Natural History," *New York Times*, June 21, 2020, www.nytimes

.com/2020/06/21/arts/design/roosevelt-statue-to-be-removed-from-museum-of
-natural-history.html.

Chapter 47: Police Brutality

200 **"IF SOMEONE PUTS HIS HAND ON YOU":** Malcolm X, "Message to the Grass Roots," November 10, 1963, in *Malcolm X Speaks: Selected Speeches and Statements*, ed. George Breitman (New York: Grove Weidenfeld, 1990), 12.

200 **"YOU'RE NOT IN ALABAMA—THIS IS NEW YORK":** James L. Hicks, "Riot Threat as Cops Beat Muslim: 'God's Angry Men' Tangle with Police," *New York Amsterdam News*, May 4, 1957, reprinted in *The Portable Malcolm X Reader*, ed. Manning Marable and Garrett Felber (New York: Penguin Books, 2013), 85.

202 **"THE GESTAPO TACTICS OF WHITE POLICE":** All of Malcolm's words are from "Moslems Await 'D-Day' in N.Y. Court," *Pittsburgh Courier*, May 24, 1958, 7.

202 **TERRORIZED JEWS AND OTHERS IDENTIFIED AS POLITICAL ENEMIES:** United States Holocaust Memorial Museum, "The Gestapo: Overview," Holocaust Encyclopedia, last edited March 10, 2021, encyclopedia.ushmm.org/content/en/article/gestapo.

Chapter 48: March on Harlem

203 **"THAT MAN BELONGS IN THE HOSPITAL":** *Autobiography*, 269.

Chapter 49: That Much Power

205 **"HARLEM'S BLACK PEOPLE WERE LONG SINCE SICK AND TIRED":** *Autobiography*, 269.

205 **"ALL AVAILABLE COPS":** Hicks, "Riot Threat," 86.

206 **"NO ONE MAN SHOULD HAVE THAT MUCH POWER":** Hicks, "Riot Threat," 87.

206 **A JURY AWARDED HIM $75,000:** *Hinton v. City of New York*, 13 A.D.2d 475 (N.Y. App. Div. 1961); and "Awards 75G to Victim of Cop Beating," *Daily News* (New York), May 6, 1960.

206 **THE LARGEST POLICE BRUTALITY JUDGMENT:** *Autobiography*, 270; and Clarence Taylor, *Fight the Power: African Americans and the Long History of Police Brutality in New York City* (New York: New York University Press, 2019), 81.

Chapter 50: Hate That Hate

210 **CALLED MEMBERS OF THE NATION OF ISLAM "BLACK SUPREMACISTS":** *The Hate That Hate Produced*, special report produced by Ted Yates, reported by Louis Lomax, and narrated by Mike Wallace, WNTA-TV Channel 13, New York, televised July 22, 1959, YouTube video, at 26:45, youtu.be/BsYWD2EqavQ.

212 **"HATE-MESSENGERS":** Words of White critics are listed in *Autobiography*, 274.

212 **"BY NO MEANS DO THESE MUSLIMS REPRESENT":** *Autobiography*, 275.

212 **"THE GUILTY, TWO-FACED WHITE MAN":** Malcolm's responses to White reporters come from *Autobiography*, 276–77.

213 **"BECAUSE IF YOU ARE WELL KNOWN":** *Autobiography*, 305.

213 **"A REMARKABLE MAN":** *The Hate That Hate Produced* at 11:05.

Chapter 51: Howard

215 **IN THE 1800s, WHITE PEOPLE DID NOT ALLOW:** See Samara Freemark, "The History of HBCUs in America," American Public Media Reports, August 20, 2015, www.apmreports.org/episode/2015/08/20/the-history-of-hbcus-in-america.

216 **"DON'T YOU BELIEVE THERE ARE ANY *GOOD* WHITE PEOPLE?":** This conversation is from *Autobiography*, 329–30.

216 **"AS-SALAAM-ALAIKUM, BROTHERS AND SISTERS":** Stokely Carmichael, *Ready for Revolution: The Life and Struggles of Stokely Carmichael (Kwame Ture)*, with Ekwueme Michael Thelwell (New York: Scribner, 2003), 257. Carmichael styled this greeting as "Salaam aleikum"; this book uses Malcolm's standard spelling.

217 **"TO US, THE NATION OF ISLAM WAS MR. MUHAMMAD":** *Autobiography*, 332.

217 **"MINISTER MALCOLM IS TRYING TO TAKE OVER THE NATION":** Rumors are from *Autobiography*, 334–35.

218 **"THOSE MUSLIMS *TALK* TOUGH, BUT THEY NEVER *DO* ANYTHING":** *Autobiography*, 334.

218 **"FOR ALL THE WORLD TO SEE, AND RESPECT, AND DISCUSS":** *Autobiography*, 334.

218 **ROSA PARKS STEPPED FORWARD ONE HUNDRED DAYS:** "Emmett Till's Death Inspired a Movement," National Museum of African American History & Culture, Smithsonian, accessed March 29, 2024, nmaahc.si.edu/explore/stories/emmett-tills-death-inspired-movement.

Chapter 52: Debate

220 **"A REPUBLICAN, DEMOCRAT, CHRISTIAN OR JEW":** Malcolm X, Howard University lecture, October 30, 1961, Malcolm X Collection, box 5, folder 15, Schomburg Center for Research in Black Culture, New York Public Library, quoted in *Portable Malcolm X Reader*, 185.

221 **"IT ROCKED ME LIKE A TIDAL WAVE":** *Autobiography*, 330.

221 **"I BELIEVED SO STRONGLY IN MR. MUHAMMAD":** *Autobiography*, 330.

Chapter 53: Planting Seeds

223 **"OFF OF GIFTS FROM WHITE PEOPLE":** The following remarks from Malcolm X and Bayard Rustin's debate at Howard are from Malcolm X, Howard University lecture, and "1,500 Hear Integration–Non-Segregation Debate," *Chicago Defender*, November 11, 1961, both sources quoted in Marable, *Malcolm X*, 186–87.

224 **THE UNITED STATES ORGANIZED A FAILED INVASION OF CASTRO'S CUBA:** "The Bay of

Pigs," John F. Kennedy Presidential Library and Museum, accessed March 29, 2024, www.jfklibrary.org/learn/about-jfk/jfk-in-history/the-bay-of-pigs.

224 **"MY STAND IS REALLY THE SAME":** Stokely Carmichael's recollection of Malcolm X's words at Howard comes from Carmichael, *Ready for Revolution*, 260.

224 **"HOWARD WILL NEVER BE THE SAME":** "1,500 Hear Integration–Non-Segregation Debate," *Chicago Defender*.

225 **HELP CHANGE THE CIVIL RIGHTS MOVEMENT:** "The Foundations of Black Power," National Museum of African American History & Culture, Smithsonian, accessed June 7, 2024, nmaahc.si.edu/explore/stories/foundations-black-power.

225 **"BLACK IS BEAUTIFUL":** See "Black Is Beautiful: The Emergence of Black Culture and Identity in the 60s and 70s," National Museum of African American History & Culture, Smithsonian, accessed March 29, 2024, nmaahc.si.edu/explore/stories /black-beautiful-emergence-black-culture-and-identity-60s-and-70s.

225 **"WHEN YOU GO TO THESE COLLEGES AND UNIVERSITIES":** Elijah Muhammad to Malcolm X, February 15, 1962, Malcolm X Collection, box 3, folder 8, Schomburg Center, quoted in Marable, *Malcolm X*, 202.

225 **FEW PEOPLE IN THE UNITED STATES WERE BEING REQUESTED TO SPEAK MORE:** The *New York Times* conducted a study of college students' social and political activity in 1962 and found that Malcolm was "in strong demand for his shock speeches" that spring. Only Republican senator Barry Goldwater, conservative magazine editor William F. Buckley Jr., and Martin Luther King Jr. were more sought after as speakers. Nan Robertson, "Campuses Show New Interest in Political and Social Issues," *New York Times*, May 14, 1962.

Chapter 54: Invasion

227 **"THE 'CLEAN CUT' NEGRO, WELL-DRESSED AND GROOMED":** "You're a Muslim If You're Well-Dressed, Clean-Cut," *Muhammad Speaks*, June 1962, 11.

227 **LOS ANGELES POLICE PROBABLY ADVISED SAN DIEGO POLICE:** Frederick Knight, "Justifiable Homicide, Police Brutality, or Governmental Repression? The 1962 Los Angeles Police Shooting of Seven Members of the Nation of Islam," *Journal of Negro History* 79, no. 2 (Spring 1994): 187.

227 **"WE HAVE BEEN WATCHING IT WITH CONCERN":** William H. Parker, interview by Donald McDonald, *The Police: One of a Series of Interviews on the American Character* (Santa Barbara, CA: Center for the Study of Democratic Institutions, April 1962), 18.

228 **"THAT EXISTS TO REACH AN UNCHURCHED GENERATION":** RTLA Church, accessed April 1, 2024, rtla.churchcenter.com/home.

229 **"LET'S TEAR THOSE PRETTY SUITS OFF THOSE [N-WORDS]":** "Muslim Defense Hits Police Testimony," *California Eagle* (Los Angeles), May 23, 1963, 4.

229 **WITHOUT MEDICAL TREATMENT:** Karl Evanzz, *The Judas Factor: The Plot to Kill Malcolm X* (New York: Thunder's Mouth Press, 1992), 119.

Chapter 55: Response

231 **"THE HONORABLE ELIJAH MUHAMMAD TEACHES US":** Payne and Payne, 426.

231 **"EYE FOR AN EYE"** and **"A HEAD FOR A HEAD, AND A LIFE FOR A LIFE":** Payne and Payne, 425, 426.

232 **"IN THE NAME OF ALLAH, THE BENEFICENT, THE MERCIFUL":** All the following quotes come from Malcolm X, speech at Ronald X's funeral, Los Angeles, May 5, 1962, "Who Taught You to Hate Yourself?," YouTube video, youtu.be/kboP3AWCTkA.

Chapter 56: Barred

235 **"A VERY BEAUTIFUL THING":** "Mayor Warns Public on Muslim's Boss," *Los Angeles Evening and Sunday Herald Examiner*, June 6, 1962, E1.

235 **"HATRED"** and **"GLAD FEELINGS OVER DEATH":** Jack V. Fox, "Black Muslim's Speech Angers Bunche," *Pontiac Press* (Michigan), July 12, 1962, 33.

235 **BOMBED A BLACK CHURCH IN BIRMINGHAM:** "16th Street Baptist Church Bombing (1963)," National Park Service, accessed April 1, 2024, www.nps.gov/articles /16thstreetbaptist.htm.

236 **"FARCE ON WASHINGTON":** *Autobiography*, 320, 324.

Chapter 57: Grass Roots

237 **"YOU DON'T CATCH HELL":** The quotes from this speech can be found in Malcolm X, "Message to the Grass Roots," November 10, 1963, in *Malcolm X Speaks: Selected Speeches and Statements*, ed. George Breitman (New York: Grove Weidenfeld, 1990), 4, 8–11.

Chapter 58: Hurt

242 **"I DON'T THINK I COULD SAY ANYTHING":** *Autobiography*, 340.

242–243 **"THE MAN WHO HAD GIVEN ME WINGS":** *Autobiography*, 344.

243 **"WELL, SON":** *Autobiography*, 344.

243 **HAD ITS AGENTS AND INFORMANTS INSIDE THE NATION:** The FBI's actions to drive a wedge between Malcolm and Elijah are discussed in Karl Evanzz, "The FBI and the Nation of Islam," in *The FBI and Religion: Faith and National Security Before and After 9/11*, ed. Sylvester A. Johnson and Steven Weitzman (Oakland: University of California Press, 2017), 161–62; and Manning Marable, *Malcolm X: A Life of Reinvention* (New York: Penguin Books, 2012), 278.

Chapter 59: Roost

245 **WORLD'S MOST FAMOUS ARENA:** "History of Madison Square Garden," Madison Square Garden, Madison Square Garden Entertainment, accessed April 1, 2024, www.msg.com/madison-square-garden/history.

246 **KENNEDY HAD CALLED ON CONGRESS TO PASS CIVIL RIGHTS LEGISLATION:** John F. Kennedy, "Special Message to the Congress on Civil Rights and Job Opportunities," June 19, 1963, in *Public Papers of the Presidents of the United States: John F. Kennedy, 1963* (Washington, DC: US Government Printing Office, 1964), 483.

246 **"FANATIC, INFLEXIBLY DOGMATIC"** and **"HOORAY, HOORAY!":** These and the following quotes from the question and answer session appear in "Malcolm X Scores U.S. and Kennedy: Likens Slaying to 'Chickens Coming Home to Roost,'" *New York Times*, December 2, 1963, timesmachine.nytimes.com/timesmachine/1963/12/02/89980478.pdf.

Chapter 60: Betrayal

249 **"DID YOU SEE THE PAPERS THIS MORNING?":** For the entirety of this conversation between Malcolm and Elijah, see *Autobiography*, 348.

250 **"IF HE SUBMITS":** *Autobiography*, 349.

250 **"IF YOU KNEW WHAT THE MINISTER DID":** *Autobiography*, 349.

251 **"THE THING TO ME WORSE THAN DEATH WAS THE BETRAYAL":** *Autobiography*, 352.

Chapter 61: Silent

253 **PROBABLY MADE MILLIONS FOR THE NATION OF ISLAM:** Benjamin Karim, *Remembering Malcolm*, with Peter Skutches and David Gallen (New York: Carroll & Graf, 1992), 122. Karim, also known as Benjamin 2X, was one of Malcolm's assistant ministers in Mosque Number Seven.

Chapter 62: Betrayal Again

255–256 **ELIJAH PUBLICLY RENAMED CASSIUS MUHAMMAD ALI ON MARCH 6, 1964:** Associated Press, "Clay Honored by Black Muslims," *Capital Times* (Madison, WI), March 7, 1964.

Chapter 63: Ready

257 **"THE PRESS IS SO POWERFUL":** Malcolm X, "At the Audubon," December 13, 1964, in *Malcolm X Speaks*, 93.

258 **"NO MAN":** M. S. Handler, introduction to *Autobiography*, ix–x.

259 **"AT NO TIME DID HE TRANSGRESS AGAINST MY OWN PERSONALITY":** Mike Handler's quotes in this section come from the introduction, xi, xiii.

259 **"MALCOLM WILL NEVER BETRAY US":** Handler, introduction, xiv.

259 **MIKE GREW UP IN THE MIDWEST:** Handler's biographical details are drawn from Robert D. McFadden, "M. S. Handler, a Times Reporter Who Covered World War II, Dies," *New York Times*, February 11, 1978, www.nytimes.com/1978/02/11/archives/ms-handler-a-times-reporter-who-covered-world-war-ii-dies-reported.html.

Chapter 64: Speak

261 **"I HAVE REACHED THE CONCLUSION":** This and the following quotes from Malcolm are from M. S. Handler, "Malcolm X Splits with Muhammad," *New York Times*, March 9, 1964, www.nytimes.com/1964/03/09/archives/malcolm-x-splits-with -muhammad-suspended-muslim-leader-plans-black.html.

263 **"YOU KNOW, IT WAS LIKE HAVING TEA WITH A BLACK PANTHER":** This and Handler's assessment that the black panther is "beautiful" and "dangerous" are from Handler, introduction, ix.

Chapter 65: MLK

265 **ALL BUT FOUR WERE WHITE MEN:** Exceptions were Asian American senators Hiram Fong and Daniel Inouye and White senators Margaret Chase Smith and Maurine Neuberger. See 110 Cong. Rec. S6415 (March 26, 1964); and *Biographical Directory of the United States Congress*, bioguide.congress.gov/search.

265 **MORE THAN HALF OF THOSE AMERICANS WERE WOMEN:** US Census Bureau, "Table 2. Estimates of the Total Resident Population of the United States, by Age, Color, and Sex, July 1, 1964," in *Current Population Reports: Population Estimates*, series P-25, no. 293, 12, October 21, 1964, www2.census.gov/library/publications/1964 /demographics/P25-293.pdf.

265 **ABOUT 12 PERCENT OF THOSE AMERICANS WERE PEOPLE OF COLOR:** US Census Bureau, "Table 2," in *Current Population Reports*, October 12, 1964. This percentage is based on the estimated population of "non-white" people in 1964. At the time "non-white" in the census meant Black, Native, and Asian people. Latino people who did not self-identify as Black or Indigenous were classified as White. The 1964 report did not break down the population estimates by race and ethnicity.

265 **RACISM KEPT BLACK PEOPLE FROM VOTING:** "Voting Rights Act (1965)," National Archives, accessed June 7, 2024, www.archives.gov/milestone-documents/voting -rights-act.

265 **RACISM KEPT BLACK PEOPLE OUT OF PLACES:** "Civil Rights Act (1964)," National Archives, accessed June 7, 2024, www.archives.gov/milestone-documents/civil -rights-act.

265 **RACISM KEPT BLACK PEOPLE OUT OF PUBLIC FACILITIES:** "Jim Crow Laws," *American Experience*, "Freedom Riders," aired April 1, 2023, PBS, www.pbs.org/wgbh /americanexperience/features/freedom-riders-jim-crow-laws/.

265 **BLACK PEOPLE HAD TO RIDE IN THE BACK:** These examples of racist treatment come from Stephen A. Berrey, "Obstacles to Freedom: Life in Jim Crow America," in *Understanding and Teaching the Civil Rights Movement*, ed. Hasan Kwame Jeffries (Madison: University of Wisconsin Press, 2019), 63.

266 **GO TO SCHOOL IN THE OLDEST BUILDINGS WITH THE OLDEST BOOKS:** LeeAnn G. Reynolds, *Maintaining Segregation: Children and Racial Instruction in the South, 1920–1955* (Baton Rouge: Louisiana State University Press, 2017), 63–66.

266 **CAME IN RESPONSE TO ALL THE RACIST VIOLENCE:** For the rationale behind Kennedy's proposal of a civil rights bill, see Mary Dudziak, *Cold War Civil Rights: Race and the Image of American Democracy* (Princeton, NJ: Princeton University Press, 2011), 115–51.

266 **"NO MEMORIAL ORATION OR EULOGY":** Lyndon B. Johnson, "Address Before a Joint Session of the Congress," November 27, 1963, in *Public Papers of the Presidents of the United States: Lyndon B. Johnson, 1963–1964*, vol. 1 (Washington, DC: Government Printing Office, 1965), 9.

267 **"WELL, MALCOLM, GOOD TO SEE YOU":** Quotes and details from this meeting come from Ted Knap, "Malcolm X Crashes King Press Session," *Pittsburgh Press*, March 27, 1964, 6; and Patrick Parr, "Malcolm X and Martin Luther King Jr. Shake Hands," *American Prospect*, February 26, 2021, prospect.org/civil-rights/malcolm -x-and-martin-luther-king-jr-shake-hands/.

267 **THE LONGEST FILIBUSTER WITH MULTIPLE SPEAKERS IN US HISTORY:** Ali Swenson, "Post Touting Longest Filibuster Gets Some Facts Wrong," Associated Press, June 1, 2022, apnews.com/article/fact-check-longest-filibuster-democrats-civil-rights-act -674586601064; and "Landmark Legislation: The Civil Rights Act of 1964," US Senate, accessed April 2, 2024, www.senate.gov/artandhistory/history/common /generic/CivilRightsAct1964.htm.

267 **THE SECOND FILIBUSTER LASTED SIXTY DAYS:** "Landmark Legislation," US Senate.

267–268 **THE SIXTH CIVIL RIGHTS ACT IN US HISTORY:** *Historical Dictionary of the U.S. Congress*, comp. Scot Schraufnagel (Lanham, MD: Scarecrow Press, 2011), s.v. "civil rights acts."

268 **"HOW CAN ANYONE BE SO NAIVE AS TO THINK":** Malcolm X, "Appeal to African Heads of State," July 17, 1964, in *Malcolm X Speaks: Selected Speeches and Statements*, ed. George Breitman (New York: Grove Weidenfeld, 1990), 76.

Chapter 66: Human Rights

269 **"THIS AFTERNOON WE WANT TO TALK ABOUT THE BALLOT OR THE BULLET":** All the quotes from this speech come from Malcolm X, "The Ballot or the Bullet," April 12, 1964, transcript, American Radio Works, americanradioworks.publicradio.org/features /blackspeech/mx.html. You can listen to Malcolm's hour-long speech at public radio station KPFA's Malcolm X Digital Archive, kpfa.org/player/?audio = 358353.

273 **GET HIS "SPIRITUAL SELF STRENGTHENED":** James Booker, "Seek to Evict Malcolm X from Home in Queens," *New York Amsterdam News*, April 18, 1964, quoted in Manning Marable and Garrett Felber, eds., "Malcolm X in Ghana," in *The Portable Malcolm X Reader* (New York: Penguin Books, 2013), 327.

Chapter 67: Departure

276 "he has followed you in the press very closely": *Autobiography*, 368.

Chapter 68: Equal

277 "people white, black, brown, red & yellow": Malcolm X, diary, April [15], 1964, in *The Diary of Malcolm X: El-Hajj Malik El-Shabazz, 1964*, ed. Herb Boyd and Ilyasah Al-Shabazz (Chicago: Third World Press, 2013), 4.

278 "muslims from everywhere, hugging, embracing": Malcolm X, diary, April [15], 1964, 4.

278 "the whites don't seem white": Malcolm X, diary, April 17, 1964, 5.

278 "not being able to speak the language": Malcolm X, diary, April 20, 1964, 15.

Chapter 69: Hajj

279 "powerfully built man": *Autobiography*, 381.

279 "why didn't you call before?": *Autobiography*, 381.

279 "never have i met a more educated, intellectual": Malcolm X, diary, April 17, 1964, 6.

280 would be considered mena, people of middle eastern and north african descent: Rachel Marks, Nicholas Jones, and Karen Battle, "What Updates to OMB's Race/Ethnicity Standards Mean for the Census Bureau," US Census Bureau, April 8, 2024, www.census.gov/newsroom/blogs/random-samplings/2024/04/updates-race-ethnicity-standards.html; and Karen Zraick et al., "No Box to Check: When the Census Doesn't Reflect You," *New York Times*, February 25, 2024, www.nytimes.com/interactive/2024/02/25/us/census-race-ethnicity-middle-east-north-africa.html.

280 "mecca is as ancient as time itself": Malcolm X, diary, April 18, 1964, 11.

280 "all sexes, sizes, colors": Malcolm X, diary, April 18, 1964, 12.

Chapter 70: All the Same

283 "never have i witnessed such sincere hospitality": The text of Malcolm's letter can be found in *Autobiography*, 390–93.

285 "had been a chronology of—changes": *Autobiography*, 390.

Chapter 71: Omowale

287 "refugee night": Alice Windom to Christine Johnson, May 21, 1964, Julian Mayfield Papers, Schomburg Center for Research in Black Culture, New York Public Library, quoted in Payne and Payne, 443.

287 **RIGHT NOW, MORE THAN ONE HUNDRED MILLION REFUGEES:** "Refugee Statistics," USA for UNHCR (United Nations High Commissioner for Refugees), accessed April 3, 2024, www.unrefugees.org/refugee-facts/statistics/.

287 **IN PLACES LIKE PALESTINE:** Mohammed Hussein, Mohammed Haddad, and Jadd Chahal, "Nowhere Safe in Gaza," *Al Jazeera*, March 4, 2024, interactive.aljazeera .com/aje/2024/displacement-israel-war-on-gaza-no-safe-place/.

288 **MEANING "THE SON WHO HAS COME HOME":** *Autobiography*, 403. Other translations include "the son (or child) who has returned." Manning Marable, *Malcolm X: A Life of Reinvention* (New York: Penguin Books, 2012), 314.

Chapter 72: Ghana

289 **FIRST GROUP OF AFRICAN PEOPLE SOUTH OF THE SAHARA DESERT:** "Ghana Country Profile," BBC News, April 14, 2023, www.bbc.com/news/world-africa-13433790.

290 **"ITS PURPOSE IS TO UNITE AFRO-AMERICANS":** Malcolm X, announcement of Organization of African-American Unity, June 24, 1964, in FBI file on OAAU, sec. 1–6, 1964–1967, 81, archive.org/details/per_fbi-file-organization-of-african-american -unity_fbi-file-on-the-organiza_1964–1967/.

290 **"WHO HAVE LOST THEIR PLACE IN SOCIETY":** Organization of Afro-American Unity, Statement of Basic Aims and Objectives, New York, June 1964, in FBI file on OAAU, 86.

290 **"MOVING MY FAMILY OUT OF AMERICA MAY BE GOOD FOR ME PERSONALLY":** Malcolm X, diary, May 11, 1964, 48.

290 **PRESIDENT NKRUMAH WELCOMED AFRICAN AMERICANS:** Karl Evanzz, *The Judas Factor: The Plot to Kill Malcolm X* (New York: Thunder's Mouth Press, 1992), 85; Payne and Payne, 442; and Michelle D. Commander, "Ghana at Fifty: Moving Toward Kwame Nkrumah's Pan-African Dream," *American Quarterly* 59, no. 2 (June 2007): 424–26.

292 **"WE HAD SOME" GOOD WHITE PEOPLE:** Vicki Garvin, interview with Les Payne, February 1993, quoted in Payne and Payne, 444.

Chapter 73: President Nkrumah

296 **CIA HELPED GHANAIAN ARMY AND POLICE OFFICIALS:** Seymour M. Hersh, "C.I.A. Said to Have Aided Plotters Who Overthrew Nkrumah in Ghana," *New York Times*, May 9, 1978, www.nytimes.com/1978/05/09/archives/cia-said-to-have-aided-plotters -who-overthrew-nkrumah-in-ghana.html; and Susan Williams, *White Malice: The CIA and the Covert Recolonization of Africa* (New York: PublicAffairs, 2021), 494–97.

Chapter 74: Changes

299 **HE STOPPED IDENTIFYING AS A BLACK NATIONALIST:** Payne and Payne, 453–54.

299 **CAUSED HIM TO QUESTION THE SEXIST IDEAS:** Payne and Payne, 454–55.

300 **URGED MALCOLM TO RETHINK CAPITALISM:** Payne and Payne, 454.

300 **"I SAW ALL _RACES_, ALL _COLORS_":** Malcolm's speech on the "Letter from Mecca" can be found in _Autobiography_, 416.

301 **CALLED THEMSELVES THE BLOOD BROTHERS:** _Autobiography_, 402.

Chapter 75: Secret Meeting

304 **"DISCUSSION OF GENERAL FUTURE OF CIVIL RIGHTS":** FBI New York office to director, coded teletype, June 13, 1964, in "Malcolm X," pt. 15 of 38, 54, FBI Records: The Vault, vault.fbi.gov/Malcolm X/Malcolm X Part 15 of 38; and Marable, _Malcolm X_, 343.

304 **BELGIAN AND AMERICAN AGENTS WERE INVOLVED:** Williams, _White Malice_, 379–90.

Chapter 76: Court Case

306 **THE FIRST OF HUNDREDS OF DEATH THREATS:** Marable, _Malcolm X_, 341.

Chapter 77: African Unity

309 **THIRTY-FOUR AFRICAN INDEPENDENT NATIONS:** The facts in this paragraph come from "Africa's Summit Conference," editorial, _New York Times_, July 24, 1964, www .nytimes.com/1964/07/24/archives/africas-summit-conference.html.

309 **"YOUR EXCELLENCIES":** This and the following quotes come from Malcolm X, "Appeal to African Heads of State," July 17, 1964, in _Malcolm X Speaks: Selected Speeches and Statements_, ed. George Breitman (New York: Grove Weidenfeld, 1990), 72–77.

311 **FEDERAL GOVERNMENT HAD NOT FORCED STATES:** Malcolm X, "Appeal to African Heads of State," 76; and "Brown v. Board of Education," Legal Defense Fund, accessed April 4, 2024, www.naacpldf.org/brown-vs-board/.

311 **"DEEPLY DISTURBED":** Organization of African Unity, "Racial Discrimination in the United States of America," Resolution 15, in _Resolutions Adopted by the First Ordinary Session of the Assembly of Heads of State and Government Held in Cairo, UAR, from 17 to 21 July 1964_, African Union, au.int/sites/default/files/decisions /9514–1964_ahg_res_1–24_i_e.pdf.

311–312 **CONNECTED WITH JOMO KENYATTA OF KENYA:** Payne and Payne, 452.

312 **GOT INTO THE AFFAIRS OF THESE NATIONS:** For a history of the CIA's interference in Africa, see Williams, _White Malice_.

Chapter 78: Gaza

313 **SOME JEWS WANTED THEIR OWN JEWISH HOMELAND IN PALESTINE:** Liora Halperin, "Origins and Evolution of Zionism," Foreign Policy Research Institute, January 9, 2015, www.fpri.org/article/2015/01/origins-and-evolution-of-zionism; and Alan R.

Taylor, "Zionism and Jewish History," *Journal of Palestine Studies* 1, no. 2 (Winter 1972): 35–40.

313 **THE BRITISH OCCUPIED PALESTINE:** Timothy Bella, "The Gaza Strip and Its History, Explained," *Washington Post*, October 9, 2023, www.washingtonpost.com/world /2023/10/09/gaza-strip-israel-hamas-explained.

313 **"A NATIONAL HOME FOR THE JEWISH PEOPLE":** Arthur James Balfour (British foreign secretary) to Lionel Walter Rothschild, November 2, 1917, (note containing what's known today as the Balfour Declaration), quoted in Rashid Khalidi, *The Hundred Years' War on Palestine: A History of Settler Colonialism and Resistance, 1917–2017* (New York: Metropolitan Books, 2020), 23–24. You can see the note here: www .un.org/unispal/wp-content/uploads/2017/05/Balfour_declaration_unmarked.jpg.

313 **SO-CALLED CHRISTIAN EUROPE OF JEWS:** Yousef Munayyer, "It's Time to Admit That Arthur Balfour Was a White Supremacist—and an Anti-Semite, Too," *Forward*, November 1, 2017, forward.com/opinion/386480.

313 **ANTISEMITIC EUROPEANS BELIEVED:** Omer Bartov, "Antisemitism, Then and Now: A Guide for the Perplexed," *Nation*, May 10, 2024, www.thenation.com/article /society/antisemitism-ancient-modern-biden-israel.

313 **HARMED THEIR JEWISH NEIGHBORS:** Jonathan Schneer, *The Balfour Declaration: The Origins of the Arab-Israeli Conflict* (London: Bloomsbury, 2011), 9.

313 **DIDN'T FEEL THAT THE COUNTRIES WHERE THEY LIVED WERE THEIR HOMES:** Theodor Herzl, *A Jewish State: An Attempt at a Modern Solution of the Jewish Question*, 3rd ed., trans. Sylvia D'Avigdor, ed. Jacob de Haas (New York: Federation of American Zionists, 1917), 2–6; and Anne Perez, *Understanding Zionism: History and Perspectives* (Minneapolis: Fortress, 2023), 20–24.

314 **"IF YOU WERE AN AMERICAN":** The quotes in this paragraph come from Malcolm X, "Message to the Grass Roots," November 10, 1963, in *Malcolm X Speaks: Selected Speeches and Statements*, ed. George Breitman (New York: Grove Weidenfeld, 1990), 4, 9.

314 **FLEEING TO PALESTINE FROM AROUND THE WORLD:** Khalidi, *Hundred Years' War*, 27, 39–41.

314 **PALESTINIANS TRIED TO STOP:** "The Nakba Did Not Start or End in 1948," *Al Jazeera*, May 23, 2017, www.aljazeera.com/features/2017/5/23/the-nakba-did -not-start-or-end-in-1948; Alex Winder, "Great Palestinian Rebellion, 1936–1939: A Popular Uprising Facing a Ruthless Repression," Interactive Encyclopedia of the Palestine Question, accessed October 28, 2024, www.palquest.org/en/highlight /158/great-palestinian-rebellion-1936-1939; and Seth Lipsky, "What Happened in Hebron?" *Tablet*, August 19, 2009, www.tabletmag.com/sections/israel-middle -east/articles/what-happened-in-hebron.

314 **BUT THE BRITISH BACKED THE ZIONISTS:** Winder, "Great Palestinian Rebellion 1936– 1939"; Khalidi, *Hundred Years' War*, 31–32, 42, 44–45; and Linah Alsaafin, "Did British Mandate Pave Way for Israeli Occupation?," *Al Jazeera*, October 27, 2017,

www.aljazeera.com/news/2017/10/27/did-british-mandate-pave-way-for-israeli -occupation.

314 **TO MURDER SIX MILLION JEWS:** United States Holocaust Memorial Museum, "How Many People Did the Nazis Murder?," Holocaust Encyclopedia, accessed October 15, 2024, encyclopedia.ushmm.org/content/en/article/documenting-numbers -of-victims-of-the-holocaust-and-nazi-persecution.

315 **ABOUT TWO-THIRDS OF THE POPULATION:** *Supplement to Survey of Palestine: Notes Compiled for the Information of the United Nations Special Committee on Palestine* (Jerusalem: Government Printer, 1947; repr., Washington, DC: Institute for Palestine Studies, 1991), 11, table 5.

315 **UNITED NATIONS ALLOCATED 55 PERCENT:** Eve Spangler, *Understanding Israel/Palestine: Race, Nation, and Human Rights in the Conflict*, 2nd ed. (Leiden, NL: Brill, 2019), 10.

315 **STARTED DRIVING PALESTINIANS OUT:** Spangler, *Understanding Israel/Palestine*, 137– 38; Marwan Darweish, "The Nakba: How the Palestinians Were Expelled from Israel," *The Conversation*, May 11, 2023, theconversation.com/the-nakba-how-the -palestinians-were-expelled-from-israel-205151; and "Gaza War: What Is the History of the Israel-Palestinian Conflict?" Reuters, October 1, 2024, www.reuters.com /world/middle-east/what-is-history-israel-palestinian-conflict-2024-05-14.

315 **MURDERED:** Ilan Pappé, *A History of Modern Palestine* (Cambridge: Cambridge University Press, 2022), 128; and Mike Curtis, "When Britain Aided Israel's 'Ethnic Cleansing' of Palestine," Declassified UK, November 7, 2023, www.declassifieduk .org/when-britain-aided-israels-ethnic-cleansing-of-palestine.

315 **THE NAKBA:** Joseph Krauss, "Palestinians Mark 76 Years of Dispossession as a Potentially Even Larger Catastrophe Unfolds in Gaza," AP News, May 14, 2024, apnews.com/article/b5cea9556e516655c25598d5dbe54192.

315 **EXPANDED ITS TERRITORY TO 77 PERCENT OF PALESTINE:** "Key Topics: History," United Nations Information System on the Question of Palestine, United Nations, accessed November 13, 2024, un.org/unispal/history/.

315 **AROUND 750,000 PALESTINIANS WERE EXPELLED:** Spangler, *Understanding Israel/Palestine*, 137–38.

315 **MANY MORE PALESTINIANS HAVE DIED:** "Total Casualties, Arab-Israeli Conflict (1860–present)," Jewish Virtual Library, American-Israeli Cooperative Enterprise, accessed November 9, 2024, www.jewishvirtuallibrary.org/total-casualties-arab -israeli-conflict; Ola Awad, "Conditions of the Palestinian People via Statistical Figures and Findings, on the 76th Annual Commemoration of the Palestinian Nakba," Palestinian Central Bureau of Statistics, May 15, 2024, www.pcbs.gov.ps /post.aspx?lang=en&ItemID=5750#; United Nations Office for the Coordination of Humanitarian Affairs, "Data on Casualties" (occupied Palestinian territory since 2008), accessed November 9, 2024, www.ochaopt.org/data/casualties; and Brendan Rascius, "Have More Palestinians or Israelis Died in War? Half of Americans

Don't Know, Poll Says," *Miami Herald*, March 22, 2024, www.miamiherald.com /news/nation-world/national/article286996080.html.

315 **1,200 ISRAELIS AND NON-ISRAELIS:** Thomas Mackintosh and Alex Boyd, "Israel Marks Year Since Hamas Attack as Fighting Rages on Multiple Fronts," BBC News, October 7, 2024, www.bbc.com/news/articles/c4g57q20l1vo.

315 **RESCUED VERY FEW HOSTAGES:** Tia Goldenberg, "Could Mass Protests in Israel over the Hostages Persuade Netanyahu to Agree to a Cease-Fire Deal?" AP News, September 3, 2024, apnews.com/article/d041f4fc2519597a15be95ad837e0df8; and Lauren Izso et. al, "Grief and Fury on Israel's Streets, as Hostage Killings Pile Pressure on Netanyahu to Secure Ceasefire Deal," CNN, September 2, 2024, www.cnn.com/2024 /09/01/middleeast/israel-hostage-protests-strike-netanyahu-intl-latam.

316 **KILLED MORE THAN FORTY THOUSAND PALESTINIANS:** Mackintosh and Boyd, "Israel Marks Year Since Hamas Attack."

316 **A GENOCIDE:** Raz Segal, "A Textbook Case of Genocide," *Jewish Currents*, October 13, 2023, jewishcurrents.org/a-textbook-case-of-genocide; Nicole Narea, "Is Israel Committing Genocide? Reexamining the Question, a Year Later," Vox, October 25, 2024, www.vox.com/politics/378913/israel-gaza-genocide-icj; and "Rights Expert Finds 'Reasonable Grounds' Genocide Is Being Committed in Gaza," UN News, news.un.org/en/story/2024/03/1147976.

316 **ISRAELI BOMBS DESTROYED MOST OF GAZA:** Haley Ott, Julia Ingram, and Layla Ferris, "Destruction in Gaza Caused by Israel-Hamas War Mapped Using Satellite Data," CBS News, October 8, 2024, www.cbsnews.com/news/israel-hamas-war -gaza-destruction-mapped-using-satellite-data; and Raja Abdulrahim et al., "Gaza in Ruins After a Year of War," *New York Times*, October 7, 2024, www.nytimes.com /interactive/2024/10/07/world/middleeast/israel-gaza-destruction-hamas-war.html.

316 **MADE BY THE UNITED STATES:** David Gritten, "Gaza War: Where Does Israel Get Its Weapons?," BBC News, September 3, 2024, www.bbc.com/news/world-middle-east -68737412; and Antoinette Radford, "Who Supplies Israel with Weapons?," CNN, October 16, 2024, www.cnn.com/2024/10/16/middleeast/where-israel-get-its-weapons.

316 **NOT ALL JEWS HAVE IDENTIFIED AS ZIONISTS:** Chris Walker, "Jewish-Led Protesters Storm Wall Street, Demanding Arms Embargo on Israel," Truthout, October 15, 2024, truthout.org/articles/american-jews-storm-wall-street-demanding-arms -embargo-on-israel; and "Our Vision," Jewish Voice for Peace, accessed October 16, 2024, www.jewishvoiceforpeace.org/resource/our-vision.

316 **LIKELY BOMBED OR RAIDED THIS HOSPITAL:** Frances Vinall and Mohamad El Chamaa, "Mapping the Damage to Gaza's Hospitals: Battered, Abandoned and Raided," *Washington Post*, May 21, 2024, wapo.st/3BorX09.

316 **HOUSED PALESTINIANS WHOM ZIONIST SOLDIERS:** Sammy Westfall and Niha Masih, "What Is Happening in Gaza's Khan Younis, as Israel's Offensive Heads South," *Washington Post*, December 12, 2023, www.washingtonpost.com/world/2023/12 /12/what-is-khan-younis-gaza-israel-palestine.

316 **NEARLY ALL OF GAZA'S 2.3 MILLION PEOPLE:** Joseph Krauss and Sarah El Deeb, "Gaza Is in Ruins After Israel's Yearlong Offensive. Rebuilding May Take Decades," Associated Press, October 9, 2024, www.ap.org/news-highlights /spotlights/2024/gaza-is-in-ruins-after-israels-yearlong-offensive-rebuilding-may -take-decades.

316 **MANY FLEEING PALESTINIANS ENDED UP:** Westfall and Masih, "What Is Happening in Gaza's Khan Younis."

316 *WE MUST RETURN:* Poem by Harun Hashim Rashid in Malcolm's travel diary, undated, Malcolm X Collection, microfilm reel 9, Schomburg Center for Research in Black Culture, New York Public Library, quoted in Hamzah Baig, "'Spirit in Opposition': Malcolm X and the Question of Palestine," *Social Text* 37, no. 3 (September 2019), 61.

316 **"THE SPIRIT OF ALLAH WAS STRONG":** Malcolm X, diary, September 5, 1964, in *The Diary of Malcolm X: El-Hajj Malik El-Shabazz, 1964*, ed. Herb Boyd and Ilyasah Al-Shabazz (Chicago: Third World Press, 2013), 115.

317 **ITS PLANS:** "Palestine National (qawmi) Charter," May 28, 1964, Interactive Encyclopedia of the Palestine Question, www.palquest.org/en/historictext/9613 /palestine-national-qawmi-charter.

317 **"NEW KIND OF COLONIALISM":** This and following quotes come from Malcolm X, "Zionist Logic—Malcolm X on Zionism," *Egyptian Gazette*, September 17, 1964, transcribed at Malcolm-X.org, www.malcolm-x.org/docs/gen_zion.htm.

Chapter 79: Full Circle

319 **"THEY REFUSED TO INSURE MY LIFE":** Benjamin Karim, *Remembering Malcolm*, with Peter Skutches and David Gallen (New York: Carroll & Graf, 1992), 181.

320 **"LIKE A MAN WHO'S ALREADY DEAD":** Theodore Jones, "Malcolm Knew He Was a 'Marked Man,'" *New York Times*, February 22, 1965, 1.

Chapter 80: Tiring

322 *"WHAT WERE THE REASONS BEHIND ELIJAH MUHAMMAD BEING AGAINST YOU":* This question and Malcolm's answer appear in "Malik Shabazz (Malcolm X): Some Questions Answered," distributed by the Islamic Centre of Geneva, reprinted in Payne and Payne, appendix, 529–30.

323 **SOME PEOPLE THINK THE FRENCH GOVERNMENT LEARNED OF A CIA PLOT:** Karl Evanzz, *The Judas Factor: The Plot to Kill Malcolm X* (New York: Thunder's Mouth Press, 1992), 278.

323 **"SERIOUS MISTAKE":** Herman Ferguson (Malcolm's friend), interview by Russell J. Rickford, February 12, 2000, quoted in Russell J. Rickford, *Betty Shabazz: A Remarkable Story of Survival and Faith Before and After Malcolm X* (Naperville, IL: Sourcebooks, 2003), 222.

Chapter 81: Rehearsal

325 **"A PROBLEM FOR ALL HUMANITY"**: Malcolm X, speech, Harvard Law School Forum, December 16, 1964, in *Malcolm X: Speeches at Harvard*, ed. Archie Epps (New York: Paragon House, 1991), 173.

326 **"THIS IS THE ERA OF REVOLUTION"**: The quotes in this paragraph and Malcolm's clarification that "some of you might be all right" come from his speech at the "Homecoming Rally of the OAAU," November 29, 1964, in *By Any Means Necessary: Speeches, Interviews, and a Letter*, ed. George Breitman (New York: Pathfinder Press, 1970), 138, 141, 151.

327 **"WE ARE TODAY SEEING A GLOBAL REBELLION OF THE OPPRESSED"**: Martin Paris, "Negroes Are Willing to Use Terrorism, Says Malcolm X," *Columbia Daily Spectator*, February 19, 1965, 3.

327 **OFFICER NAMED GERRY FULCHER SECRETLY LISTENED**: Marable, *Malcolm X*, 355–57. For more information about Gerry Fulcher and his assignment to secretly listen to Malcolm's conversations for the NYPD, see Gerry Fulcher, oral history interview by Dr. Manning Marable, October 3, 2007, transcript, tape 2, p. 12–tape 3, p. 11, in *Portable Malcolm X Reader*, 411–26.

328 **"GET YOUR HAND OUTTA MY POCKET!"**: This quote and Malcolm's reply come from Evanzz, *Judas Factor*, 292.

328 **"I JUST THINK I SAW A DRESS REHEARSAL FOR THIS MAN'S ASSASSINATION"**: Gene Roberts, interview with Les Payne, February 1992, quoted in Payne and Payne, 467.

328 **SHARPLY *REDUCED* THE NUMBER OF POLICE**: Payne and Payne, 467; and Tamara Payne, "Who Killed Malcolm X?" *Nation*, December 9, 2021, www.thenation.com /article/society/malcolm-x-assassination-investigation.

Chapter 82: 2:30 A.M. AGAIN

329 **"HAVE ANY OF *ELIJAH MUHAMMAD'S* FOLLOWERS LEFT THE *MOVEMENT* WITH YOU"**: These questions and answers are from "Malik Shabazz (Malcolm X): Some Questions Answered," 531–32.

Chapter 83: Father to Son

333 **"IT COULD HAVE BEEN DONE BY ANY ONE OF THE MANY"**: Associated Press, "Malcolm X's Home Is Bombed: Black Nationalist Leader, Family Flee Unhurt," *Chicago Tribune*, February 15, 1965, 3.

334 **"TO GET PUBLICITY"**: "Malcolm Accuses Muslims of Blaze; They Point to Him," *New York Times*, February 16, 1965, www.nytimes.com/1965/02/16/archives /malcolm-accuses-muslims-of-blaze-they-point-to-him.html.

335 **"WAKE UP, BROTHER"**: Richard Benfield, "His Work Will Go On, Wife Says," *Record* (Hackensack, NJ), February 22, 1965, 5; and Alex Haley, epilogue in *Autobiography*, 470.

Chapter 84: Audubon

338 WASHINGTON HEIGHTS: Information about the neighborhood's population comes from "The History of Washington Heights," Nuestro Stories, December 7, 2022, nuestrostories.com/2022/12/the-history-of-washington-heights/; and CoreData.nyc, "Washington Heights/Inwood MN12," NYU Furman Center, accessed April 5, 2024, furmancenter.org/neighborhoods/view/washington-heights-inwood.

339 "WHY DIDN'T YOU TELL ME?": This conversation comes from Benjamin Karim (Benjamin 2X), interview with Les Payne, May 1992, quoted in Payne and Payne, 472.

340 "LOOK AT HIM": Richard Harris, interview with Les Payne, August 5, 1995, quoted in Payne and Payne, 512.

Chapter 85: Hold It, Hold It

341 "HOW ARE YOU GOING TO OPEN UP?": Karim, *Remembering Malcolm*, 189.

342 "MAKE IT PLAIN" and "I NOW INTRODUCE TO YOU": Karim interview, quoted in Payne and Payne, 475.

342 "AS-SALAAM-ALAIKUM": The account of Malcolm's assassination, including Malcolm's and Betty's words, comes from Payne and Payne, 476–79. Spelling has been standardized.

343 "MALCOLM X HAS BEEN SHOT AND I THINK HE'S DEAD": Aubrey Lewis (FBI agent), interview with Les Payne, quoted in Payne and Payne, 482.

Chapter 86: Ancestor

345 THOMAS JEFFERSON, WHO ENSLAVED MORE THAN SIX HUNDRED BLACK PEOPLE: Thomas Jefferson Foundation, "Slavery FAQs–Property," Thomas Jefferson's Monticello, www.monticello.org/slavery/slavery-faqs/property/.

345 "WE HOLD THESE TRUTHS TO BE SELF-EVIDENT": Quotes from the Declaration can be found in "Declaration of Independence: A Transcription," July 4, 1776, America's Founding Documents, National Archives, www.archives.gov/founding-docs/declaration-transcript.

346 TWO DECADES IN PRISON FOR A MURDER THEY DID NOT COMMIT: Ashley Southall and Jonah E. Bromwich, "2 Men Convicted of Killing Malcolm X Will Be Exonerated After Decades," *New York Times,* November 17, 2021, www.nytimes.com/2021/11/17/nyregion/malcolm-x-killing-exonerated.html.

347 ABOUT THIRTY THOUSAND PEOPLE CAME: Rickford, *Betty Shabazz*, 247.

347 "MANY WILL SAY TURN AWAY": Ossie Davis, "Our Shining Black Prince," eulogy at the funeral of Malcolm X, Faith Temple Church of God, February 27, 1965, in *Malcolm X: The Man and His Times*, ed. John Henrik Clarke (New York: Macmillan, 1969), xii.

The Schomburg Center, now home to the Malcolm X Collection, in Malcolm's address book, circa 1958 to 1961

CREDITS